"President Trump's Catholic supporters descended from immigrants we used to call 'white ethnics.' So, the white Catholic embrace of Donald Trump in 2016 raised eyebrows in the Church and among political and cultural observers. Whether you find this development exciting or embarrassing, Professor Steven Millies explains how and why it happened with rigor and insight. Drawing on his years of careful learning and study, Millies has written an important book on the Catholic vote in the Trump Era."

—Jacob Lupfer
Political Analyst

"Though often labelled the 'swing vote' in US national elections, the Catholic vote has long confounded political analysts. That has never been more true than since Catholic voters helped anchor Donald J. Trump's unexpected 2016 presidential victory. Millies skillfully puts the Trump victory in the context of a nearly half-century long evolution of Catholic voting, and in so doing he showcases more clearly than others what underlies the motivations of politically-engaged Catholics. Much more than a conventional political analysis, Millies's book goes deep into Catholic history, tradition, and theology to provide a deep understanding of the various forces that drive Catholic voting. Highly recommended."

—Mark J. Rozell
Dean of the Schar School of Policy and Government
George Mason University

"*Good Intentions* should be required reading for those who want to understand the complex and unique history of the relationship between Catholics and politics in the United States, from *Roe v. Wade* to the election of Trump. Millies's book will greatly help our understanding of the dramatic expansion of the gap between liberals and conservatives in these last two decades, especially within the wider context of the history of the intra-Catholic division in American cultural and political life."

—Massimo Faggioli
Professor of Historical Theology
Villanova University

"*Good Intentions* traces recent US Catholic history to illuminate the contours of the contemporary public church and present political moment. Steven Millies's engaging narrative deftly navigates enduring tensions at intersections of theology, law, and politics in view of the impact of cultural and religious polarization in the postconciliar church. His subtle, interdisciplinary analysis offers valuable insights into questions of conscience, political engagement, and Catholic identity that will prove helpful to those interested in forging a path forward beyond the binary thinking and divisive patterns he identifies."

—Kristin E. Heyer
Professor of Theological Ethics
Boston College

"The American Catholic population has never been more divided: half voted for Donald Trump while half voted for Hilary Rodham Clinton. How did our divisions become so deep and bitter? Steven Milles's perceptive history allows us to make sense of the past, and to move toward common ground in the future."

—Cathleen Kaveny
Libby Professor of Law and Theology
Boston College

Good Intentions

A History of Catholic Voters' Road from *Roe* to Trump

Steven P. Millies

LITURGICAL PRESS
Collegeville, Minnesota

www.litpress.org

Cover design by Monica Bokinskie. Photo by Steve Fontanini. Copyright © 1976. *Los Angeles Times*. Used with permission.

1 2 3 4 5 6 7 8 9

Library of Congress Cataloging-in-Publication Data

Names: Millies, Steven P., author.
Title: Good intentions : a history of Catholic voters' road from Roe to Trump / Steven P. Millies.
Description: Collegeville, Minnesota : Liturgical Press, 2018. | Includes bibliographical references and index.
Identifiers: LCCN 2018010654 (print) | LCCN 2017053396 (ebook) | ISBN 9780814644904 (ebook) | ISBN 9780814644676
Subjects: LCSH: Catholics—Political activity—United States—History—20th century. | Catholics—Political activity—United States—History—21st century. | Voting—United States—History—20th century. | Voting—United States—History—21st century. | Elections—United States—History—20th century. | Elections—United States—History—21st century.
Classification: LCC BX1407.P63 (print) | LCC BX1407.P63 M55 2018 (ebook) | DDC 324.9730088/282—dc23
LC record available at https://lccn.loc.gov/2018010654

for Mary Ruth Singer and Scott Singer,

and for all of the lay women and men
working every day to make
their parishes and their country
great

Contents

Acknowledgments

While I was a graduate student at The Catholic University of America in Washington, DC, I had an unusual opportunity to observe many of the Catholic bishops of the United States up close. From 1997 to 1999, I was a student member of the university Board of Trustees. Because it is "the bishops' university," bishops make up half of the Catholic University board. During one of those years, I sat in executive committee meetings in addition to the full board meetings. I also sat on a trustees' committee that hired the university's fourteenth president. In meetings and over dinners, on coffee breaks and during short rides in cars or on shuttle buses, I got to know many of those bishops. That's not to say we became friends. However, it is to say that I came to know those bishops as people a little bit. While it all was happening, I knew I was getting a rare and privileged glimpse of something. I was determined to observe and remember everything I could. I have been and I remain intensely grateful to Catholic University and to those bishops for that illuminating experience.

Not surprisingly, I found that our nation's bishops are good men. Some more than others, of course. But every one impressed me with his holiness and his intelligence. Quickly, though, I came to appreciate something else about them. It surprised me a little, but on reflection it should not have. The lay trustees on the board generally were successful people from the worlds of finance or law. They were people accustomed to a lot of responsibility for others and for overseeing large assets. In my time with them, I came to see our bishops as not really being very different from those lay trustees. Catholics sitting in the pews of our local parishes generally don't think of our shepherds as being like CEOs, managing hundreds of employees or millions (even billions) of dollars in assets. But of course, they are. Much of their time is devoted to tasks that are not really spiritual in any way. That realization came to me as a revelation twenty years ago, as I think it would come to most lay Catholics. The church defines the role of the bishop in three ways—teaching, sanctifying, and governing. Bishops do all three. But day in and day out, even they would agree that governing occupies the bulk of their time.

I owe a debt of thanks to the many Catholics in my parish and in other parishes who sometimes have reminded me that I have had an unusual and privileged experience of glimpsing how the church in the United States is led, and by whom. I have had a peek behind the curtain that has shown me something many people who have known bishops know. But most people in the pews have not known bishops. This book came from conversations with those Catholics who attend Mass regularly, who believe in the Gospel and in the teachings of the church, who support their bishops, but who have been frustrated and bewildered because their bishops' behavior can seem so strange sometimes—especially when they are dealing with political issues. This book is for them, and it comes with my gratitude for how those people have reminded me that we cannot give in to our bewilderment and frustration. In fact, this book is my effort to do on a larger scale what I have tried to do many times in conversations that I have had in parking lots and narthexes. I cannot dispel all of the frustration, even for myself. But years of study and experiences like the one I've described provide a way I can help to banish the bewilderment. Maybe, once we understand a little bit more about what has motivated the bishops—which, to no small degree, is what they share in common with most American Catholics—we can overcome at least some of the frustration. With gratitude to the many lay Catholics I've talked to and the countless others I never will meet who fit the description I've given here, this book comes as a reply to the questions people ask me most often and as an affirmation that I am with them, in common cause, to make the most of the lay apostolate in our church.

Liturgical Press and especially Hans Christoffersen were generously receptive to this idea for a little book. The proposal for this book came together rather quickly after the 2016 election and Hans could not have been more encouraging and helpful as this book has come to its completion. The early writing went very quickly, and then in the summer I suddenly found myself with a new job in a new city, while still holding my old job in another part of the United States. To say the pace of my writing slowed would be an understatement. Hans and Liturgical Press were patient and generous. My task as an author had become unavoidably difficult, but my friends at Liturgical Press made it as easy as it could be. I could not be more grateful.

I also owe a word of gratitude to my new colleagues at Catholic Theological Union in Chicago, whose encouragement and flexibility with my needs as I take up my new position there have helped give me the time I needed to complete this work. In a special way, let me thank Mark Francis, CSV, Barbara Reid, OP, Ton Sison, CPPS, Bob Schreiter, CPPS, Scott Alexander, Steve Bevans, SVD, Andy Cirillo, Peter Cunningham, and Jessica Curbis, all of whom have made my transition easier.

I received very important assistance from Dr. Matt Thornburg, a colleague at the University of South Carolina Aiken, and Phillip McHood, a political science major at USC

Aiken. Some of what a reader finds in this book depends on a sort of data analysis I am unqualified even to consider doing. Phillip McHood is the sort of student any professor wants to find in his class, and he offered diligent assistance with 2016 election data without which I could not have completed this book. Matt had no reason to help out, yet his expertise and generosity made it possible for both Phillip McHood and me to complete our tasks.

My wife, Mary Claire, and our children, Nora and Andrew, provided the support that made this book possible. They have suffered for it, too. As I was scrambling to write in early mornings, on weekends, and in otherwise spare moments, my wife and children lost access to my time and attention to this book. I cannot give it back. But I can—and I do—hope that this work, as much as the work we lay women and men all do, can bear some fruit. Finally, the better world we want for our families and the reign of God itself depends on our working to bring them forth.

Steven P. Millies
Chicago, Illinois
October 24, 2017
Feast of St. Anthony Marie Claret
Bishop, Missionary, and Educator
amid political turmoil

Introduction

The earliest exit polling reports about the 2016 presidential election told a story that was at once completely unsurprising and, at the same time, head-scratchingly strange: Donald Trump had won the White House with a majority of American Catholic voters.

The picture that emerged later, as more detailed studies of the 2016 presidential vote became available, was more complicated. In April 2017, the Center for Applied Research in the Apostolate at Georgetown University used better data to determine that "Catholics voted for Clinton 48 percent & Trump 45 percent." A later study of the election—the most comprehensive one available, with over 64,000 respondents—more or less bears out this picture of the result.

Among Catholic Voters	
Donald Trump	49 percent
Hillary Rodham Clinton	46 percent

The difference is statistically quite small, and so this is a virtual tie between Clinton and Trump among Catholic voters in 2016.[1]

In one sense, perhaps it is not so surprising after all if Catholics preferred Donald Trump about as much as they preferred Hillary Rodham Clinton. Neither candidate reflected an appealing perspective on social or political questions for Catholics. The 2016 election offered Catholics a vexing choice. Then again, the nature of making political choices never has been such that any candidate for office should excite easy enthusiasm among voters who take Catholic faith seriously when making decisions on the ballot. George W. Bush was pro-life, but he launched an elective war that was condemned by Pope John Paul II. Barack Obama protected abortion rights, but he made healthcare more accessible for millions of vulnerable people. So while we may be tempted to say that Clinton and Trump offer us a special case in the 2016 election, neither one clearly appealing to Catholic voters, perhaps that does not make the 2016 election such a special case after all. No recent election—and few elections ever—have offered faithful Catholics an obviously suitable candidate. If we are tempted still to say that there was something different, unprecedented, about the 2016 presidential election, we need to look elsewhere for an explanation.

Of course, an explanation is not difficult to find. The difference was Donald J. Trump himself. Trump's victory represents an unprecedented development in American politics. Not only is he the first person to become president without any previous experience of public service, but Trump is also the first to be elected by the American people without a clear public policy roadmap. Ronald Reagan's campaign in 1980 released economic models that justified his hopes for a tax reform. Bill Clinton offered clear proposals to streamline government and cut the deficit. Perhaps most voters did not read the white papers filled with policy specifics that the campaigns released, but the policy specifics existed. Journalists at least read them and, even if those public policy papers were filtered for voters through the media, still specific policy proposals were part of the decisions voters made even if only indirectly. A mark of Donald Trump's political inexperience as much as his keen ear for our political moment, the Trump campaign was notoriously short on policy specifics. A wall would be built, and Mexico would pay for it. Little was offered to explain how. Obamacare would be repealed and replaced with something better that voters would "love," but never a word about what that was. A master showman for as long as he dominated New York City society and tabloid headlines, Trump and his campaign played to his strength. Attention-getting promises have one overriding purpose: to get attention. And, every modern campaign has done its share of attention getting. What was different in 2016 was that many voters did not look any further than the spectacular promises. The reality show Trump was hosting was enough for many voters—indeed, more voters than ever before were unbothered by the lack of details. It suited what their expectations from politics had become.

Then there was the matter of character and temperament. Trump claimed he could "stand in the middle of Fifth Avenue and shoot somebody and I wouldn't lose any voters." His voters almost literally have proved him right. John McCain was held captive as a prisoner of war by the North Vietnamese; he refused early release and endured years of abuse he might have escaped so that he could stay with his comrades. For Trump, McCain was not a hero, yet veterans preferred him by a two-to-one margin over Hillary Rodham Clinton. Trump launched a days-long Twitter outburst against Ghazala and Khizr Khan, parents of a fallen soldier, after they spoke at the Democratic National Convention. Military families continued to support Trump. Donald Trump was overheard on tape boasting about sexual assault. Evangelical Christians and many Catholics still supported the twice-divorced acknowledged adulterer. Simpler gaffes and less outrageous scandals were enough to threaten or derail entirely other presidential campaigns at earlier moments in our history—even quite recently. Nothing seems bad enough to turn away Trump's supporters. The sheer number of his scandals somehow has conspired to make Trump scandal-proof.

If we try to imagine why the lack of any serious specifics about policy or why such obvious deficiencies of character and temperament did not disqualify Trump from election among so many voters, finally perhaps we arrive at the most useful explanation for why 2016 seemed so different. A change has taken place among voters in American life. The politics of grievance, grudge, and revenge always have been with us. The problem was so present in the 1790s that George Washington cautioned against it in his Farewell Address.[2] No moment in American history has been untainted by arguments so heated that they became personally divisive and destructive. Yet, in the last few decades the problem has intensified. By 2016, that intensity altered the dynamics of our national politics so much that Donald Trump could be elected president of the United States. And even though they only preferred him about as much as Hillary Rodham Clinton, Catholics played an important part in the growing, destructive divisiveness of American political life that made Trump's nomination and election possible.

The story of the 2016 presidential election must be told through this perspective on what made it different. In turn, that is a story of how something has changed among the American people. Finally, because they have come to occupy such a prominent role in American life, numerically and as a social influence, the 2016 election is a story in no small part about Catholic voters. Over the last several decades of American life, it has become common to speak of a culture war that is under way. That culture war is marked by the outlines of an argument over moral questions in American social and political life, and Catholics have been a part of that argument for as long as it has been under way. Those moral issues, especially abortion, became a preoccupation of Catholic political attention. But this story is not only that simple. In part, the determination among Catholics to press cultural arguments has owed to a particular, peculiar history shared by American Catholics who descend from the Catholic immigrants who came to the United States in the late nineteenth and early twentieth centuries. Those circumstances in which Catholicism has been expressed in the United States throughout the twentieth century have played an important role in shaping the Catholic engagement with American politics as we know it today.

For those reasons, this book is not so much a political analysis or an examination of American politics in the light of Catholic social teaching. It is both of those things in places, as much as this book also addresses some specialized topics in law and sociology. But in fact this book is a history, and its purpose is to tell a story that is complex. We might easily take our beginning here from the American founding or from the nineteenth-century entry of Catholic immigrants into the United States. Chapter 1 will set our stage with a survey of Catholicism in the early United States because the questions raised by the election of 2016 are so big and so broad that we cannot overlook the past. We take our more proper and specific beginning from the US Supreme Court's *Roe v. Wade* decision in 1973, which is where chapter 2 begins, as we will trace the changes in how Catholics engage US politics from that point as an important moment that set the culture war into motion. *Roe* arrived at the moment when Catholics in the United States had, by many measures, reached their peak cultural influence. The Supreme Court's decision unsettled American Catholics' sense of where they fit into American life and, amid rising divisions in American life that emerged through the Cold War and from the tumult of the 1960's, *Roe* marked the beginning of a long road of increasing polarization toward the 2016 election. Chapter 3 takes up that story in the decade after *Roe* amid the first skirmishes between Catholic politicians and Catholic bishops over the role of Catholic faith in public life. Chapter 4 takes up a period of time from the 1990s to the early 2000s when the polarization we now recognize became entrenched both in American politics and in the church, with clear lines drawn between a culture of life and a culture of death and little discernible space between them where a more moderate or nuanced position could be found. In chapter 5 we will see some of the ways that the divisions over culture reached their peak in the years since the presidential election of 2004, and in chapter 6 we examine some of the perverse consequences of that polarization, especially after the economic crisis of 2008, in the light of Christianity's always-fraught relationship with the world.

All along the way, the US Catholic bishops will remain important figures in the story of the road that leads from *Roe* to the election of Donald Trump. Like the American Catholics they lead, there is not much evidence that the bishops are enthusiastic or happy about the place in which we all find ourselves. Like other Catholics, some are so concerned about issues like abortion that they have made a series of political calculations for many years, all of which have aimed at something good but that now have culminated in the election of Donald Trump. Many are uncomfortable with where a near-single-issue focus has led us. This was a road on which Catholics embarked with the best of intentions. The US Catholic bishops and the people they lead wanted to promote the dignity of human life, and they have sought to advance a consistent ethic of human life all along.[3] But this road American Catholics have walked since *Roe* is not the only way to advance the cause of life. There always are alternatives. To reconsider our path and find another requires us first to retrace our steps and learn how we have gotten to where we are.

Chapter 1

Catholic and American

It is an irony of history that the first Mass in what is now the continental United States was celebrated in 1509 by Spanish explorers in the party of Juan Ponce de León. While the United States ultimately would declare their independence from an English king and the influence of English-speaking Irish immigrants would shape Catholicism in the US, the story of Catholicism in the US begins with Spain.

The irony is more than an amusing curiosity. It raises issues central to the story of American Catholicism. It reminds us that every Catholic on these shores is a newcomer, and the story of American Catholicism is a story of immigrants even from the beginning. In a way, it also underscores the strange position of Catholics as outsiders throughout most of American history. As Protestantism came to the Massachusetts Bay and Jamestown settlements some time later, dominating respectable American culture for centuries that followed, Catholics long would labor to establish their bona fides as Americans, striving to find their place in an establishment disposed to regard them as interloping newcomers with their strange papist beliefs. The irony is all the greater since it is clear that the Spanish brought Catholicism to the American shores decades earlier than Protestantism arrived.

That striving is important to the story of American Catholicism. Catholics have been big city mayors and governors, cabinet officers and members of Congress, justices of the Supreme Court, vice president, and president. Yet somehow, the challenge of being American always plagues Catholics. Seventy million Catholics fill every level of American society, Catholics make up the largest religious denomination in the United States (the most-churched developed nation in the world), yet the question of integrating into American life never goes away. A barrier seems to separate Catholicism and Americanism, and there have been many attempts to explain it. Cardinal Francis George of Chicago observed that Americans are inevitably "culturally Calvinist," owing perhaps to America's pilgrim origins at Plymouth Rock, and no matter how far they have come, how much more diverse the United States has become, that includes Catholics. Perhaps, like Judaism, Hinduism, Islam, and many other ancient faith traditions, Catholicism is too big to integrate fully into American history and culture.

In a peculiar way, that has been a strength of American Catholicism. European Catholics have spent the centuries since the Reformation on the defensive, in retreat. The European forebears of America's immigrant Catholics did not need to grapple with the fretful compromises of worldliness like the followers of such Reformers as Luther, Calvin, or Henry VIII did. Outsider status may have helped American Catholics, with no historically inspired expectations of political hegemony, to imitate better the example of the early church. As St. Paul admonished the Christians of Rome not to conform themselves to the world and St. Augustine reminded Christians they only are pilgrims on a sojourn in the world, American Catholics have been a people apart.[1] Their relative isolation nurtured something unique. American Catholicism is different from Catholicism in other parts of the world, and it has given gifts to the church that, perhaps, could not have come from another people.[2]

It is this struggle between American Catholics and their national home both to preserve and to overcome that defined the experience of Catholics in the United States both in and out of politics throughout most of American history. Yet, naturally, politics is an important sphere of life in which values are contested and decisions have far-reaching social and moral consequences. Especially as American Catholics emerged from the Catholic ghetto in the 1960s and entered the American mainstream during the 1970s, the question of distinctiveness began to present leaders within the Catholic Church with a crisis. In early days, perhaps the crisis was more subtle—felt or sensed, rather than known. Still, the fact was that it was growing easier for American Catholics to distinguish their commitments of faith from their public acts as citizens or as elected officials. It is important to say that neither the Democratic Party nor the Republican Party ever offered Catholics a comfortable home in terms of issue positions. Yet, the group behavior of Catholics for a long time reflected a struggle all their own to accommodate their beliefs to their political alternatives among candidates and parties. Once Catholic political behavior became indistinguishable from that of non-Catholics, an obvious conclusion to draw was that Catholics were not struggling in quite the same way anymore. Being Americans had won out over being Catholics for some number of Catholics, or at least it might have seemed that way to American bishops as the 1970s began.

To approach the choices made by American bishops since the 1970s as they have taught Catholics about social or political questions requires that we should understand some of that background. Before we can understand why the decades since *Roe v. Wade* have unfolded in the way that they have among American Catholics, we need to see clearly how the landscape had changed between American Catholics and non-Catholics, between Catholic bishops and the people in the pews, across a long arc of American history.

A Catholic Ghetto

Catholics briefly had a home in the United States when George Calvert, the 1st Baron Baltimore (1579–1632), received the charter for the Maryland colony from King Charles I in the years leading up to the violent outbreak of the English Civil War. England would be overcome by religious conflict throughout the next four decades as Anglican and Calvinist Protestants vied for hegemony. Those bloody years eventually would give birth to a tradition of religious toleration, but not right away and not really for everyone. The author of religious toleration in the English-speaking world, John Locke, extended toleration widely but not to Catholics.[3] Even on the other side of the Atlantic, Calvert's colony for refugee English Catholics would not be safe for long. By 1644, Puritans who had settled in Providence (later renamed Annapolis) began to exert territorial pressure as the Maryland colony became a theatre of the English Civil War. When the Civil War ended in 1688 with the accession of William of Orange (the Glorious Revolution), Catholics began to suffer legal proscriptions in what had been founded as a safe haven for them. Catholic worship was forbidden and, in 1704, the Puritan government passed an "Act to Prevent the Growth of Popery."

By the late eighteenth century, as the United States declared independence in 1776 and began its government under the Constitution in 1789, the situation for Catholics was little easier. Barely 1 percent of the whole United States worshipped as Catholics, most of them concentrated in Maryland (where, perhaps, they amounted to 10 percent of the population). At the time of Independence, Maryland's Charles Carroll (1737–1832) became the only Catholic to sign the Declaration. Yet even as Carroll affixed his name to Jefferson's parchment, the Mass still had to be celebrated privately and Catholics were taxed onerously at double the rate for other Marylanders.[4] Prejudice against Catholics in Revolutionary America was so widespread, the eminent historian of Catholicism in America, John Tracy Ellis, recorded that there were outbursts of anti-Catholicism even in Washington's Continental Army.[5] Catholics found a comparatively peaceful home elsewhere in Pennsylvania, where the Quaker William Penn had founded his colony on principles of toleration, and in the mid-1700s the Jesuits began sending missionaries, first to Philadelphia. The Catholic community nurtured at Philadelphia by the missionary Jesuits would mark a turning point in American Catholic life.

The Jesuits had provided a lifeline to persecuted Catholics in nearby colonies, giving twelve priests to the sixteen thousand Catholics of nearby Maryland and operating a number of schools there. At one of those schools in Cecil County, a young cousin of Charles Carroll fell under the influence of the Jesuits. He would go on to be educated at the Jesuit college in St. Omer (Belgium) before joining the Society of Jesus himself. John Carroll, SJ (1735–1815) would become not only the first bishop of Baltimore, but the first American bishop in 1789. Vigorous Catholic support for the War for Independence had created a friendlier climate for Catholics in the new United States, and by the time of the Constitutional Convention in 1787 many states already had loosened the laws persecuting Catholics. Up to this time, Catholics had feared that the appointment of a bishop to America by the pope would stir a backlash. The appointment of the first Anglican bishop of the United States in 1783 began to raise Catholic hopes that they might be permitted a bishop of their own, and Carroll, as the superior of all of the missions in the US, appealed for a bishop to Rome. An eye-catching detail in Carroll's request may surprise contemporary readers, however. Aware of American suspicions about the influence of the pope, Carroll thought it wiser for the priests of the United States to elect their first bishop from among their own number. Sensitive to the circumstances, Pope Pius VI agreed. John Carroll was elected to be the first Bishop of Baltimore by the priests of the United States, carrying twenty-four of twenty-six votes.[6]

Catholicism would grow slowly at first in the United States during the next century. It is difficult to describe the numbers meaningfully in the early part of the nineteenth century. Census data would not make any effort to track religious affiliation until 1850, and then it relied on reporting from churches. As a result, estimates tended to be "incredibly inflated."[7] We cannot be precise about the numbers, but in a greater sense the statistical picture does not really require us to be precise. The scale of the late-nineteenth-century growth of Catholicism in the United States, owing to the waves of Catholic immigrants who entered the US after the Civil War as industrialization got under way and created an unquenchable demand for labor, brought rapid and geometric growth. By 1870, the percentage of Catholics in the United States had doubled the number before the Civil War.[8] By the dawn of the twentieth century Catholics were 17 percent of the population, nearly quadrupling in fifty years, and that percentage would still increase throughout the 1900s.[9]

But numerical progress was not the same as social progress. Especially as Catholicism came to be identified with the strange new immigrant cultures entering the United States from Ireland, Italy, Bohemia, and elsewhere, prejudice against Catholics grew worse for a long while as their numbers grew larger. Nativism took hold early in the nineteenth century, when "native"-born Americans struck out against the immigrant Catholics whom they regarded as foreign strangers. An Ursuline convent in Massachusetts was burned in 1834. Ugly tracts were published against Catholics.[10] In 1844, riots in Philadelphia saw two Catholic churches burned along with the homes of many Irish immigrants. By the 1850s, the Know-Nothing movement took hold. Several anti-Catholic secret societies (for example, the United Sons of America in Pennsylvania, or the Order of United Americans in New York) formed whose members, when questioned, replied that they "know nothing," a term that stuck as a label. The Know-Nothings claimed the name and formed a political party with brief success. A short while later, in the immediate aftermath of the Civil War, the so-called Christian Knights of the Ku Klux Klan emerged to terrorize not only freed slaves, but also immigrants, Jews, and Catholics. The Klan was founded in the South, though it was active as far north as Michigan and Pennsylvania in the later decades of the nineteenth century.

It may, for these reasons, seem understandable that American Catholics did not spend the 1800s emerging from the shadows so much as scrambling deeper into them. Catholic communities around the United States built for themselves a parallel social, economic, medical, and educational world that was unknown anywhere else in Catholic experience. Catholic schools offer the best example. John T. McGreevy opens his book *Catholicism and American Freedom: A History* by recounting a Boston episode both extraordinary and typical ("The Eliot School Rebellion" in 1859, as it was known) wherein the hands of a ten-year-old Catholic boy, Thomas Whall, were struck by a school official with a cane "for half an hour" because he would not recite the King James Bible translation of the Ten Commandments, as the law required in a public school.[11] A conflict opened between Catholics and Protestants in Boston that saw hundreds of Catholic students discharged from public schools, transfixed the community, and was preached about from practically every pulpit in Boston. Little surprise that the beginning of the twentieth century saw seventy-six parish schools established across the Archdiocese of Boston, which became one of the largest Catholic school systems in the United States. The pattern, of course, would be replicated elsewhere, and not only in schools. Catholics in the United States spent much of the late nineteenth century constructing their own separate world, one in which their children and their sick would be cared for away from the harsh conditions of Gilded Age capitalism and the unwelcoming attitudes of their fellow citizens.

Yet, it should be remembered that turning inward by constructing a Catholic ghetto was not just a response to unwelcoming conditions faced by so many ethnic groups who brought their Catholic faith to the United States in the late 1800s. In fact, it was an affirmation of an already-ingrained instinct among American Catholics. While we might name many leaders of American Catholicism in the nineteenth century, it would be good at this point to remember two for how they help us understand the unusual and distinct flavor of American Catholicism.

The first is Orestes Brownson (1803–1876). Brownson was a convert, received into the Catholic Church when he was forty-one years old. By profession, Brownson was a teacher before he was ordained as a Universalist minister in 1826. He fell out with the Universalists after he became interested in social reforms, and he moved to Unitarianism because they would tolerate his desire to work among, with, and for laborers to seek economic and social reforms. To that end, he began publishing a magazine that brought him wide renown. His literary interests gradually drew him into the orbit of Catholic thinkers, leading to his conversion in 1844. Brownson, we might say, was the first widely known convert to Catholicism in the United States, and that gave him an outsider's perspective on how his fellow Catholics approached being Americans. Brownson found it perplexing that so many in the Catholic world sought "to keep Catholics a foreign colony in the United States."[12] Even in those long-ago days, the impulse to maintain a Catholic identity as "a people apart" was strong. Brownson's most important book, *The American Republic* (1866), went further to argue that it is "the special mission of the United States . . . to continue and complete in the political order the Graeco-Roman civilization" that was continued in the Catholic Church through the Middle Ages and gives to the US its foundation in "real catholic, not sectarian principles" that permit the church to "exert her free spirit, and teach and govern men by the Divine law."[13] Catholicism and American political life, far from being different, in fact reinforced and needed each other. Brownson lies buried today in the Basilica of the Sacred Heart at the University of Notre Dame.

As much as Brownson believed in a Catholic Church in the United States "no longer . . . encumbered with the obsolete forms of the Middle Ages," one open to "what is true and just . . . [in] Liberalism and Socialism," Father Isaac Hecker (1819–88) also strained against the fearful tendencies of the Catholic ghetto.[14] Hecker founded the Paulist Fathers, the first religious community of men to originate in the United States. Although born in New York, Hecker was something of a missionary to American Catholics. He had a boundless confidence not just in Catholicism, but specifically in the American church. In 1870, Hecker wrote that "Europe may find not only her political regeneration in the civilization on the other side of the Atlantic, but also the renewal of Catholicity."[15] Hecker was unabashed to see the future of Catholicism in the United States, and he was bold to call American Catholics out of their ghetto.

Looking back from the perspective of today, it is difficult not to hear something prophetic in Brownson's and Hecker's confidence. Their determination to bridge the distance between Catholic faith and American principles seems to have anticipated the American contribution to debates about religious liberty in the twentieth century and the way that

Catholics leaped into the mainstream of American life. At the same time, among Catholics of the 1800s in America or elsewhere, Brownson and Hecker were unusual. The path to acceptance would be bumpy and it would plunge the church in the United States into controversy. It also sketched out the shape for how American bishops would lead their people.

A Flock of Shepherds

Jesuit Father Thomas J. Reese agreed with the judgment of historians that the church in the United States is unusual in global Catholicism at least in one way, its bishops have worked closely together since the time of Bishop John Carroll.[16] The apostles called by Jesus in the early church gathered around one table at the Last Supper and made decisions together in the Acts of the Apostles. By the Middle Ages, a bishop of Rome had become the "first among equals" who made decisions for the whole church while bishops, who had acquired lands and temporal power, took on more the character of individual princes who rarely interacted than that of the Apostles who shared all things "in common" (Acts 2:44).

The isolation of medieval bishops was as much an accident of history as was the close collaboration of American bishops that emerged from a unique set of circumstances in the United States. Almost from the beginning, the bishops of the United States were close collaborators mostly because they each had vast responsibilities in new dioceses that reached over state boundaries at a time before rapid forms of transportation or easy communication, and because their problems in that situation were so similar. Apart from exchanges of letters, in the years between "1783–1884, the entire American Church met in three general chapters of the clergy, a synod, a bishops' meeting, seven provincial councils that were also national councils, and three plenary councils."[17] That was an extraordinary amount of contact among Catholic priests and bishops in those years that made the church in the United States something unusual, and something that would exert an influence on global Catholicism. But perhaps it also is worth describing what those meetings were.

A general chapter of the clergy referred to a meeting of priests. A chapter meeting might invite every priest, but more typically priests in individual regions would choose representatives who would attend the chapter on their behalf. A synod is a "conference of the bishops of a nation" that discusses "religious and other matters," and whose decisions must be approved by the Holy See. A synod also might be called a national council. A provincial council is a meeting of the bishops in a province. Each archbishop governs his own archdiocese, but his archdiocese is the center of an ecclesiastical province that includes other, usually smaller dioceses. (For example, today the Archdiocese of Baltimore is the center of a province that includes the Dioceses of Arlington, Richmond, Wheeling-Charleston, and Wilmington.) A provincial council, therefore, would be a meeting of the bishops in a province. A plenary council calls together the bishops of a nation in the way a synod does, but it must be called by the Holy See and a representative from Rome presides over a plenary council.[18]

While all of the meetings among American bishops were important, perhaps none was more important than the three plenary councils that met in Baltimore during the nineteenth century. The First Plenary Council of Baltimore (1852) produced twenty-five decrees that included the first provision for widespread seminary education in the United States and issued requirements for the administrative organization of dioceses that still are in place today. The Second Plenary Council of Baltimore (1866) dealt with a range of technical issues—matters of canon law—and also encouraged American Catholics in the veneration of Mary and the saints. That Second Plenary Council may be more important to recall as the first gathering of several bishops who would leave a deep mark on the church in the United States, including Father James Gibbons, who made his first acquaintance with the American bishops at that meeting. Later, as Archbishop James Gibbons, he would oversee the Third Plenary Council of Baltimore (1884) as the apostolic delegate, the pope's representative. Eventually, Gibbons would become a cardinal and the most important voice in American Catholicism. That Third Plenary Council was a significant event in the history of American Catholicism, not only because it founded a national Catholic university, encouraged the creation of parish schools, and consecrated the United States to the Immaculate Conception, but also because it occurred on the threshold of a uniquely American controversy in the church.

The Americanist Crisis—what one leading historian of American Catholicism called *The Great Crisis in American Catholic History*—began from an almost trivially small event. In 1891, a French theologian wrote an introduction to a French-language biography of Isaac Hecker, one that suggested that Hecker's American-influenced theological ideas denied the authority of the church. The essay sparked quick and furious controversy not just in Rome but throughout the world, mostly because the controversy was not about Hecker at all. Abbé Felix Klein, the author of that essay, hijacked Hecker's ideas to continue an old argument about the role of the church in the Catholic nations of Europe, particularly France. It was a touchy subject in the nineteenth century, so soon after the French Revolution had ransacked sanctuaries and seized church lands as part of its effort to banish religion from public life. Hecker's ideas, particularly his convictions about religious freedom, seemed to cast

Americans on the side of European secularists (modernists) in Klein's telling of them. Before long, Hecker's defenders were labeled Americanists, and Americanism was a great crisis in the church that questioned seriously for the first time whether the church could accept an American-style separation of church and state.

The Americanist controversy divided even American bishops. Some bishops defended the American separation of church and state. They included Archbishop John Ireland (1838–1918) of St. Paul, Bishop John Keane (1839–1918), rector of The Catholic University of America, Bishop Denis O'Connell of Richmond (1849–1927), Bishop John Lancaster Spalding of Peoria (1840–1916), and Cardinal James Gibbons (1834–1921), the archbishop of Baltimore. Others who were suspicious of the new constitutional arrangements in America included Archbishop Michael Corrigan of New York (1839–1902), Bishop William McCloskey (1823–1909) of Louisville, Bishop Bernard McQuaid (1823–1909) of Rochester, New York, and Archbishop Patrick Ryan (1831–1911) of Philadelphia. The Americanist controversy drove to the heart of the questions facing Catholics in the United States. Could Catholics accept a system of government that did not recognize the authority of the church? Was the American-style separation of church and state beneficial for Catholics, somehow different from European ideas about secularism? At the same time, Americanism also raised questions for Roman authorities. For centuries in Europe, the church always had been able to assume it would occupy a privileged place in social and political life. The decades since 1789 had plunged that idea into doubt, and the church was unsettled by the change. Could this new American arrangement suggest a new way for the Catholic Church to think about its place among the nations of the world?

At first the church chose caution. Americans like O'Connell, Ireland, and Gibbons who favored the American-style separation of church and state found themselves out in the cold when Pope Leo XIII published his apostolic letter *Testem Benevolentiae* (1899). Pope Leo called attention to "certain things which are to be avoided and corrected," among which he included the idea that there could be "a church in America that is different from that which is in the rest of the world," and that "the passion for saying and reviling everything, the habit of thinking and of expressing everything in print . . . [has] cast such a deep shadow on men's minds" that the authority of the church is more needed than ever before. *Testem Benevolentiae* offers a rather stunning rebuke against the American political system, its protections of speech and press, and its protections against a religious power to censor. Subsequent decades would see the church develop its thinking about civil liberties dramatically and in a different direction. Yet, as the twentieth century dawned, Pope Leo's letter nurtured suspicion of prominent American bishops in Rome as much as it would hang over US–Vatican relations until the Reagan administration, when the United States would open full diplomatic relations with the Holy See for the first time in US history.

John Tracy Ellis presents *Testem Benevolentiae* in a more moderate light, noting that "each side maintained it had been vindicated," with one side acclaiming the condemnation of heresy while the other, like Gibbons, cheerfully observed that the celebration of dangerous errors Pope Leo condemned had "nothing in common with the views, aspirations, doctrine and conduct of Americans." In fact, Ellis concluded, "From the perspective of over a half century . . . [not] a single American Catholic was known to have left the Church because he refused to give up the errors which the pope had reproved."[19] Historical opinion generally agrees today that Pope Leo misjudged what Americans were saying amid his own anxieties about conditions in Europe, and the whole Americanist episode amounted to what one historian has called a "phantom heresy," a misunderstanding.[20] It did not seem that way in 1899 when, for example, Archbishop John Ireland spent a "gloomy spring in Italy" following publication of *Testem*, haunted by "insinuations from [Vatican] officials" and watching the resolve of fellow American bishops like Keane and O'Connell waver.[21] Those seemed like dark days. Still, from where we are today, what was important was that the episode had brought American bishops together to defend themselves in a way that would galvanize a sense of community among them throughout the twentieth century. After the Third Plenary Council, the bishops had agreed to hold a meeting each year.[22] These regular meetings soon would become formalized.

Events that would diminish the effects of *Testem* intervened only two decades later with the American entry into World War I. The Wilson administration and their congressional supporters were eager that Catholics should support the war, and they appealed to the bishops in the hope that they would win support from ordinary Catholics. In response, Paulist Father John Burke formed the National Catholic War Council in 1917 to coordinate the bishops' efforts to aid the war effort with the federal government. Supported by Cardinal Gibbons and other key members of the American hierarchy, Burke's success at developing a bishops' national response to an important issue impressed everyone. Made bold by success, Burke sought permission from the bishops to create a permanent organization. In particular, Burke zeroed in on a point that would shape the future of Catholicism in the United States. Burke realized that a national organization for bishops headquartered in Washington could help the bishops become an effective group of lobbyists. "Without a voice in Washington," Burke worried, the Protestant churches already working as a Federal Council of Churches would go unchallenged as "the ruling power in all legislation that affected religious and moral interests," leaving "the field clear to our opponents and the opponents of our Church."[23]

The National Catholic Welfare Council (NCWC) was born in 1919, providing a new purpose for annual bishops' meetings after the war's end, and a permanent staff was hired to oversee the NCWC's work on a full-time basis. In short order, Catholic Relief Services and the Catholic Health Association would begin to take their earliest shapes as the bishops directed the charitable good works they had begun during World War I domestically toward the needs of Americans at home. The NCWC would not have an entirely easy time. There was no other organization of bishops like it in any other nation in the world. The NCWC was so exotic that Pope Pius XI made a brief and unsuccessful effort to suppress it in 1922, shortly after his election. The Holy See relented to American appeals that the NCWC was necessary to press Catholic interests in the United States, although Pope Pius did manage to compel a name change: the National Catholic Welfare *Council* became the National Catholic Welfare *Conference*, its third name in five years. Even so, the conference would stabilize and grow during the next forty years.

The most significant changes to the national bishops' conference came in the years immediately following the Second Vatican Council, when the conference took its definitive and contemporary shape. The documents of Vatican II clarified the status of national bishops' conferences. It was in *Lumen Gentium*, the Dogmatic Constitution on the Church, where the relationship was described between a bishop's authority in his own diocese, in collaboration with other bishops regionally or nationally (such as in conferences), and globally as the whole college of bishops in union with the pope. In the Decree on the Pastoral Office of Bishops in the Church (*Christus Dominus*), the Council fathers observed:

> It is often impossible, nowadays especially, for bishops to exercise their office suitably and fruitfully unless they establish closer understanding and cooperation with other bishops. Since episcopal conferences—many such have already been established in different countries—have produced outstanding examples of a more fruitful apostolate, this sacred Synod judges that would be in the highest degree helpful if in all parts of the world the bishops of each country or region would meet regularly. (37)[24]

Despite the reservations of Pope Pius XI and the suspicions that swirled during and after the Americanist controversy, and despite (or perhaps because of) the newness and unusualness of the Catholic Church in the United States, Americans led the way into the establishment of national bishops' conferences that were found to be so useful as now to be institutionalized permanently by the Council.

The NCWC was renamed again in 1966, becoming the National Conference of Catholic Bishops (NCCB), and over the next five years the NCCB set about the difficult task of writing statutes by which to be governed and of reorganizing its staff. While another name change still lay ahead—today, the organization is known as the United States Conference of Catholic Bishops (USCCB)—the conference had reached its mature shape since the final adoption of those revised statutes in 1972 under the leadership of the conference's general secretary, Bishop Joseph Bernardin.[25] Already in the years between the Second Vatican Council and the final adoption of those statutes in 1972, the conference had been engaged in lobbying efforts, issuing statements against states that relaxed their legal restrictions on abortion. The bishops' conference became a well-organized, carefully structured organization, capable of applying political pressure, just as the United States Supreme Court neared its decision in the 1973 *Roe v. Wade* case. The Catholic voice would be heard by officials in Washington, and Catholic women and men who vote would hear a consistent message about the issues of the day in the pews of their local parishes. The bishops' conference had become an effective way to leverage the roles played by bishops together in the national conference and alone, singly in their home dioceses.

The conference was not only a lobbying organization, of course. The national conference still supported the efforts of Catholic schools, Catholic hospitals, and Catholic charity as it had since the first organization of the conference in 1922. In fact, since the Third Plenary Council brought the bishops together to promote the building of parish schools, there had been increasing coordination of national efforts to see to the needs of Catholics from the cradle to the grave (literally, with the development of Catholic cemeteries). Those institutions had become the ramparts of a Catholic subculture in the United States under the administration of the NCWC between 1922 and 1966, a response to the suspicion and rejection that had greeted Catholics in American life since the days of Charles Carroll's Maryland colony. Those were the years John Tracy Ellis had described as characterized by a "pervading spirit of separatism" during which Catholics "suffered from the timidity that characterizes the effects of a ghetto they have themselves fostered."[26] Their bishops fostered it with them. Yet, as Catholics emerged from that ghetto in the 1960s and began to enter the mainstream of American life, the bishops' conference turned outward with them. Not only did institutions like Catholic schools and hospitals begin increasingly to serve non-Catholic populations, but the bishops' conference became more activist with regard to social and political questions, moral issues in American life. In other words, this emergence from the ghetto occurred just at the moment when *Roe* splashed abortion into the center of national political debate. The bishops' conference made the transition right alongside the emergence of the abortion issue, and just as it confronted ordinary Catholics. Those forces converged in 1973.

Catholic Identity

Russell Shaw is a Georgetown-educated journalist. He got his start working for the Archdiocese of Washington's (District of Columbia) newspaper, but went to work shortly thereafter for the NCWC in the early 1960s. When the conference became the NCCB/USCC in 1966, Shaw became the director of publications for the National Catholic Education Association before returning to work for the conference in 1969, where he remained for most of the next twenty years overseeing publications and media relations. Shaw was in charge of communicating the conference's message to the world during the earliest years when the national conference had taken its mature shape and had become an important actor in national political debates, and while American Catholics had become more acceptably mainstream than any Catholics before them in American history. Perhaps it should not surprise us that Shaw has written a book.

In *American Church: The Remarkable Rise, Meteoric Fall, and Uncertain Future of Catholicism in America*, Shaw deals with many of the topics covered here so far.[27] Indeed, in many ways, his purpose is not so different from the intentions of this book. Shaw accounts for where Catholics stand in American life and how they got there. He describes the early colonial experiences of Catholics and reviews the Americanist controversy and the role that bishops' meetings played throughout the history of American Catholicism. Shaw gives us another perspective as well, however. It may be his most important contribution to a conversation about American Catholics, even if it was an inadvertent contribution.

Shaw was born in 1935. He was raised inside the ramparts of a Catholic enclave and formed his earliest ideas about the world and the church from that perspective. His recollections of being like "most kids growing up American Catholic in the 1940s" are affectionate. They include memories of his own parish neighborhood in the Mount Pleasant section of Washington, where the Knights of Columbus erected a statue of Cardinal Gibbons in a public park, and where he experienced "the celebration of the Eucharist in its pre–Vatican II form."[28] More interesting for us than Shaw's recollections of his personal past are his descriptions of the changes that came in the 1960s and 1970s, changes he observed up close at the national conference.

Shaw laments the cultural and sexual revolutions of the 1960s, mostly for how they "bowled over" Catholics who "succumb[ed] to an aberrant zeitgeist."[29] He questions John F. Kennedy's pledge to voters in 1960 ("Whatever issue may come before me as president . . . I will make my decision . . . in accordance with what my conscience tells me is in the national interest, and without regard to outside religious pressures") as defining the national interest according to "the private judgment of the president without reference to moral principles from religious sources."[30] Perhaps most revealing of all is what Shaw described as a "blunder":

> At the American bishops' post–Vatican II meeting held in Washington, DC, in November 1966, the bishops, acting with little or no advance public notice, abolished the rule requiring Catholics to abstain from meat on Fridays. A small thing in itself, fish on Friday nevertheless had been a highly visible feature of Catholic religious identity for generations, helping to set Catholics apart from others and making a statement to the world: "We're Catholics, and we aren't like everyone else." Now abruptly abolishing Friday abstinence sent a very different message: Things the Church previously had emphasized could be discarded like a pair of worn-out shoes.[31]

Shaw appears to give great weight to the custom of Friday abstinence and sees danger in abandoning it. Like the disciplines of Lent, Friday abstinence certainly is a beneficial penitential practice. But it remains true that those practices are not the same as being Catholic. They are not *essential* to the faith. They are only customs grown up over long usage, still as susceptible to change as priestly celibacy or the distinctive clothing worn by members of religious communities and priests (the habit, the Roman collar, the cassock). Our faith is found in the Creed, the dogmas and doctrines of the church. For many Catholics in the United States like Shaw, the importance of these customs has become magnified not because they are essential to Catholic faith, but precisely for the reason that Shaw named so specifically. They say, "We're Catholics, and we aren't like everyone else."

It is a peculiar and distinctive feature of Catholicism in the United States, which developed in opposition to a prevailing Protestantism, to think in terms of identity like this, to define Catholic faith *against* other things rather than to conceive of it as *for* something. That judgment is not a novel one. Charles R. Morris described "The foundations of American Catholicism" and the attitudes of bishops like Gibbons and Ireland—"*in* America, vehemently *for* America, but never *of* America."[32] We find that sensibility also in the descriptions of Jay P. Dolan ("religious and ethnic conflict tended to harden the lines of the Catholic cultural ghetto . . . [shaping] Catholicism into a very ethnocentric and religiously exclusive community"), John T. McGreevy ("Catholics obviously lived *among* Americans, but were they *of* them?"), and Timothy B. Neary ("Roman Catholics . . . remained segregated in clearly defined ghettos").[33] As the twentieth century unfolded, open prejudice against Catholics continued to be acceptable in the most respectable circles. Paul Blanshard, an editor at *The Nation*, published a series of bestselling books in the 1950s and 1960s that described Catholics in terms that would be familiar today if they were used to describe Muslims:

> What would happen to American democracy if our alleged twenty-six million Catholics grew to be a majority in the population and followed the direction of their priests? . . . The democratic *form* of our leading institutions might not be altered very much. Probably the most striking effect of Catholic control would be apparent in the *spirit* of those institutions and the *use* to which they would be put. . . . There is no Catholic plan for America distinct from the Catholic plan for the world. . . . [T]he master plan is only one plan and the world-wide strategy is directed from Rome. In a Catholic world *every* national government would establish the Roman Catholic Church in a unique position of privilege, and support its teachers and priests out of public revenues.[34]

Blanshard laid out a series of constitutional amendments allegedly sought by Catholics that sound a lot like more contemporary claims about *Shari'a* law. Much like those inflated claims about Muslim plots today, the treatment of Catholics throughout American history—especially in the mid-century—had an effect. It both made Catholics determined to prove themselves as Americans and, simultaneously, cultivated a sense of being permanent outsiders.[35]

During the Cold War, working-class Catholics found an opportunity to prove their patriotism, and they seized it. Following the New Deal years and World War II, the elite institutions of the white Anglo-Saxon Protestant establishment increasingly came to be thought of as liberal. In the fever of the 1950s Red Scare, to be liberal was the next thing to socialism. Those were the days when Senator Daniel Patrick Moynihan (himself an Irish Catholic) observed that "Harvard men were to be checked; Fordham men would do the checking." Suddenly, Catholics were to be trusted to be good Americans *because* of their faith, not despite it. In 1960 Jesuit Father John Courtney Murray published his landmark book *We Hold These Truths: Catholic Reflections on the American Proposition*, in which he argued that the same principles of the natural law taught for centuries by the Catholic Church "furnished the basic materials for the American consensus": drawing from the same faith in a "truth that lies beyond politics," Catholicism and the US Constitution pose no serious conflict with one another.[36] John F. Kennedy overcame the long-standing suspicions and fears surrounding Catholics to become president of the United States, and it seemed that Catholics finally had arrived. In many ways they did. Yet, in another very important sense, nothing fundamentally changed at all.

Study after study for more than twenty years has confirmed the same result—there is no such thing as a "Catholic vote." Catholics do vote, but their voting behavior is not distinctively different from any other group of Americans. They vote for Republicans or Democrats in nearly the same proportions as other groups of Americans. That would appear to confirm how much Catholics have entered the mainstream and lost their distinctiveness. But something more subtle is at work. In the years following JFK's election, the Second Vatican Council, the Vietnam War, Watergate, and everything else that divided the United States so firmly into conservative and liberal camps, the polarization among Americans more widely imprinted itself on Catholics.[37] Like their fellow Americans, Catholics also are polarized and, now, the question of Catholic distinctiveness is a division within the Catholic community of the United States. It can be heard in Russell Shaw's laments about meatless Fridays and it can be seen in the differences among parishes that conform to the pre–Vatican II liturgical practices and those who embraced the reforms of the Council. Some Catholics cannot distinguish their longing for the lost distinctiveness of being Catholic from *being Catholic*. Perhaps nowhere does that political division cut more deeply into the Catholic community than on the so-called culture war issues such as abortion, marriage, euthanasia, and others. And, perhaps, no result is more tragic than the feedback loop that came next: as polarization became a part of American Catholic thinking, American Catholics retained and reinforced that polarization in American politics.

The dawn of the twenty-first century found two groups of American Catholics opposed to each other. Those groups took shape during the closing decades of the twentieth century. One group of Catholics had assimilated, entered the mainstream of American life comfortably, and found ways to sort through the conflicts between faith and worldliness that arise in daily life, especially in political life, much like their forebears Hecker, Brownson, Gibbons, and Ireland. These Catholics would say they only have located a harmony between being American and being Catholic that always was there. The other group of American Catholics has resisted assimilation and has identified certain markers of a Catholic identity—from meatless Fridays to an uncompromising and specific political and legal position on abortion—as essential and nonnegotiable characteristics of an American Catholic. Distinctiveness is their preoccupation, not harmony. Where others seek to build a bridge to American life, these American Catholics seek to confront and disrupt those things in American life that do not correspond closely to church teachings. Both groups are made up of people who are intensely patriotic, devoted to being good Americans. Both are committed to their Catholic faith, one group emphasizing demands of faith that distinguish Catholics from the American mainstream while the other emphasizes how a Catholic perspective interacts and harmonizes with mainstream, American life. The irony is that, gazing across the polarizing division over Catholic identity at one another as they are, these two groups of Catholics are both engaging in a characteristically American pattern of behavior. Their Left/Right polarization has every characteristic in common with what prevails in American politics, and it is recognizable that way even to a non-Catholic. In this worst way possible, both liberals and conservatives have joined the American mainstream; they have assimilated.

The conflict over the place of Catholics in the United States has become a conflict between Catholics. It is fought less over what it means to be an American than over what it means to be a Catholic, and it has taken on the characteristics of the American political polarization. That conflict still reflects the strivings of the immigrants in the American Catholic past, the struggle to bring the old world to the new world and to overcome the differences between them. As that conflict has transformed across decades of American history, the US bishops and their conference have grown and matured in their own approach to American life and the problem of Catholic identity.

This new phase of the conflict over how to be Catholic in the United States has not taken shape apart from the bishops. They are Americans, too, and their responses are conditioned by the same history and memories. We know that "culture has a historical character," and the American bishops belong to American Catholic history and culture as much as any of us.[38] In their ministry, bishops must take "a deeply balanced approach" that proclaims the Gospel authentically in ways that are suited to "the social and cultural conditions in which they live."[39] The challenges facing American bishops against the historical background of American Catholicism are daunting. Those challenges presented themselves in the early 1970s as the *Roe* decision was published. Those were the earliest moments of maturity for the new national conference, and they came in a cultural moment fraught with destabilizing changes. The Second Vatican Council had upended church life while dizzying social upheavals unfolded and, for good measure, the Vietnam War and the Watergate scandal were undermining American confidence in basic institutions. Catholics were among those Americans being buffeted by change and scandal, and it could not fail to influence and shape how American bishops replied to the new challenges facing them.

The history of striving and struggling to integrate into American life and to be heard had shaped Catholic life in the United States for a long time before *Roe*. That history would, in turn, shape the responses of the bishops, individually and as a group, in the decades that followed *Roe*. The influence can be seen reflected in the language of the conference's 2016 *Faithful Citizenship* statement in which the bishops describe a "dual heritage as both faithful Catholics and American citizens" and highlights its "distinctive call" that comes in a distinctly Catholic voice that proclaims how "the Catholic community brings important assets to political dialogue about our nation's future."[40] "[P]olitics in our country often can be a contest of powerful interests, partisan attacks, sound bites, and media hype," the bishops write, and that is far from the "responsible citizenship" and "participation in political life" cultivated by "the Catholic Tradition."[41] The bishops are not saying anything particularly surprising about American politics. The contrasts they are offering would describe politics in any place or time. They echo St. Augustine's laments about the late Roman Empire because politics and human nature are always the same. What is unusual is the emphasis on being different—not from what is worldly in any ordinary or general sense, but on Catholic distinctiveness from what is American. In fact, it is not a mere distinctiveness but a suggestion that Catholic faith may even be essential to a better sort of citizenship. As Harvard men were to be checked, Catholics with well-formed consciences have a deeper insight than their non-Catholic fellow Americans.

A stew of ingredients had simmered together in the kettle for a long time when abortion bubbled to the surface in 1973. Abortion emerged to be the central issue in the encounter between American Catholics and their country because it raises essential questions in moral theology and constitutional law, but also because it arrived at a moment in American Catholic history when the bishops were equipped and felt so emboldened as to address it directly. Like a crack in a piece of ice or a window, abortion sits at the central point of impact but its fracture lines spread out away from abortion to touch the other culture war issues of euthanasia, marriage, religious liberty, the death penalty, war, and peace. Yet, the emphasis in each political cycle's argument since *Roe* has never strayed from abortion. On the question of abortion, Catholics have differed with one another about the right way to be Catholic in ways that mirror the polarization outside the church even as the argument over abortion also is tinged with the same old Catholic struggle to integrate with American life.

From the beginning of the national debate about abortion in 1973, the abortion question has been about more than just the moral and legal status of unborn children. As expansive as that issue is in its reach across the political debate, it has had an inverse tendency to reduce and simplify political conversations down to one issue. Voting only on the issue of abortion has been under discussion at least since the second presidential election cycle after *Roe*, in 1980.[42]

If perhaps half of American Catholics embarked on the 2016 election feeling moved more by the promise of a pro-life justice on the US Supreme Court than by any other consideration, they were responding to something under way since the *Roe* decision but also from long before *Roe*. So were their bishops. To understand that better demands an even deeper examination of the history of being Catholic and American since *Roe*.

Chapter 2

Personal and Political

The Catholic archbishop of Cincinnati was an unlikely prospect to become a leading voice in a national political debate, but Joseph Bernardin was not a normal bishop. As 1973 began Bernardin had been close to national issues for six years, throughout his short time as a bishop. Brought to the national conference in Washington, DC, as its general secretary in 1968, Bernardin had been charged with adapting the conference and its 1922 governing documents to the new mandates of the Second Vatican Council. That made Bernardin one of the most visible Catholic bishops in the United States. Before he came to Washington, Bernardin had signed one of the first pastoral letters against the Vietnam War and he had marched in the funeral of Martin Luther King Jr. while he was a bishop in Atlanta. Bernardin knew how to handle controversy. Yet even he was unprepared for what was coming.

It was a sign of Bernardin's rising prominence and the increasing political importance of American Catholics that Richard Nixon asked Bernardin to speak at an inaugural prayer service on January 21, 1973. The US Supreme Court announced its decision in *Roe v. Wade* the next day. Throughout his career, Bernardin was known for his careful and measured public remarks. Bernardin chose every word carefully. Yet, Bernardin's public statement following the *Roe* decision was quite stark:

> The Supreme Court's decision yesterday on abortion is a genuine tragedy for this country. The arguments used for the position taken, which severely limits a state in restricting the evil of abortion, completely overlook a God-given right which cannot be violated by any human authority: the right to life of the unborn fetus. . . . In taking this position, we are not attempting to impose a "sectarian" belief on the rest of the community. We are dealing here with a moral value—the right to life—which transcends denominational lines. . . . No human agency has the right to change the basically evil character of an action. This decision, then, in no way affects the moral teaching that abortion is an evil. . . . Our prophetic voice must continue, now with greater urgency, to sensitize the consciences of people to the evil of unrestricted abortion.[1]

There was no room for subtlety or nuance in a statement like that. The word *evil* appeared four times. There is no mistaking Bernardin's meaning, or his own apparent, personal shock at the *Roe* outcome.

The *Roe* decision did not, in fact, completely overlook the interests of the unborn fetus. This is one of the more common misunderstandings of the Court's decision. Prior to *Roe*, abortion was regulated separately by each individual state. Some states made abortion a criminal act for which a physician could be punished. At the time of the *Roe* decision, thirty-seven states still had tight restrictions on abortion, though that number had been shrinking. *Roe* took abortion out of the states' hands. The Court found that the US Constitution's protections for a physician's medical judgments and a woman's personal rights were greater than the states' power to restrict abortion. Further, the Court recognized that a pregnancy could be divided into thirds, three trimesters. In the first trimester, states were not permitted to restrict abortion, but in the second and third trimesters the states increasingly were permitted to protect the interests of the unborn fetus.[2] Thus, as a pregnancy progresses, the protection of the woman's and the physician's rights scale down while the rights of the unborn child scale up. *Roe* removed restrictions on abortion during the first third of a pregnancy, but left them largely intact for the remainder of a pregnancy, balancing the rights of an unborn child with those of a pregnant woman or her physician.

The legal and constitutional issues at work in *Roe* are more subtle than our contemporary political debate generally permits them to seem. And short of a constitutional amendment or a Supreme Court decision that not only reverses *Roe* but finds some protection for unborn children in the Constitution (which today protects by name the rights of "All persons *born* or naturalized in the United States" [emphasis added]), no action of the US Supreme Court can end legal abortions definitively in the United States. State governments still will be able to permit abortion, and citizens still can travel freely between states to procure abortions if they wish to. The preoccupation with *Roe* in our politics among Catholics has come to dominate our conversations not because there is some clear legal and political way forward to protect human life but, rather, because there is no clear legal and political solution. No matter how challenging abortion is in that way, it remains the case that abortion sits in a messy, uncertain position between the law and politics on one side, and our most essential moral and religious concerns on the other side. American Catholics, descended from immigrants who were rejected for so long and who faced so much prejudice, embarked on the 1970s with the confidence of those who had "made it." The Second Vatican Council had brought the church together with the modern world, and Catholic intellectuals like John Courtney Murray had built convincing arguments that the distance between being Catholic and being American was not really so great after all. The *Roe* decision brought the confidence of those American Catholics—and their bishops—to a sharp, sudden halt.

Still, the newfound confidence of Catholics in American life did shape the ensuing debate over *Roe*. Armed with a new sense that they did have a place in the American public square, Catholic bishops, at first reluctantly and later with greater determination, embarked on a path to change the laws of the United States by means of public persuasion. They raised awareness among voters, sought to influence legislators and other officials, and, in short, they took on many of the characteristics of lobbyists and interest groups. That approach quickly went beyond abortion and encompassed other moral issues as well as the practical needs of Catholic institutions such as schools and hospitals. There is, in fact, nothing wrong with Catholics or Catholic bishops expressing their ideas and needs through the institutions of a free system of government.

Time would tell whether that was the most prudent way for Catholics to seek what they want.

The Right to Life

Somewhat improbably from our perspective today, the national political debate over abortion was slow to get under way. As incredible as it is to imagine, abortion did not even come up in a press conference President Richard Nixon held eight days after the *Roe* decision. The morning after that press conference, Nixon spoke at the National Prayer Breakfast, where, once again, abortion did not even come up.[3] In the earliest moments after *Roe v. Wade*, there is little evidence that most Americans thought about abortion in the same cataclysmic terms as today. Even as late as 1982, a study concluded that "a congressional candidate's abortion stance will not affect his general election chances."[4] Yet, there was not silence about abortion everywhere in the United States in the early days that followed *Roe*.

Within days of the decision, Rep. Lawrence Hogan of Maryland introduced language for the first proposed constitutional amendment that would have superseded the Court's *Roe* decision. Eleven other constitutional amendments would emerge as lawmakers in both parties rushed to express their outrage at *Roe* on the record in those days before abortion would become a polarizing point of division between the parties. That would come soon. But in those early days, Catholic lawmakers thought much the same way that their bishops did. They were shocked and outraged at a sudden change in the laws of the United States that ran so contrary to their most essential moral instincts. Over time, we might perhaps say that political instincts overcame moral scruples and, in some cases, we should allow that this was true. But it may be more true to say that a perceptible movement from the Democratic Party to the Republican Party was under way among many Catholic voters before the *Roe* decision. Fewer and fewer Catholics in elected office would be Democrats after the 1970s because of abortion, but also because of forces that already were under way.[5]

Still, another set of players was entering the picture as these changes were under way. Some accountability must also rest with the US bishops. Peter Steinfels has observed, "When it came to abortion, church leaders never made themselves perfectly clear on the room between moral principle and specific strategies in politics or policy."[6] Steinfels's claim opens up a perspective on how the US bishops joined the political battle over abortion during the early days when the right to life first was given political definition and how the bishops' approach helped to shape what would come later.

Perhaps not surprisingly, Catholic bishops did not offer much that was specific in the debate over a human life amendment, or the scope of a right to life, in these early days of the debate. As teachers of faith and morals, the

Catholic bishops were quite articulate about the broad questions of whether "the unborn child is a person," or expressing "a commitment to the preservation of life to the maximum degree possible."[7] But policymaking is about details and the messy particulars that come about in human circumstances. Did the bishops intend that no exceptions should ever be permitted, even in cases where a mother would die? What sorts of punishments did the bishops have in mind to enforce the requirements of a constitutional amendment? How severe would those punishments be? Would those punishments target women procuring abortions? Physicians who perform them? If both, would their guilt weigh equally? Broad principles about the sanctity of human life do not translate neatly into the complexity of public policy.[8] Yet, in their public comments for the media as well as in their congressional testimony supporting a human life amendment to the Constitution, bishops did not offer more than broad, principled objections. Catholic lawmakers and other public officials whose roles demanded that they answer questions about details in policymaking were left by their bishops largely to fend for themselves once the debate passed the broad principles and entered the difficult realm of details. For public officials who were Catholic, the debate over *Roe* quickly fell victim to the issue's uncertain position between faith and politics. Perhaps that was inevitable, and so the partisan division over abortion occurred inevitably when Catholic faith could not provide the guidance that policymaking needed. Whether inevitable or not, however, it would be difficult to assert that the bishops played no role in the how the partisan division over the abortion issue unfolded. The bishops were consistently a part of the debate even in those early days, yet for all of their consistency they did not offer much guidance about *how* a Catholic public official should be against abortion.[9]

Indeed, the bishops had embarked upon the public debate about abortion years before the *Roe* decision. In 1965, Father James McHugh joined the staff of the bishops' conference. A sociologist, McHugh had been working with Catholic nurses' and physicians' organizations in the Archdiocese of Newark when he left New Jersey to complete a degree at The Catholic University of America. He joined the staff as Director of Family Life in 1965 and, by 1967, the bishops formed the National Right to Life Committee (NRLC) with McHugh as the first director. Forming the NRLC reflected the bishops' growing concern about the full range of issues affecting the family as much as it also reflected the somewhat uncertain position of church organizations relative to political action. Of course, the First Amendment laid out the most basic rules of the road concerning both the fundamental separation of church from state and the rights of American citizens (including religious believers) to participate in decision-making. The picture had grown somewhat murkier in the unfolding legal environment affecting the relationship of money to politics.

The twentieth century saw Congress begin to take a sustained interest in campaign finance for the first time in American history. By 1943, with passage of the Smith-Connally Act, Congress specifically excluded labor organizations from contributing to political campaigns. In order to remain involved in political life, unions created separate organizations called political action committees that would receive contributions from unions and, in turn, make contributions to political campaigns that supported labor. The solution was a work-around. If the law forbade unions from giving to pro-union candidates, the unions would create a third-party committee who would make the contribution for them. By 1954, Congress passed the Johnson Amendment, which empowered the Internal Revenue Service to revoke the tax exemption of any religiously affiliated organization found to be "carrying on propaganda or otherwise attempting to influence legislation," or otherwise "participate in, or intervene in . . . any political campaign on behalf of any candidate for political office."[10] After 1954, the bishops found themselves in a situation not unlike the unions. The Catholic Church surely had positions on important issues it wanted to advance in public debate even in the 1950s. The Johnson Amendment made that more complicated.

We should observe that the bishops accepted the Johnson Amendment and its requirements with equanimity and even some enthusiasm. In 1969, the conference saw a policy of "neutrality" and "mutual abstention" that keeps "politics out of religion and religion out of politics" as healthy in light of "the constitutional separation of Church and State."[11] Perhaps this caution about political activity was a result of Catholics' fraught immigrant past in the United States and the concern that their fellow Americans would target Catholics again if the church became too involved in public affairs. In any event, even as the bishops were accepting of the requirement, the Johnson Amendment created complications. The "concept of neutrality is an extremely elusive one," and it raises "as many questions as it answers."[12] In order to work within the messy complexity demanded by the law and, at the same time, to address political issues effectively, the bishops elected to follow the example of labor organizations. The NRLC, a separate committee that would become separately incorporated by 1973, was created in order to put the bishops at arm's-length from political activity in much the same way that political action committees distanced labor organizations from political activity. In a way, creating the NRLC followed the pattern established in 1966 when the bishops created two organizations from the same national conference of Catholic bishops: the National Conference of Catholic Bishops (NCCB), which dealt with internal matters such as liturgy and the selection of bishops, and the United States Catholic Conference (USCC), which dealt with the secular world outside the church. Already with the USCC, and for a long time on a more ad hoc basis, the bishops had done some lobbying on such issues as government support for Catholic schools. The creation of the NRLC, an organization legally separate from the church, was something categorically different. Using a legal fiction drawn from the political world, the bishops had become lobbyists.[13]

The decision was not uncontroversial, even among the bishops or at the conference. In early days immediately following *Roe*, Russell Shaw, who at that time was charged with media relations for the NCCB/USCC as the director of the Office of Information, preferred a strategy that would "educate and motivate individual people against abortion," rather than going over the heads of the voters with a focus on lawmakers.[14] Later, as the bishops considered concrete steps, Bishop Walter Curtis said bluntly, "It is not the proper task of this Conference to lead a lobbying effort."[15] Perhaps that opposition was provoked by Father McHugh himself, who advocated, in as many words, a "public affairs [i.e., lobbying] program" aimed at Congress to win a constitutional amendment that would reverse the *Roe* decision.[16] The McHugh approach would win out, however, and the overall effort would begin to resemble a more ordinary political lobbying effort as soon as Cardinals Krol, Cody, Madeiros, and Manning testified before the Senate in 1974. The US bishops would become conscious wielders of political influence, endeavoring to pressure lawmakers with the moral influence Catholic bishops exert over faithful voters. An overall approach to the abortion controversy was taking firm shape in the middle of 1973.

It is important to note that the bishops' reaction was understandable. Not only did *Roe* upset bishops like Joseph Bernardin, the rest of the other bishops, and faithful

Catholics more generally: the decision came as a startling blow to Catholic confidence in the United States that had so recently accepted Catholics. But there is another factor we have not named. In 1968, at the persistent urging of Krakow's Cardinal Karol Wojtyła (the future Pope John Paul II), Pope Paul VI overruled a panel of lay theologians and married couples to affirm the church's teaching against artificial contraception in his encyclical letter *Humanae Vitae*.[17] *Humanae Vitae* unleashed a sort of debate inside the church in the United States that had never been imaginable before, and the climate grew quite difficult for bishops. Lay Catholics' reaction against *Humanae Vitae* was swift and immediate, probably because most of them had expected the teaching to be changed. Rather consistently, research has found that significant majorities of married Catholic couples use artificial contraception despite what the church tells them in *Humanae Vitae*.[18] That rejection has not been without support from theologians, either. A generation of leading theologians in and out of the United States was building their careers on reexamining long-standing church teachings. Many of them were priests. Swiss Father Hans Küng questioned the primacy of the pope, while Father Edward Schillebeeckx, a Dominican from Belgium, began probing the assumptions of Christology, the teachings about the divine nature of Jesus. The 1970s had begun in a climate of questioning long-settled matters of practice among Catholicism around the globe. It was no different in the American theological community. Even before *Humanae Vitae* was announced, Father Charles Curran was dismissed from his position on the theology faculty at The Catholic University of America in 1967, largely because his work was at odds with the teaching against artificial contraception.[19] As horrified as they were by the *Roe* decision, however, American bishops may also have sensed an opportunity in it.

The Catholic response to *Roe* was characterized by "unusual unity" in an otherwise fractious climate in which questioning was becoming rampant.[20] The *Roe* decision touched a nerve among Catholics, whose instinctive revulsion crossed party lines in those early days and was shared nearly universally. A 1971 letter from Senator Edward M. Kennedy in reply to a question about abortion illustrates the point. Kennedy later would join the most ardent defenders of abortion rights in the US Senate. In 1971, he was less guarded about his own "personal feeling that the legalization of abortion on demand is not in accordance with the value which our civilization places on human life."[21] As the abortion debate grew more political and legally complex, Kennedy's public position differed from his private view. But prior to the formation of the abortion maelstrom in American politics, we can see how even Ted Kennedy's Catholic faith had formed in him a disposition toward the sacredness of human life that doubted how legal abortion possibly could have a place in American law. That baseline of unity must have seemed like a welcome relief to the nation's increasingly beleaguered bishops. Feeling the closeness of the years spent in a tightly knit community of immigrant Catholicism slipping away from them both while Catholics entered the American mainstream and as that mainstream of American life grew stranger to Catholic sensibilities, the immediate aftermath of *Roe* must have appeared to offer the opportunity to reverse the trend. American Catholics, perhaps, would join together—under their bishops' leadership—to reverse *Roe* either by constitutional amendment or by some other political means. Or, at least, it may have seemed that way.

In the end, embarking on that lobbying campaign and joining the political fray, the bishops would overplay their hand.[22] Not only would they fail to overturn *Roe*, but the bishops' political action would alter the relationship between Catholicism and American life for decades.

1976: "The Worst Year Ever"

In the climate of questioning that had settled over the church after *Humanae Vitae*, perhaps it was not the most prudent notion. Yet, the bishops had determined to observe the American bicentennial with a national conference on justice. A project dear to Detroit's Cardinal John Dearden, the president of the bishops' conference, "A Call to Action" (CTA) was intended "to measure the progress of the Church in the United States toward a true pastoral presence and an effective engagement in public policy."[23] In several ways, timing offers the necessary context. CTA came in tandem with the American Bicentennial to underscore the depth of American Catholics' commitment to their home country and the length of the history of Catholicism in the United States. At the same time, in the atmosphere following *Humanae Vitae* and the Second Vatican Council's effort to address the church in the modern world, a conference broadly treating a topic like justice would only naturally invite spirited debates. Over one thousand lay delegates came together in Detroit to meet with their bishops and to have that discussion for three days in July 1976. The results were not what Dearden and the other bishops had hoped. The lay delegates at CTA approved measures that called for the end of priestly celibacy and the ordination of women. The outcome forced Dearden and the vice president of the national bishops' conference, Archbishop Joseph Bernardin, into the uncomfortable position of defending CTA, which they had planned and which had produced those controversial outcomes. But for as much as the bishops may have felt that CTA left egg on their collective face, it was not even the main reason why Russell Shaw referred to 1976 as "The Worst Year Ever" for American Catholicism.[24] As uncomfortable as CTA was, the presidential election would be even more uncomfortable.

As difficult as it has become to identify the characteristics of a "Catholic vote" in American politics, it was not always so difficult. The immigrant roots of most American Catholics who dwelled in the big cities of the Northeast and the industrial Midwest created a strong identification between Catholics and the Democratic Party that lasted from before the 1928 presidential campaign of Al Smith to the 1960 election of John F. Kennedy. The acceptance of Catholics into the American cultural mainstream also brought Catholic voters into a pattern parallel to the rest of the American mainstream. "When political observers speak of a monolithic Catholic vote," one recent study concluded, "such a presumption is a myth that harkens back to the days of Kennedy and Roosevelt."[25] But it should seem unsurprising that, only thirteen years after the death of President Kennedy, the political assumptions of the 1976 presidential election still were shaped by that myth. Even if a distinct Catholic vote was already a myth by the time of the 1976 campaign, it was only natural that everyone involved should believe that they still could rely on Catholic voters to be motivated and unified by their Catholic faith at the ballot box. As they embarked on the 1976 election already playing the role of lobbyists in national politics, certainly that included the US Catholic bishops.

We should say that the bishops did not spend 1976 attempting to elect or to defeat a particular presidential candidate. In fact, the bishops played the central role thrust upon them in the campaign with some evident distaste. Still, in this first presidential election since the *Roe* decision and amid their efforts to build support for a human life amendment to the Constitution, the political fray drew in the bishops with an almost physical power that they could neither overcome nor temper. The shape of the bishops' involvement was determined long before it began, when the bishops determined to behave like political activists in the months following *Roe*, and that involvement would shape American politics and the political expectations of American Catholics for two generations. The key critical assumption that laid at the heart of the bishops' motivations was that, even amid the disorientation that followed *Humanae Vitae*, there was a residuum of unity among American Catholics that could bring them together in opposition to abortion. If they could tap that moral unity to oppose *Roe*, perhaps the bishops also could quell the questioning that was emerging across a range of other issues in church life.

As the 1976 presidential campaign took shape, the prospects for Catholics on the abortion issue looked good. Governor Jimmy Carter of Georgia, the eventual nominee of the Democratic Party so long supported by Catholic voters, described himself as a born-again Christian. The term had some newness and unfamiliarity in mid-1970s America. In some ways, it was Jimmy Carter who popularized the term *born-again* to most voters. The *Oxford English Dictionary* does not find the description in use before 1961, and Carter was the first national political figure to identify with the term, which would shortly become rather synonymous with the Moral Majority, whose Christian voters would elect Ronald Reagan in overwhelming numbers against Carter in 1980. Later the term would be supplanted in ordinary usage by referring to these Christians as evangelicals. Because he was a born-again Christian, there were ample reasons to expect that Carter would oppose *Roe* and, considering the weakness of Gerald Ford's unusual political position as the only unelected president in American history who followed a historic Republican presidential scandal, there was every reason to expect that the Democrat would win the election. For the US bishops, who hoped to see *Roe* somehow reversed, the 1976 election would have looked like an opportunity once Carter had locked up the Democratic nomination in mid-June.

But Carter had problems inside the Democratic Party, which had followed the turbulent currents of the 1960s into a more liberal and overall northern direction. The "solid South" had supported the Democrats since Reconstruction, and no candidate from the Deep South had been nominated for the presidency since Zachary Taylor in 1848. Carter, a born-again Christian from Georgia with support from conservative white Democrats, set off alarm bells within an increasingly liberal Democratic Party. As Carter's campaign steamrolled through the late months of spring, an "Anybody-But-Carter" movement grew among northern liberal Democrats such as Jerry Brown and Frank Church. Other constituencies within the Democratic Party—particularly civil rights groups and the emerging women's movement—expressed some alarm at Carter's nomination. Jimmy Carter embarked on the summer of 1976 with a clear but not untroubled path to the White House.

Carter's summer of 1976 was devoted to unifying these Democratic constituencies behind his campaign. Carter had announced his support for an Equal Rights Amendment earlier in the year, but he continued to face opposition among women and spent the weeks leading to the convention in meetings hoping to avert a floor fight over the role of women in the Democratic Party.[26] Despite an exemplary record on civil rights issues in Georgia, which included a losing 1966 campaign for governor against Lester Maddox, Carter committed a gaffe in April 1976 when he spoke against federal integration policies to say that the federal government should not disturb the "ethnic purity" of established neighborhoods. The episode awakened fears among African American voters about a Southerner in the White House, and Carter spent much of the next several weeks engaged in damage control, meeting with civil rights leaders. Yet Carter himself assessed his greatest weakness approaching the general election campaign to be the "religious issue."[27] By the "religious issue," Carter did not refer to his being a Southern Baptist or a born-again Christian. He meant, rather, the softness of his support among opponents of abortion and, especially, among Catholics.

Jimmy Carter's problems within the Democratic Party placed him in a difficult position on abortion. Since he already faced difficulty among women, abortion effectively compelled him to choose between women's groups and pro-life groups, which, within the Democratic Party, meant Catholics. The platform committee began to meet on June 11, drafting a document that would later be adopted by the Democratic National Convention that would nominate Carter and would "almost certainly reflect the views of former Gov. Jimmy Carter of Georgia."[28] There would be no avoiding getting pinned down on abortion. The language chosen by the committee for the platform eventually said, "We fully recognize the religious and ethical nature of the concerns which many Americans have on the subject of abortion. We feel, however, that it is undesirable to attempt to amend the Constitution to overturn the Supreme Court decision in this area."[29] To say the least, the US bishops were unsatisfied. The president of the bishops' conference, Archbishop Joseph Bernardin, called the abortion plank "irresponsible," and later went on to express concern that "this action by the Democratic platform committee may have the effect of increasing feelings of frustration and alienation from the political process felt by many Americans."[30] To put it more bluntly, Catholics might bolt.

Carter scrambled, and what came next bore the graceless marks of rush and panic. Carter insisted, "the wording of the Democratic party plank was . . . not in accordance with my own desires, [but] I do not favor a constitutional amendment which would prohibit all abortions. . . . I think abortion is wrong and I think government ought not do anything ever to encourage abortion."[31] The US bishops, unsurprisingly, were unmoved by the suggestion that the Democratic nominee had been sidelined by his party's platform committee, and the bishops did not fail to notice that Carter went on to affirm the plank's spirit of recognizing the moral difficulty in the abortion question while dodging any responsibility for government to engage the moral question. Carter's tap-dancing may, from our perspective today, appear to be cynical in a typical way. But if we take seriously the idea that politics is complex and more than one issue is always in play, the impossibility of Carter's position becomes clearer. Jimmy Carter certainly wanted to be president of the United States, and we may feel certain he must have been motivated by many hopes across a range of issues facing Americans in 1976. The emergence of abortion as an issue that might split the Democratic coalition endangered Carter's ambitions and his best intentions as much as it would do to anyone in his position. To salvage any chance to be elected and to be an effective political leader, Carter had to find a way to hold that coalition together any way he could.[32]

At the same time, the US bishops were behaving in a peculiar way. As the Carter campaign scrambled to find a way to hold on to Catholic voters in a series of frantic phone calls and clumsy gestures toward Catholic leaders that Democratic vice-presidential nominee Walter Mondale agreed were "annoyances," the bishops' conference was flexing political muscle in an unprecedented new way.[33] The Carter campaign initiated a series of contacts with Bishop James S. Rausch on July 20, culminating in an August 31 meeting between Carter, Archbishop Bernardin, New York's Cardinal Terrence Cooke, and Youngstown's Bishop James Malone. In the six weeks leading up to the August 31 meeting, Rausch had played a critical role as the general secretary of the bishops' conference.

Something important to recall about the bishops' conference harkens back to the difficulty of knowing what is meant when we attribute something to "the bishops." The work of the national bishops' conference is a very small part of any Catholic bishop's life.[34] Ordinarily, a bishop has responsibility for a diocese. The larger his diocese or archdiocese the greater the demands, and even a small diocese is a vast organization. Bishops and archbishops also have responsibilities to Vatican congregations, the committees of bishops in the Vatican made up of bishops who live in Rome and bishops from around the world. A cardinal has an even greater set of responsibilities to the Roman congregations and to the pope. For an average US bishop, the work of the bishops' conference is very remote from their day-to-day work. For that reason, the conference has a full-time staff that deals with national issues concerning the bishops on their behalf. Bishops, generally, are quite content to leave such matters to the conference staff, and, especially where the specialized competencies that deal with law and political questions are concerned, most bishops lack the training and the experience to do anything other than depend on the conference.[35] The conference staff is led by a general secretary, who, in 1976, was Bishop Rausch.

Bishop James Rausch had been assistant general secretary to Bernardin before succeeding Bernardin as general secretary in 1972. With Bernardin, Rausch had implemented changes to the bishops' conference's statutes that modernized the organization and brought it into line with the Second Vatican Council's requirements. Now the leader of the conference's staff, Rausch was already taking a more involved role in national politics than Bernardin had taken as general secretary. In his years as general secretary, Bernardin communicated brief, written statements to Congress on pieces of legislation of concern to the bishops, or he sent representatives to testify. By the time of the 1976 election, Rausch already had personally testified three times before congressional committees. Rausch's full statements to the committees were very professional pieces of advocacy, detailed policy briefs built on church teaching and careful economic or legal analysis, not short statements. The difference between Bernardin's and Rausch's approaches as general secretary certainly was due in part to Bernardin's having led the conference through a transition. Bernardin's time as general secretary was marked by modernizing the conference so that it could engage more directly the social and political questions that concerned Catholics. In 1976, with Bernardin the president of the conference (elected by the nation's bishops) and Rausch as general secretary, the conference was less preoccupied with reorganizing itself and it was freer to be an advocate with government for the poor, the sick, the worker, and so forth. Still, as much as Rausch's and Bernardin's circumstances as general secretary were different, which may explain a difference in approach, it also is true that Rausch appeared unafraid to lead the conference in a more muscular posture toward national political questions.

In testimony before the House subcommittee on Resources, Food, and Energy, Rausch described the success of the conference's lobbying efforts after the House voted for cuts in US support for the World Bank's International Development Agency. Rausch reminded the subcommittee about the influence the bishops had over millions of Catholic voters.[36] In the summer of 1973, when CBS sought to re-air two episodes of *Maude* dealing with abortion, Rausch and the conference "organized" a protest that put pressure on advertisers to prevent the reruns. Rausch told the *New York Times*, "advocacy of abortion is unacceptable in a situation comedy format," and, flexing the muscle of Catholic viewers and consumers through the conference, Rausch had gotten a CBS executive to acknowledge airing the episodes was an "error."[37] So, when Bishop Rausch cautioned vice-presidential candidate Walter Mondale that the Carter campaign had given the impression that "'Catholics don't count,'" and Catholics would "remain firm in their commitment to this issue [abortion] and the centrality it plays in the election year," he was playing a sort of political hardball he had been playing for a few years as general secretary of the conference.[38] The conference had embarked on playing the political game when Father McHugh persuaded the bishops to embark on a "lobbying effort" in 1973, and by 1976 President Ford's staff would observe that the church had become "aggressive" in its campaign against abortion.[39] The aggressiveness was apparent in an August 18 news release from the bishops' conference that praised the Republicans for their platform's abortion plank and called on Americans to "urge all candidates for political office to commit themselves" to a constitutional amendment overturning *Roe*, the very thing Carter had been resisting.[40] Rausch had been in conversations with the Democrats since July 20, and Carter's campaign would have recognized this press release for the warning shot that it was.

Rausch's contacts with the Carter campaign led the executive committee of the bishops' conference into two fateful meetings in 1976, one with Jimmy Carter and the other with Gerald Ford. The Carter meeting took place on August 31. Along with Rausch, Archbishop Bernardin and the rest of the executive committee met with Carter at the Mayflower Hotel and, as Russell Shaw recounts it, "the meeting did not go well."[41] Governor Carter hoped to reach an accommodation short of a constitutional amendment and a change to the plank in the Democratic platform. He "reminded the bishops that he personally shared their conviction that abortion was immoral," but Carter could not agree with them about the politics of abortion.[42] Bernardin read from a prepared statement that quickly made it clear how Carter's position was unacceptable to the bishops. The meeting led nowhere, and when Bernardin encountered the press outside the hotel matters quickly grew even worse.

The bishops "stepped out of the funeral parlor quiet of the meeting room into the accident scene excitement of journalists at work."[43] It is not difficult to imagine the media frenzy over this high-level meeting between church leaders and a presidential candidate. Archbishop Joseph Bernardin pronounced the bishops to be "disappointed with the Governor's position," and he reiterated the call for a constitutional amendment.[44] Perhaps unsurprisingly, a controversy began to form almost immediately. The next day's newspapers pounced, and a media storm began to swell. The *New York Times* story emphasized how Carter still relied on his "personal opposition to abortion," but quoted Bernardin to say that "personal opposition is not enough."[45] The *Washington Post* cast the story in terms of two ships passing in the night, with "Bernardin, an outspoken advocate of government prohibition of abortion, [saying] he was 'disappointed,'" while Carter called the meeting "productive."[46] Rausch complained that "the media contributed to the impression that the meeting was much more confrontational than it was," and that was fair.[47] There is no evidence that the meeting was confrontational in any way. On the other hand, there was no getting past how badly the meeting went.

There are good reasons to think the bishops bore most of the blame. An agenda that the Carter campaign prepared described their expectation for an "informal" meeting.[48] Carter began with a brief presentation that touched on several issues on which he shared common ground with the bishops.[49] The bishops "listened in silence," and when Bernardin read from his two-page prepared text that addressed only abortion Carter was "startled" and "stunned as Bernardin said that until the bishops and the candidate resolved the abortion issue, there was no point in going forward on other topics."[50] Having committed to playing political hardball, the bishops chose an all-or-nothing strategy that left Carter no alternative to total surrender on the abortion issue. The platform was written, the Democratic National Convention was over, and it was nearly Labor Day: all of the exit doors were closed, and Carter was locked into his position. Forced by the bishops to choose between core Democratic constituencies—Catholics and women's groups—Carter opted to bet that the bishops did not speak for most Catholics. He obtained reassurances from Catholic Democrats such as Senators Frank Church and Ted Kennedy that they would campaign for him, and they believed most Catholic voters would weigh all of the issues. Adam Walinsky, who had worked for Robert Kennedy, had already written to Carter that his "Catholic problem" could not "be solved by meetings with the staff of the Bishop's [*sic*] conference" because "there is no single 'representative,' broker, nor any collection, who can" speak for all Catholics.[51] Now Walinsky's and the others' advice would guide Carter. The bishops' voice would be minimized. In fact, they had minimized their own ability to influence Carter when they tried to force an all-or-nothing choice on him.

At the same time, there was another actor at work besides the bishops and the Carter campaign. The *New York Times* may have gotten it just right with a September 5 headline: in a close election, "Ford Hopes Linked to Catholic Vote."[52] "'We think they're [Catholics] up for grabs,' a senior Ford campaign official said of the urban Catholics," and only days after the disastrous meeting between the bishops and Carter, the Ford campaign was prowling for Catholic voters. Of course, the Carter campaign could not have failed to be aware that their "Catholic problem" was an opportunity for Republicans. A July 20 memorandum describing how "a situation . . . could be exploited by the opposition to develop doubts in the mind of Catholic voters; enough doubt to vote for President Ford," was circulated within the campaign, and a September 16 letter to Carter from Indiana Senator Birch Bayh confirmed a widespread sense that

"Ford campaign tactics will keep national focus on the abortion issue."[53] At the same time, there were those within the bishops' conference who foresaw danger in how the bishops had embarked on a campaign of political pressure tactics. The *New York Times* quoted anonymous sources inside the conference to observe that key staff members had "hinted they would resign" over what seemed to them like "a dangerous involvement in partisanship and an unjustified narrowing of the church's social concerns" down to one issue, abortion.[54] Another member of the conference staff, Father Bryan Hehir, wrote a prescient memorandum to Bernardin, agreeing with the sources in the *Times* that "today it is widely believed we are [a one issue Church]," and foresaw that "the political dimensions of the abortion issue will feedback into the Church." As Hehir saw it, "we are perceived as being *against* Carter," and the partisan feedback not only would throw a partisan light on Catholics, allying them with Republicans, but that partisanship would overtake the church and "recreate the *Humanae Vitae* turmoil."[55]

Quite without intending it, time would prove quickly that the bishops had fallen into just the trap Hehir feared. The bishops met with President Ford at the White House on September 10. Bernardin again read a statement, though the bishops' greater comfort on the abortion issue with Ford permitted Bernardin to raise the broad set of issues that Carter only hoped to talk about on August 31.[56] Ford responded to Bernardin with a five-page thank-you letter that not only emphasized his agreement with the bishops' call for a constitutional amendment and described his cosponsorship of an amendment when he was a member of the House of Representatives, but also went on to pledge support for Catholic schools, for "relieving hunger and malnutrition in the world," and for their shared "moral ideals."[57] As Bernardin had pronounced the bishops to be "disappointed" after the meeting with Carter, he told a scrum of reporters that the bishops had been "encouraged" by their meeting with Ford, prompting at least one bishop to lament publicly that "the leadership of the Catholic Church and the church itself were scarred . . . with wounds incurred from two words. . . . The words were 'disappointed' and 'encouraged.'" Those two words "had made us look like a one issue church," a perspective so pervasive that in a Labor Day homily Newark Archbishop Peter L. Geraty rejected forcefully the idea that "the Catholic Church is a one-issue Church."[58]

There were other implications that turned out to be, by turns, both ominous and farcical. Meeting both with Ford and Carter might have satisfied the most minimal standard to appear to be nonpartisan, but their advocacy about abortion and the bishops' public disappointment certainly appeared to tilt the bishops toward one candidate. The Internal Revenue Service had already sent an inquiry to the bishops' conference on August 2, raising eleven separate questions about the conference's Pastoral Plan for Pro-Life Activities. The IRS put the conference on notice that its federal tax exemption was threatened by its undisguised political advocacy, and the conference was in danger of crossing a line away from being a religious organization toward a political organization. On September 16, the conference's own lawyers agreed with the IRS in a memo that advised the bishops they had obligated themselves to meet with any third-party presidential candidates who desired a meeting now that they had met with Ford and Carter, to avoid any appearance of partisanship that might change their tax status. Those requests for meetings poured in.[59] But that flood of third-party candidates was not the only Pandora's Box unlocked by the bishops' conference.

The events of August and September of 1976 unleashed divisions among the bishops, within the community of American Catholics, and across the whole span of national politics in the United States. The next several years would see those divisions play out in the bishops' conference, and they would influence its development as an organization that was still quite new at the time of the 1976 election. Among Catholics, the divisions over abortion politics would come to preoccupy political decision-making for the next two generations and, for as significant as Catholics are proportionally among American voters, these events certainly did affect American political life most frequently (but not always) at the presidential level.

The conference may not have wanted to play kingmaker. Once they embarked on a course of political advocacy, however, inevitably they began to play the role. It is not possible to advocate forcefully for an issue position and not to prefer a partisan outcome when there is partisan disagreement. If the Republicans generally are pro-life and the Democrats are generally pro-choice, and the bishops have a preference, then they prefer one outcome. They are partisans. The bishops have spent decades resisting that implication, but it remains as logically inevitable as it was during the 1976 election, or in 1973 when Father McHugh urged this approach.

Schisms

The pro-life movement was only beginning to take its contemporary shape in the mid-1970s. Abortion itself was not new, of course. But it was natural that the changed legal and political landscape that followed the *Roe* decision should intensify and alter the opposition to abortion. There was, of course, a pro-life movement before *Roe*. Daniel K. Williams has observed in his book *Defenders of the Unborn* (Oxford, 2016) that the Catholic Church in the United States had been driving the adoption of state laws against abortion for many years before *Roe* was decided. Williams verifies that, before the *Roe* decision, the pro-life movement was not dominated by socially conservative activists in the Democratic Party. Overall, opposition to abortion was found among "Catholic Democrats who were committed to New Deal . . . ideals such as a living wage and the legal recognition of workers' rights, both of which Pope Pius XI had endorsed, [and] led them to give enthusiastic support to President Franklin Roosevelt and his Democratic successors from Harry Truman to Lyndon Johnson."[60] This tends to confirm what the bishops said throughout the 1970s and in their quarrel with the Carter campaign: abortion was not "a Catholic issue," it needed to be seen in the larger context of the bipartisan, fully "American liberal values of human rights," just as Catholic bishops in the United States had been asserting since the *Roe* decision that "unless America is prepared to protect unborn human lives, it cannot with confidence guarantee protection to any life."[61] It seems clear that abortion became an issue for political conservatives after the *Roe* decision. For Williams, the Supreme Court's ruling marked the moment when Catholic voters migrated from the Democrats to the Republicans, changing the politics of abortion decisively, and when abortion politics began to play a larger role in the national political debate. It does not seem sensible, though, to think of this as Catholic voters becoming more conservative because they changed political parties, or as the movement of Catholic voters changing the Democrats and the Republicans. The picture is both more complex and simpler.

The shifting of political coalitions in American politics during the last third of the twentieth century involved Catholics, but it was not only about Catholicism. Civil rights, the emergence of the United States as a global power in the postwar era, the Cold War, and the social conflicts of the 1960s all conspired together as a whole pattern to realign American politics during the years between the Kennedy and Reagan presidencies. That realignment was under way almost a decade before *Roe*. Simply to say that Catholic voters and their parochial concerns transformed American political life overlooks a lot. At the same time, because of the social and political position Catholics occupied in American life as the 1960s became the 1970s, all of the reasons why the Carter campaign spent so much time chasing Catholic voters tell us how central Catholics were to the change effected in American political life from the 1968 Nixon campaign to the 1980 Reagan campaign. As the Democrats began to lose a century-old grip on the Solid South, Catholic voters in northern states became more essential to the success of Democrats who hoped to win the White House.[62] Those Catholics, as Daniel K. Williams described, increasingly identified with Republicans on economic issues as they also responded to Republican rhetoric about urban decay while they watched their old ethnic neighborhoods changing around them. The 1976 campaign made clear, though, how well the Republican Party understood that opposing *Roe* was the key to depriving Democrats of the northern Catholic votes that they needed to balance losses in the South. Jimmy Carter managed to get by in 1976, but the decades that followed illustrated how difficult that would be for Democrats. Social issues from abortion to bussing to crime would define the difficulty.

The growth of an alliance between Catholic voters in the north and Southern Christians, who primarily identify as evangelicals, did not grow up overnight. But that growth began after the 1976 election, and events drove the alliance. The US Supreme Court had begun to play a larger role in American political life with *Brown v. Board of Education of Topeka* in 1954. Through the 1950s and the 1960s the Supreme Court addressed a range of American hot-button issues ranging from criminal justice to contraception. The emergence of a newly assertive Supreme Court coincided with the social changes in the United States that unsettled so many working-class Catholics, people who felt they had finally just been accepted into the American mainstream at a moment when that mainstream appeared to be abandoning its commitment to the world of values they could recognize. A sense of growing cultural distance from elite institutions in the United States triggered an old immigrant instinct, to withdraw into the safe enclave of ethnicity, religious faith, and traditional values. And while Catholics did not retreat to their old parishes and neighborhoods in the 1970s, they did begin to retreat from the Democratic Party and other institutions that, more and more, seemed out of touch with them.

That cultural distance centered on what seemed like a lack of authenticity or sincerity. The Supreme Court had been saying, in such decisions as *Mapp v. Ohio* (1961) and *Miranda v. Arizona* (1965), how the law sometimes demanded that criminal defendants known to be guilty should go free.[63] Now, as *Roe* was decided, Catholic public officials spoke about their "personal opposition" to abortion without any indication that they would act against the *Roe* decision. That was, in fact, the particular objection of the bishops' conference:

> It has become rather commonplace of late for some elected officials and candidates for public office to allege personal opposition and personal disagreement with the Supreme Court's abortion ruling—but to couple this with opposition to amending the Constitution to correct the situation they say they oppose. I do not think many Americans find this either persuasive or responsible.[64]

Perhaps it was the climate of those Cold War years during which Catholics climbed into the American mainstream as much as anything else. The struggle against communism had helped to make Americans out of Catholics, but it also was framed in the absolute terms of good versus evil in the

American imagination. The effect seems to have been particularly powerful among many Catholics.[65] After *Roe*, those Catholics and their leaders found no more room for subtlety or nuance about a complex, difficult political question like abortion than they did about Soviet communism. Rather, as a result of thinking in binary, polarized terms throughout the Cold War, abortion became a question of being with-us-or-against-us. That sort of thinking had been at work in American politics for three decades by the time of the 1976 election, since the beginning of the Cold War, and as we look back it is difficult to separate Cold War absolutism from the beginnings of the culture war in American political life, in which abortion always has been the most important issue. Just as, at one time, the pervasive fear that there was a "red under every bed" and betrayal lurked all over the United States during a Red Scare, now it seemed that the politicians who mouthed their opposition to violent crime or abortion really were against ordinary Americans, after all. This began to look very much like a sort of treachery that needed to be exposed.

Describing American social and political life in terms of a culture war began in the decade following the 1976 election. The *Oxford English Dictionary* recognizes the first use of "culture war" in this context in 1987. By 1988, one book described culture wars in terms of a "conservative restoration" and, by 1989, George Weigel wrote that Catholics were engaged in a "culture war."[66] In 1991, James Davison Hunter defined the phenomenon with his culture war thesis. Hunter described the cooperation between traditional Catholics, evangelical Protestants, and orthodox Jews in that struggle between good and evil after the fall of the Soviet Union in terms of a "New Ecumenism," or "a new form of cooperative mobilization, in which distinct and separate religious and moral traditions share resources and work together toward common objectives."[67] In particular, those objectives pertained to a cultural "realignment . . . at the deepest and most profound levels . . . over the very meaning and purpose of the core institutions of American civilization."[68] Use of the phrase "culture war" gathered momentum through the unfolding of the 1990s and, given the similarities between the absolutism of Cold War politics and the absolutism of abortion politics, it is difficult not to notice that talk of a culture war exploded into wide usage just as the Cold War was ending, as though the instinct for polarized, twilight struggle between good and evil needed some outlet to satisfy itself once the Soviet threat evaporated.[69] The succession from the Cold War to the culture war has been the defining feature of the four and a half decades since the *Roe* decision. *Roe* was the incipient event that gave a focal point to social forces already gathering in response to the unrest of the 1960s. To some degree, those forces began as a rejection of the New Deal. That response became important for national politics in the 1976 presidential election. The bitter polarization that took shape during the 1980s quarrels over school prayer and the confirmation battle over President Reagan's nomination of Robert Bork matured at just the moment when the Cold War ended.

Yet, we should not depart from this historical description of the outbreak of the culture wars without observing that the metaphor of a "culture war" was not entirely figurative. The term has an unlovely history. In the 1870s, the Prussian Chancellor Otto von Bismarck embarked on a program to combat secularism and the influence of the Roman Catholic Church. Bismarck coined the term *Kulturkampf* (literally, "culture struggle") to describe his closings of monasteries and churches as well as the effort to drive out a Polish minority. Perhaps among some Catholics, today the phrase offers a tempting comparison that resonates with their feelings of being beleaguered in contemporary American social life. But it also is the case that some have been engaged in the culture war who took the idea of warfare a bit more seriously.

By the late 1970s, with six years of unsuccessfully opposing *Roe* behind them, some pro-life activists began to grow restive. Dissatisfied with the National Right to Life Committee's slow and steady efforts to oppose *Roe* by legislative and constitutional means, a new organization splintered off with support from the conservative think tank the Heritage Foundation. The American Life League (ALL) began developing new tactics they called the "rescue movement." They developed a tactic they called "sidewalk counseling," in which they would approach women at the entrances to abortion clinics with the hope of discouraging them. This tactic and others that more closely resembled civil disobedience—including blocking clinic entrances—brought the ALL into the courts as they tested the boundaries of free speech and freedom of assembly. Yet even more extreme tactics would follow not long after.

The early 1980s brought the outbreak of violence at abortion clinics and against abortion providers. In 1982, a doctor and his wife were kidnapped and held for days. 1983 saw a clinic burned in Hillcrest, Virginia. A Pensacola clinic was bombed on Christmas Day in 1984, and just a few months earlier a Benedictine priest who was director of pro-life activities for the Diocese of Birmingham (Alabama) assaulted and injured several workers in an abortion clinic. In 1987, there was an attempted bombing in California. That the violence would continue sporadically throughout the 1990s and even into the more recent past is unsurprising when we consider the stakes implied by the metaphor of a "war." In the early 1990s, *The Wanderer* (a publication for traditionalist Catholics) published an essay answering the question, "Can the Killing of Abortionists Be Justified?" The writer was Charles Rice, who taught at the University of Notre Dame Law School from 1969 to 2000, and his arguments are as measured and as carefully reasoned as we would feel entitled to expect. The result of those arguments is this conclusion:

> The principle of the double effect could apply to the defense of the unborn in some cases. If you were in the room with an abortionist as he was about to perform an abortion, you would have the moral right, and probably the duty, to use reasonable force to prevent that imminently threatened killing of the unborn child. Your action would be moral if you used only the force necessary to stop the killing and if your intent was to stop the killing rather than to harm the abortionist. It is most unlikely, at least, however, that deadly force would be necessary or justified even in this situation. And you surely would have no right intentionally to kill the abortionist.[70]

Again, Rice's conclusion is measured and he does not in any way support the killing of abortion providers on the grounds of legitimate defense. On the other hand, Rice has left the door open to the use of some force: violence is not off the table entirely.

Of course, Rice's arguments and the extremism of others are a little beside the point. The bishops' conference never endorsed the use of violence against abortion providers. Indeed, the conference and the National Right to Life Committee did nothing to encourage even civil disobedience, and all of their political engagements have been focused since before *Roe* on lobbying at the federal and state levels, with each branch of government, against abortion. Make no mistake, neither the conference nor any US bishop has ever called for or implied anything like violence. On the other hand, the bishops have contributed to and kept alive the atmosphere of a culture war. That metaphor does not need much elaboration either on a view of its deeper past in European history or in the light of the legacy of the Cold

War in American history. The metaphor itself is extreme, at least in the sense that it suggests a sort of all-or-nothing polarization that, for example, cannot tolerate any subtlety about being opposed to something personally while finding no practical political or legal alternative. The Catholics who belonged to older immigrant groups, their children, and their grandchildren in the urban centers of the Great Lakes, Northeastern, and mid-Atlantic regions of the United States have responded, and have kept the culture wars alive in their political behavior over the last four decades. New divisions in American life have brought about the increasing polarization that characterizes our politics, and abortion is at the center.

Twenty-four years before Donald Trump was elected, a Republican presidential candidate said that the 1992 election was "about . . . who we are. It is about what we believe. It is about what we stand for as Americans. . . . It is a cultural war, as critical to the kind of nation we will one day be as was the Cold War itself."[71] That candidate did very well among Catholic voters. His name was Patrick J. Buchanan. In 2017, the *New York Times* called Buchanan "the First Trumpist," a sentiment with which Buchanan agreed: "I was all for Trump."[72]

Chapter 3

Consistent Ethics

No one really expected Cardinal Karol Wojtyła to be elected pope in 1978. He had done well in the August 1978 balloting after Pope Paul VI died. But Wojtyła was Polish, and no non-Italian had been elected since 1522. The cardinals chose an Italian that summer, electing Cardinal Albino Luciani to be Pope John Paul. Wojtyła returned home to Poland and put thoughts of being the first non-Italian pope since Adrian VI out of his mind. Those who were near to Wojtyła when word arrived only five weeks later that Pope John Paul had died recall how "shaken" he was by the news and, perhaps, by its implications.[1] Eighteen days later, Wojtyła was elected by the cardinals. When he accepted the papacy, Wojtyła inherited a large organization loaded not just with the baggage of Pope Paul or Pope John, but also with the baggage of centuries. The early dashing of his hopes to take the name Stanisłaus ("too nationalistic") was a signal that the church would not bend very easily even to a pope's wishes.[2] The world would know him as Pope John Paul II.

But Pope John Paul II would occupy the papacy for more than twenty-six years, the second longest reign since Saint Peter. John Paul II's long pontificate eventually did enable him to leave a deep imprint on the church. One of the most important and far-reaching changes that would come took place relatively early. As with much else about the papacy, John Paul II had inherited an apostolic delegate to the United States whom he had not chosen. Pope Paul had named Archbishop Jean Jadot to be apostolic delegate to the United States in 1973. Like the national conference of bishops, the apostolic delegate played a complex and sometimes confusing role in church life. At one level, the apostolic delegate was a diplomat.[3] He was the representative from the Holy See to the United States of America. At a deeper level, the apostolic delegate was the pope's spokesman to the bishops of the United States who played a role in the work of the bishops' conference and the selection of bishops, and who also briefed Vatican officials about matters inside the American church. Jadot played all of those roles vigorously. A 1977 profile noted that Jadot took "a more active part in these matters than his predecessors, steering a difficult course between the role of policy shaper and the pitfall of exceeding his mandate by appearing too meddlesome."[4] While Jadot "scrupulously refrained from involvement in specific causes and politics in the American church," press accounts did record that Jadot's efforts to steer the US bishops toward the middle did not please everyone.[5] The *New York Times* noted that Jadot had been "caught in the middle of differences between bishops . . . when they divided over the results of the first national church consultation on social issues in 1976" in those meetings with Carter and Ford.[6] John Paul moved rather promptly to replace Jadot in 1980 amid growing dissatisfaction both in Rome and among some US bishops who favored more confrontation than accommodation with the secular world, especially where moral issues like abortion were concerned.

Just as the dawn of the 1980s brought a new era for the church in the United States, so also did the whole church begin to enter a new phase at the same time. Part of the reason was the new pope, whose vigorous witness to the faith was equaled only by his vigorous good health. John Paul's travels and his skillful use of the media reshaped the papacy for the twentieth century, greatly increasing the pope's influence inside and outside the church. But another force was at work too, and the dismissal of Jadot was one of many signals that suggested it. The Second Vatican Council had been over for fifteen years, and the renewal of the liturgy had been finalized just seven years before the 1980s began. The shock of the Council had passed, and the 1980s brought a second phase of the Council's reception. The tide now would turn against the bishops and other church leaders who had embraced the reforms of the Council. Pope John XXIII once joked about two types of people in the church, "those with their foot on the gas and those with their foot on the brake." The gas had been pressed since Pope John opened the Second Vatican Council. With the coming of a new apostolic delegate, Archbishop Pio Laghi, the 1980s would favor the brake. It remains common today to talk about Jadot bishops and Laghi bishops. Jesuit Father Thomas Reese described the difference this way:

> The bishops appointed under Archbishop Laghi are often compared to those appointed under Archbishop Jean Jadot, whom he replaced in December 1980. The consensus among journalists and nonepiscopal experts is that the bishops appointed under Archbishop Laghi and John Paul II are more "conservative" than bishops appointed under Archbishop Jadot and Paul VI. These labels apply primarily to church issues, not political or economic issues.[7]

To put it just a little more succinctly, the bishops appointed to the United States in the 1980s tended to be less interested in engaging the secular world in a dialogue, more interested in confronting secular culture with an "authentic" alternative rooted in traditional doctrine. Indeed, that language of authenticity marked a distinct shift in tone that came in a distinctive way as New York's Archbishop John O'Connor and Boston's Archbishop Bernard Law were installed only four days apart in 1984. Characteristically Laghi bishops, both called in their installation homilies for "authentic" faith, and they spoke about what is "absolutely indispensable to our Catholic faith: the authority of the Holy Father."[8] A new direction was being charted.

But perhaps it only was natural. Not only had the forces of polarization been unleashed by the Cold War and under way in the United States for decades at that point, but in John Paul II the church now had a leader whose life and experience had been shaped by the Cold War. As a respected biographer of John Paul has put it, "The confrontation between the Church and Poland's communist masters was a constant war, not a sporadic set of skirmishes. It was always 'we' and 'they,' 'us' and 'them.' . . . This was a nonadjudicable struggle. Somebody was going to win and somebody was going to lose."[9] Or, in the words of Archbishop Bernard Law, "we cannot tolerate the false notion that it can be 'yes' in some aspects of our life and 'no' in others."[10]

The time for debating the nuances about personal opposition and public positions was over. The time had come for consistency.

The Challenge of Consistency

Archbishop Joseph Bernardin had been bruised by the events of the 1976 presidential election. By disposition, Bernardin was a reserved person. His increasing responsibility in the church had cast greater and greater attention on him since his 1952 ordination, and he had gradually grown accustomed to it. But being at the center of a church controversy that intersected a presidential election was something else altogether. Beyond mere public attention,

1976 had placed Bernardin and the bishops' conference under a microscope. If the debate were only about whether abortion is unacceptable the matter would have been easy. Bernardin had been unreserved in his criticism of the US Supreme Court's *Roe v. Wade* decision since the first moments after its announcement. His exasperation about abortion only became more evident in his public comments throughout the rest of the 1970s.[11] But legal and political questions are different from moral questions, especially in the United States where so many citizens do not share the Catholic faith or the moral convictions that accompany it. As Bernardin learned to his chagrin during the 1976 election, articulating the Catholic position on important issues of the day is not as simple as reciting from the *Catechism* or even preaching the Gospel. Winning souls does win votes eventually, but a pastor's job is not the same as a lobbyist's. Winning souls is supposed to come first, not winning political battles. More than that, the rapidly polarizing argument over abortion threatened to consume any attention that could be given to other issues. The bishops had been working throughout the 1970s to focus attention on hunger, and they also had concerns about nuclear weapons and immigration. How could those issues, or many others, cut through all of the heat and noise of the tumult over abortion?

Perhaps that was part of the calculation when Archbishop Jadot intervened with the US bishops after the meetings with Carter and Ford in August 1976 and urged the bishops to issue a statement asserting their political neutrality.[12] The statement did not water down the bishops' strong commitment to "the need for a constitutional amendment to protect the unborn." But they went on to add that their concerns also included "unemployment, adequate educational opportunity for all, an equitable food policy both domestic and worldwide, the right to a decent home and health care, human rights around the globe, intelligent arms limitation and many other social justice issues." Finally, the bishops emphasized that "our profound concern for the specific issue of abortion is based on the fact that life is not only a value in itself but is absolutely fundamental to the realization of all other human values and human rights."[13] The bishops were drawing attention to other issues that form a whole tapestry in which abortion is a critical thread, but which all hangs together.

Bernardin left Cincinnati for Chicago in 1982, the second largest archdiocese in the United States at that time, and he went with Pope John Paul's confidence. The two had known each other since Bernardin visited Poland in 1975 and Cardinal Wojtyła visited Cincinnati during the following year. Pope John Paul had taken a particular interest in the appointment of a new archbishop for Chicago, and he appeared determined that it should be Bernardin.[14] Another signal of the pope's confidence, Bernardin was elevated to the College of Cardinals less than a year after he went to Chicago. Bernardin was not really a Jadot bishop. Jadot was appointed to the United States the year after Bernardin was named archbishop of Cincinnati, and Jadot left for Rome in 1980, so he played no role in Bernardin's appointment to either position. But Bernardin had been identified closely with Jadot, and certainly they shared the same approach to the appointment of bishops and other issues. Despite any substantive disagreements that this might imply with John Paul, Bernardin's personal relationship with the new pope had created a situation in which, especially after being appointed to Chicago, he enjoyed considerable freedom to try to remake the church's role in the political debate. Perhaps we might even say that he hoped to repair damage that had been done in 1976.

The first step the bishops took was a pastoral letter issued by the whole bishops' conference. *The Challenge of Peace* was released by the conference in 1983. A pastoral letter is a teaching document normally written by a bishop to his own diocese. Any bishop has three specific duties under canon law—in his own diocese, he dispenses the sacraments, he is a steward of the church's property, and he teaches the faith. A pastoral letter is an important tool in a bishop's teaching office. The bishops of the United States had been working together since the days of Bishop John Carroll, and they had issued pastoral letters together since the Second Plenary Council of Baltimore in 1866. The Second Vatican Council had formalized those collaborations when it created a role for national conferences of bishops to play in the church.[15] During the 1980s with *The Challenge of Peace* (1983) and *Economic Justice for All* (1986), the US bishops signaled a different approach to collaboration, in light of how the Council imagined a new role for bishops' conferences. The *Roe* decision had prompted the bishops to take a more activist posture and, while the bishops continued to take pride in the "consistency" of their opposition to abortion, their pastoral letters and other engagements with public issues began to address a wider range of issues.[16] The conference would continue to issue statements and even pastoral letters after *The Challenge of Peace* and *Economic Justice for All*. Yet, those two documents continue today to stand out as unusual for their ambition. No other document from the US bishops since the mid-1980s has been like them in scope or impact. Yet, almost as quickly as the bishops began collaborating in this way, they stopped.

When the initial decision was made to write *The Challenge of Peace*, it was in response to the election of Ronald Reagan as much as anything else. Reagan had been supported by a majority of Catholics even as he had expressed a willingness to build up American nuclear stockpiles. One influential bishop at the conference's November 1980 meeting observed that the implications of the election for the arms race had brought the world to "a point of urgent crisis."[17] The conference formed a committee to write the letter to teach Catholics in the United States about what the church says about questions of war and peace in the nuclear age, and Bernardin chaired the committee. For Bernardin, the letter represented an opportunity to speak directly to Catholic voters who had grown so preoccupied by abortion during the 1976 election that they may have forgotten other issues. Across a wide range of those issues, including nuclear weapons, abortion, and capital punishment, as well as a range of subtler threats to human life such as hunger and disease, the bishops urged Catholics to recognize how the church calls on them to "relate our concerns about war and peace to other 'pro-life' questions."[18] *The Challenge of Peace* and the 1986 pastoral letter on Catholic social teaching and the US economy, *Economic Justice for All*, both reflected a bold effort to leverage the potential of bishops' conferences in the first two decades following the Second Vatican Council, and to use the ability of bishops to speak together with one voice as a way to confront the ordinary, worldly problems of twentieth-century life. In *Economic Justice for All*, the bishops lamented "a tragic separation between faith and everyday life" (5) that emerges as the theme of both pastoral letters. As the Reagan administration dismissed the bishops as "too idealistic" or as "unwitting agents of the Kremlin," the bishops' reply challenged those certainties of the world with the confidence of faith.[19] The dignity of the human person is paramount in all cases, an interest above every other interest that is "as old as the Hebrew prophets, as compelling as the Sermon on the Mount, and as current as the powerful voice of Pope John Paul II" for Catholics.[20] Even as that was true for both of those pastoral letters as they brought the church's social message to bear on immediate problems of the world in the early to mid-1980s, the letters were only a beginning. After their publication, the challenge "to adhere consistently to the principles" found in those letters remained as a difficult problem.[21]

The conference's pastoral letters are worthy of mention not so much for any particular impact they had on American politics as for how they marked a turning point in the bishops' engagement with American politics. The two pastoral letters continued the unprecedented level of involvement in US national political questions on which the bishops embarked after the *Roe* decision. While the bishops' conference had existed in one form or another since World War I, never before the mid-1970s had the US bishops ever embarked on anything like the campaign for a constitutional amendment to overturn the *Roe* decision. With the peace pastoral letter and the economic pastoral letter, the bishops continued their political advocacy. It should be said that advocacy was in harmony with the urgings of the Second Vatican Council when the Pastoral Constitution on the Church in the Modern World called on Christians not to shirk "their earthly responsibilities" to the political community (*Gaudium et Spes* 43). It is only a natural consequence for spiritual leaders to weigh in on how the church sees the earthly questions of political life in terms of the demands of the Gospel. Still, for all of the reasons it was true in the 1976 election, taking public positions on issues like the nuclear arms race and economic policy was a risky proposition, fraught with the danger that the bishops would appear to be partisan. Very much to their credit, the bishops went to great lengths to avoid partisanship in the drafting of the pastoral letters.[22] The bishops went out of their way to steer a middle course, with only the Gospel and the social teachings of the church to guide them. Still, many people did receive the pastoral letters in a spirit of partisanship, and those partisan responses fueled a new phase in the bishops' engagement with American political questions. The bishops' position on nuclear arms in *The Challenge of Peace* and *Economic Justice for All* was much closer to the position of the Democrats, even as the bishops' consistent position on abortion reflected better the Republican platform. The effort of the bishops to remain consistent with church teaching regardless of partisan implications is evident. But that sort of consistency did not travel well outside the sanctuary of the church. One Republican congressman complained publicly that "'a consistent pro-life ethic' requires support for liberal social programs along with opposition to abortion," just as Catholic Democrats objected to the church's demands that they "impose" the requirements of their faith and oppose abortion in public policy.[23]

Consistency about church teaching across the whole range of political issues was not meant to be easy or to make anyone comfortable, of course. As the 1980s went on, it got even harder. Cardinal Bernardin engaged the difficulty even further six months after the bishops released *The Challenge of Peace*. In a lecture at Fordham University on December 6, 1983, Bernardin proposed what he called "A Consistent Ethic of Life." The Consistent Ethic reflected Bernardin's effort to continue down that middle path of consistency, disregarding the ideological commitments of Republicans and Democrats, conservatives and liberals, and simply applying the teaching of the church consistently across the range of issues concerning human life. The Consistent Ethic took *The Challenge of Peace* as "a starting point for developing a consistent ethic of life" that underscores the "*presumption* against taking human life" in every case.[24] Pope John Paul II described the new technologies that open "new opportunities for care" as they also pose "new potential to threaten the sanctity of life" in his encyclical letter *Redemptor Hominis*.[25] In a similar way, Bernardin asked, "In a time when we can do anything technologically, how do we decide morally what *we never should do*?"[26] That question encompassed abortion and nuclear war. It also encompassed "issues of genetics," "capital punishment," and "the care of the terminally ill."[27] Facing all of these challenges at once amid the blistering political debates that surround them, the church found itself needing a steady yardstick by which to evaluate the questions raised by new scientific and social developments. The Consistent Ethic was an effort to describe one. Another name for this effort caught on quickly, it stuck, and it led to frequent misunderstandings of Bernardin's purpose.

The phrase does not appear in the text of Bernardin's Fordham lecture, but the *New York Times* reported the next day that "the Cardinal said the various issues made a 'seamless garment' that deserved the utmost attention of the American Catholic church."[28] Bernardin's friend and biographer Eugene Kennedy recalled that "seamless garment" was a "shorthand usage," and it became an "ongoing source of mild frustration for Bernardin, an unnecessary loose thread teased out of the fabric of his thought by those who found it easier to criticize the inadequate simile than the substance of his reasoning."[29] Whether referring to the Consistent Ethic as a "seamless garment" frustrated Bernardin or not, Kennedy captured the spirit of theological opposition to Bernardin's Consistent Ethic. Critics worried that the Consistent Ethic made abortion and euthanasia morally equal to reporting for the draft or executing criminals after they were found guilty of murder. There is a difference, those critics said, between killing in war and executing a criminal and, in the case of abortion or euthanasia, the killing of innocents. Those critics had the full depth of the church's moral theology on their side to make those important distinctions. Yet, they were also focused on the wrong problem. Bernardin's own loose talk at the Fordham lecture about how the nuclear arms race and abortion were "linked" and the metaphor of a seamless garment contributed to the misunderstanding and made it sound as though the Consistent Ethic of Life said that those moral problems were the same. In a way, that turned out to be a fortunate problem. Those critics forced Bernardin to develop and clarify the Consistent Ethic to such a remarkable degree that it became a life's work.

Bernardin offered no fewer than ten public lectures exploring and deepening the theme of the Consistent Ethic of Life between 1983 and 1986, and then later even more. More extraordinary, he participated in an academic symposium on the Consistent Ethic. Bernardin sat while scholars probed, questioned, and refined the Consistent Ethic, and then he published their findings.[30] The fact that the Consistent Ethic does not rank moral issues according to importance does not mean that it would regard all moral issues as equal. To think in such terms only misplaces the focus of the Consistent Ethic, which is not on the particular moral issues affecting human life so much as on the criteria we use to evaluate moral questions. Bernardin's guiding star—a "*presumption* against taking human life"—is only a place to begin.

Those scholars whom Bernardin invited to critique the Consistent Ethic questioned it in historical, philosophical, theological, and interreligious terms. They raised difficult questions that made it plain that Bernardin's initial propositions about a Consistent Ethic needed a lot of work.[31] Still, the Consistent Ethic had opened a conversation among bishops, lay people, and academic experts to enlarge the church's engagement with American political questions beyond the scope of abortion at a time when the Second Vatican Council had established the basis for Catholics' playing a role in politics at an individual and institutional level. The questions facing Americans were as numerous as they were important, and the 1976 election had demonstrated how Catholics were at the height of their social and political influence in the United States. Bernardin's effort was a natural development from those circumstances, and it had one additional notable characteristic. The Consistent Ethic won praise from John Rawls, an American political philosopher whose ideas defended the notion of a neutral public square in which a strict separation between religious ideas and political ideas must be maintained. Yet, in the Consistent Ethic, Rawls acknowledged how Bernardin had identified a way for the church to join political debates that secular liberals like Rawls could not simply dismiss.[32]

Of course, the endorsements of secular liberals never were going to persuade those inside the church who saw no hope of bringing secular liberals to the Catholic way of seeing things. For them, the idea of a seamless garment offered the picture of one whole cloth, with no breaks or differentiations. It placed abortion on an equal footing with other, less fundamental threats to life. And, even if those criticisms of the Consistent Ethic could not withstand an encounter with what Cardinal Bernardin actually said, it did not matter. The people who rejected the seamless garment outright were not interested in dialogue with the world outside the church, anyway.

The 1971 Synod of Bishops had affirmed that "the Church has the right, indeed the duty, to proclaim justice on the social, national, and international level, and to denounce instances of injustice," as the US bishops had quoted it in their own 1976 statement on "Political Responsibility: Reflections on an Election Year." In that document, the bishops had urged voters to "examine the positions of candidates on the full range of issues, as well as the person's integrity, philosophy and performance," and they named a "broad range" of issues on which "the Bishops of the United States have already expressed themselves."[33] Abortion was first of those issues named. Of course, the bishops had named the issues "in alphabetical order," and not in any order of importance.[34] Other issues, such as housing, food policy, and military expenditures followed, but only alphabetically. Placing abortion at a level of importance beyond every other issue was not yet a priority for the US bishops three years after *Roe.* In 1976, in their statement of political neutrality, the US bishops again affirmed their concern on "the broad range of issues" they had "enumerated in testimony presented to the Democratic platform committee on May 20, 1976, and to the Republican platform committee on August 9, 1976."[35] Bernardin's Consistent Ethic, in a way very much like the influence Jadot had on the bishops' conference, continued to follow a trajectory down the middle of American social and political life, true to the church's teaching in a way that was critical of both parties because both parties had issue positions the church could not support.

Bernardin's Consistent Ethic was in step with everything the US bishops had been saying for decades. It simply was not in step with the new tone of the US bishops in the 1980s. The ground had shifted inside the church in the United States. Conservative activist Phyllis Schlafly condemned the Consistent Ethic, calling it "very divisive to the prolife movement."[36] Agreeing with a spokesman for the National Right to Life Committee who described how that group's members "have sharply different views on such issues as capital punishment, human rights and society's obligation to the poor," Schlafly was blunt: trying to unite people over those issues, Schlafly predicted, would "sabotage the prolife movement."[37]

We never will know if Schlafly was right, or whether something else was possible. We certainly do know that she and those who agreed with her were not interested in finding out.

Kennedy's Ghost

Abortion had made the 1976 presidential campaign difficult enough for the church without a Catholic on the ballot. Adding a Catholic contender for the White House to the potent stew of political forces at work around the abortion question for the church and for both major political parties would only make things far worse. Everyone was spared that situation in 1980, when neither the Democrats nor the Republicans nominated a Catholic. In 1984, it would be different.

Twenty-four years earlier, Senator John F. Kennedy faced considerable skepticism throughout the United States, but especially in the South when he ran for president in 1960. To quell fears among Democratic constituencies outside the urban centers of the Great Lakes and the East Coast about being an Irish Catholic, Kennedy offered a sort of a statement of religious and political faith at a September 1960 meeting of the Greater Houston Ministerial Association in Texas. He said:

> [B]ecause I am a Catholic, and no Catholic ever has been elected President, the real issues in this campaign have been obscured—perhaps deliberately, in some quarters less responsible than this. So it is apparently necessary for me to state once again—not what kind of church I believe in, for that should be important only to me—but what kind of America I believe in. I believe in an America where the separation of church and state is absolute—where no Catholic prelate would tell the President (should he be Catholic) how to act, and no Protestant minister would tell his parishioners for whom to vote—where no church or church school is granted any public funds or political preference—and where no man is denied public office merely because his religion differs from the President who might appoint him or the people who might elect him. . . . I ask you tonight to follow in that tradition—to judge me on the basis of my record of 14 years in Congress . . . instead of judging me on the basis of these pamphlets and publications we all have seen that carefully select quotations out of context from the statements of Catholic church leaders, usually in other countries, frequently in other centuries. . . . Whatever issue may come before me as President—in birth control, divorce, censorship, gambling, or any other subject—I will make my decision in accordance with these views, in

> accordance with what my conscience tells me to be the national interest, and without regard to outside religious pressures or dictates. . . . But if the time should come . . . when my office would require me to violate my conscience or violate the national interest, then I would resign the office; and I hope any conscientious public servant would do the same.[38]

Those remarks satisfied the worries of so many Democratic voters in 1960 that Kennedy was elected to the White House. But the implications of Kennedy's message would haunt Catholic politicians, Catholic bishops, and Catholic voters for generations that followed.

What certainly is clear in Kennedy's remarks is how Catholics had almost emerged from the ghetto of immigrant Catholicism in 1960, but not quite entirely. The ugliness of the anti-Catholicism dredged to the surface of American life by Kennedy's candidacy reopened wounds for many American Catholics in what was otherwise a moment of triumph.[39] After all, Kennedy was Irish. He belonged to one of those immigrant groups that had lurked at the margins of American social and political life in a Catholic ghetto. The prejudice Kennedy faced in the 1960 election was familiar to Catholics at every level of American life, and many still experienced that prejudice.[40] In a way, Kennedy charted the path out of that ghetto into the American mainstream that countless others would follow. The Kennedy campaign, after all, arrived at just the moment when Catholic anticommunism had provided the *bona fides* for Catholics to become trusted Americans. Yet, the terms for following Kennedy's path were defined in that Houston address. Access to the mainstream demanded some division of personal convictions from political responsibility, a concession to the reality that the people's representatives must represent all of the people—many of whom are not Catholic and do not agree with what the church teaches.

Especially when we consider all of the compromises demanded by the American political system in order to get anything done, we know that no one ever gets everything she or he wants. A political official might personally want a higher minimum wage, but that outcome may not be possible politically. Or a president might have moral objections about the use of American nuclear weapons. Would the American people be wrong to expect him to maintain a nuclear deterrent and put his personal objections aside to do the unpleasant things needed to provide security against the nuclear threat posed by another nation? Abortion does not pose exactly the same problem as either of those questions, of course. But like those hypothetical cases, abortion raises the problem of pluralism. Pluralism describes the situation in which many people, living together, are permitted to believe many different things. Pluralism describes America, and pluralism demands that we tolerate our differences. In a political system like the American system of government, citizens have to find a way to live together despite the fact that they believe different things about important questions. Balancing personal moral conviction against the legal and political possibilities of American government is a particular problem for public officials and, history has proved, it has especially been a problem for Catholics who hold public office. The problem arose for John F. Kennedy during the 1960 campaign. We have seen that problem return during the 1976 presidential election, when Archbishop Bernardin lamented that "personal opposition is not enough" where abortion is concerned. The 1984 presidential election would bring that problem to new, more forceful collision with the abortion issue and the US Catholic bishops.

New York's Governor Mario Cuomo spent the 1980s at the center of speculation about whether he would seek the presidency. Cuomo was the son of Italian immigrants, born in New York City's outer boroughs in working-class circumstances. In every way but one, Cuomo was like those children and grandchildren of Catholic immigrants who had risen into mainstream acceptability during the mid-twentieth century. But where so many of those other descendants of Catholic immigrants drifted from the Democratic Party to the Republican Party through the twentieth century, Cuomo became an icon of American liberalism. Rising first through New York City politics, after a failed bid for mayor of New York, Cuomo won election as governor in 1982. Almost as quickly, he became a national figure.

Certainly, Cuomo was one of the most prominent Catholics in national politics during the 1980s. His acclaim won him a coveted spot as keynote speaker of the 1984 Democratic National Convention in San Francisco. Primetime convention speaking spots did not always launch speakers into the high-altitude orbit of presidential politics. But Barack Obama gave the 2004 keynote, and Bill Clinton gained national attention with a primetime address at the Democrats' 1988 convention. The Democrats' 1984 nominee, Walter Mondale, briefly courted Cuomo for the second spot on the Democratic ticket, but the vice-presidential nomination ultimately went to Geraldine Ferraro. Like Cuomo, Ferraro was an Italian Catholic from New York and, raising the stakes for the abortion issue, Ferraro's gender brought women's issues to the fore of the 1984 campaign. Abortion would dominate the discourse of another presidential campaign, but this time a Catholic noncandidate would be the focus of the controversy. Mario Cuomo took the abortion issue and the questions surrounding a Catholic holding public office head-on.

Cuomo's efforts to explain how he applied his moral convictions as a Catholic to the duties of his public office came first in the introduction to a published diary of his 1982 gubernatorial campaign. Cuomo explained to a Harvard

University audience in July of 1984, "When the diary was accepted by Random House for publication, the senior editor . . . [said] give us an introduction that describes your philosophy in twenty-five pages, and where your philosophy comes from."[41] The introduction finds Cuomo linking together his Catholic faith and his political commitments so indistinguishably that we could be tempted to describe the connection as seamless. "I never felt the two commitments were incompatible," Cuomo wrote.[42] Cuomo described a perspective we could identify as Catholic communalism, a rather typical description of the tradition of Catholic social teaching. He emphasized themes that would recur ten days later when he spoke at the Democratic convention. Politics, Cuomo recalled, meant "trying always to arrange a package of justice, charity, and mercy, proffering it beyond the walls of our own homes, our own churches, our own lives," and he expressed an idea of "family" as "the bedrock on which my political philosophy rests."[43] Speaking also "as a Catholic governor who was elected to serve" all the people, Cuomo reflected on the "relationship between my private philosophical commitment and the law we make and enforce for the commonweal."[44] That theme also would reemerge.

Cuomo's most important contribution to the 1984 campaign came at the invitation of Notre Dame's Department of Theology, which invited the New York governor to speak on September 13, 1984. Cuomo asked,

> must politics and religion in America divide our loyalties? Does the "separation between church and state" imply separation between religion and politics? Between morality and government? Are these different propositions? Even more specifically, what is the relationship of my Catholicism to my politics? Where does the one end and other begin? Or are the two divided at all? And if they're not, should they be?[45]

The answers that Cuomo offered did not satisfy many people. Then again, the topic of his remarks had bedeviled generations of theologians and philosophers, statesmen and lawyers. Yet, in at least one way, the reception that awaited Cuomo's remarks was a bit surprising.

Overall, Cuomo followed the outlines of Kennedy's Houston remarks in 1960. As Kennedy distinguished between the private life of the Catholic believer and the public activities of an elected official, Cuomo observed that "Catholic public officials take an oath to preserve the Constitution," which includes protections for things "sometimes contradictory" to Catholic faith.[46] Cuomo made it clear, as Kennedy did, that he felt that being an elected official obliged him to honor the "consensus view of right and wrong" found in American "public morality," a term borrowed from Jesuit John Courtney Murray. Cuomo went on, further than Kennedy went, to make observations concerning abortion, which was not an issue to which Kennedy needed to address himself in 1960. Here Cuomo's remarks were astute about the limits of politics and the law, in the way we would expect a lawyer and governor of a large state to know that politics and the law are imperfect instruments for solving complex moral problems. In terms of moral theology, Cuomo's remarks were imprecise to the point of being problematic. It was no surprise that problems followed.

To the extent that Cuomo described the problem of abortion from a lawyer's and political leader's perspective, it remains difficult to quarrel with him today. Cuomo ticked off a list of possible political responses to legalized abortion that remain as unappetizing today as they were in 1984: a constitutional amendment risked another era of "Prohibition," "legislating what couldn't be enforced," and, in a way St. Thomas Aquinas had written about, inviting "disrespect for the law in general"; returning the question to the states would create a "checkerboard of permissive and restrictive jurisdictions" that would permit "millions of" abortions to continue; and cutting Medicaid funding for abortions "would not prohibit the rich and middle classes from having abortions."[47] Finally, Cuomo looked to history. Whenever abortions have been restricted or illegal, they still have gone on. This creates other problems, for even "if we could put most abortions out of our sight, return them to the backrooms where they were performed for so long," the Catholic conscience should be troubled by the abortions that would continue and the risks to mothers and children posed by unsafe medical procedures. All of this, in fact, is quite sensible and, within the perspective of American law and political reality, it is unarguably right.

Cuomo's Notre Dame remarks were more troubled on the grounds of moral theology, when he more than once failed to distinguish abortion from other issues such as the nuclear arms race and care for the poor. Here the teaching of the church is clear and, among Catholics, settled. Abortion is a grave moral evil; it belongs to a category of sins, including desecration of the Eucharist and breaking the seal of the confessional, that incur an automatic excommunication that, in ordinary cases, only can be absolved by a bishop. If a person uses artificial birth control or a couple gets a divorce, the church teaches that those things are sinful. Yet, while mortal sins, they do not incur excommunication. Cuomo's argument failed to observe that distinction. With apparent puzzlement, he lamented that "abortion is treated differently," as though the difference had no basis or justification.[48] The grave sinfulness of abortion has been a constant teaching of the church for centuries.[49] It is not really surprising that Governor Cuomo should have overlooked that distinction. He was candid to acknowledge, "I do not speak as a theologian; I do not have that competence."[50] That was an honest, even a generous admission, since it acknowledged the greater competence of others to speak about parts of Cuomo's argument. Yet, his critics did not share that same spirit of generosity. Cuomo had invoked Bernardin's Consistent Ethic in his Notre Dame remarks, in which Bernardin had preserved the distinction between abortion and the other issues along the spectrum of human life.[51] Having invoked Bernardin while being somewhat careless with moral distinctions about abortion, Cuomo's public remarks at Notre Dame also made it easier for critics of Bernardin to dismiss the Consistent Ethic. Grouping Cuomo's updating of Kennedy's 1960 remarks together with Bernardin's Consistent Ethic, critics now found themselves able to paint an opposing party that supported a "secular-separationist agenda" that would radically cut religious beliefs off from political life.[52] Critics of Cuomo's remarks such as Illinois Rep. Henry J. Hyde accused him of a "double standard" that said it was acceptable for Catholic bishops to speak out about nuclear disarmament but not about abortion.[53] Along lines forming since 1976 and firmed up with the earliest responses to the Consistent Ethic, two sides increasingly began to polarize the church in the United States.

The conflation of Cuomo's Notre Dame remarks with the Consistent Ethic led into even less charitable directions, as "Cardinal Bernardin's 'seamless garment' " was described as "the 'Cuomo cloak.' "[54] Cuomo and Bernardin were consistently lumped together: Bernardin was seen to be giving cover for Catholic Democrats who were beholden to pro-choice pressure groups, while Cuomo was seen to be dividing religious belief forcefully from public life.[55] The irony was that Cuomo's argument, different in its moral specificity from Bernardin's, was not very different from Kennedy's argument in 1960, when he said, "I will make my decision in accordance with . . . what my conscience tells me to be the national interest, and without regard to outside religious pressures or dictates." The chief difference between Cuomo and Kennedy was that Cuomo had taken up the abortion question. Kennedy was praised widely by American Catholics and their bishops as he blazed a trail into the American mainstream in 1960, while scorn was heaped on Cuomo in 1984.[56] Of course, in years following 1984, it became possible to lament that Kennedy's "words stripped the public square of religious influence and attacked the principle of pluralism and free speech."[57] It even was possible to make the link directly, to say that Cuomo's 1984 remarks "tracked back to Kennedy."[58] After abortion became so central to Catholic's consciousness of American politics, Kennedy's memory would not be spared.

Like the polarizing rhetoric of the Cold War that divided the world into an American "us" and a Soviet "them," the search for enemies outside eventually turned inward. Just as the Cold War devolved into a Red Scare, the political challenge abortion posed to Catholics, steeped in American Cold War culture, drove many to seek an ever more "consistent" Catholic witness on that lone issue. Bernardin's Consistent Ethic became a fulcrum on which the Catholic engagement with abortion pivoted from consistent ethics toward consistent politics. The pivot came in Cuomo's attempt to engage the abortion issue, and it came under the lingering shadow of the 1960 Kennedy campaign and all that came before it.

Cuomo had not set out to play this role. While many observers supposed that Cuomo must have been planning an eventual campaign for the White House, that never happened. Cuomo's own account of how his intrusion into the political debates of 1984 came about did not enter the public record until later. Charles R. Morris interviewed Cuomo for his book *American Catholic* (1997), and Cuomo recalled that the Notre Dame episode began when he did not veto a bill permitting state funds to pay for abortions. In the aftermath,

> he was at home with his wife and one of his children, watching a television interview with the archbishop [New York Archbishop John O'Connor]. "Somebody asked him whether I should be excommunicated. I thought the question was offensive, and I expected him to brush it off, the way you do with questions like that. But he *didn't*. He actually *considered* it! And gave some kind of answer that implied that maybe I should be. You can't imagine how devastating that is. To be sitting there with your wife and one of your children and have that said about you. My son—he was thirteen—said, 'Dad, is that true? Could you be *excommunicated*?' . . . I was so upset. . . . I couldn't sleep."[59]

The episode is illuminating not because it tells us something about Cuomo's motives for speaking at Notre Dame. In fact, he had already accepted an invitation to speak and called to cancel it after Archbishop O'Connor's remarks. "There had been a lot of publicity about my abortion position, and I didn't want to embarrass them," Cuomo said.[60] Rather, the picture Cuomo draws of a Roman Catholic archbishop musing about the state of someone's soul through the media tells quite a lot about how much the dialogue over abortion had deteriorated, and how badly it had corroded the internal life of the church. In any event, Notre Dame's president Reverend Theodore Hesburgh, CSC, prevailed on Cuomo to keep the speaking engagement. History tells us the rest.

That Cuomo became the main story was a little strange, since he never was on the presidential ballot in 1984. That was Geraldine Ferraro, a Democrat from Long Island and the first woman nominated by a major party. Ferraro did not avoid controversy about abortion or quarrels with Archbishop O'Connor during the campaign. Like Cuomo, Ferraro said, "I try to separate my religious views from my standing on the issues," and she met with the same reactions with which Cuomo met.[61] Archbishop O'Connor suggested

Ferraro had "said some things about abortion . . . which are not true," appearing to mean that it was not possible for a Catholic to make the distinction between personal faith and public action as a political official.[62] Ferraro hewed to the same line that Cuomo had been laying out, one that dated back to the 1976 election and the distinctions that Jimmy Carter had sought to draw. This time, even more than in 1976, the Catholic bishops were having none of it. O'Connor was joined by Boston's Archbishop Bernard Law, who released a statement in September and called abortion "the critical issue in this campaign." Law went further, saying that it is "irresponsible" to separate personal faith from public actions "on the pretext that this is only a matter of personal opinion."[63] Assertions like these anticipated a next phase in the conflict between Catholic elected officials and Catholic bishops when the bishops' efforts to influence the policy debate would become clouded by an increasingly uncomfortable appearance of political partisanship. The president of the bishops' conference, Bishop James Malone, denied the bishops had any partisan intentions in August of 1984, but Archbishop Law was somewhat less artful. Asked whether his remarks were directed toward any particular candidate, Law replied, "This statement is directed at all candidates and all voters. I think Geraldine Ferraro is a candidate."[64]

The Archbishop and the Judge

Archbishop John O'Connor remained archbishop of New York when he became Cardinal O'Connor in 1985. He would continue to be a courageous and influential spokesman for pro-life causes until his death in 2000. As the 1980s ended, the abortion debate would turn on the influence of another O'Connor.

When President Reagan nominated Sandra Day O'Connor to the United States Supreme Court, her nomination was opposed by pro-life members of Congress who suspected she would not vote to overturn *Roe v. Wade*. By 1992, that judgment proved correct when O'Connor had joined in two cases that shifted the ground of the abortion debate while yet upholding the landmark abortion decision. *Webster v. Reproductive Health Services* (1989) came as the first substantial challenge that *Roe* had received before the US Supreme Court since the 1970s. Missouri had passed a law that defined life's beginning at conception and, from there, set forth restrictions on abortion that included the allocation of state funding away from abortion services and allowed a physician to refuse an abortion if the fetus was determined to be viable.[65] In its *Webster* decision, the Court avoided ruling on the question of whether life begins at conception; however, the Court both upheld the state's authority to direct funding away from abortion services and recognized that changes in the viability standard were inevitable. Most important of all, the Court did not fundamentally disturb the central claim of *Roe* that the right to seek abortion is a private matter protected by the Constitution.

This is an important if subtle point that can be difficult to understand outside the world in which legal scholars think about the Constitution. Justice O'Connor wrote in *Webster* that the Court would violate a "fundamental rule of judicial restraint" if it reconsidered the *Roe* decision. That requires some explanation.

Judicial restraint is a recognized approach to interpreting the law. Generally speaking, it is the approach preferred by judges whom we might call conservative, who sometimes are called strict constructionists. Judicial restraint calls on judges to use judicial power sparingly, to defer to the law as they find it when a case comes before them unless there is some overwhelmingly obvious need to change it.[66] Judges like O'Connor who favor judicial restraint believe in a principle of law called *stare decisis*, which means "stand by what is decided." Once the law has been defined, whether by a legislature or by a court, the judge who believes in judicial restraint presumes that the law should be left alone as much as possible. The principle is important because it gives stability to the law. The legitimacy of the law depends in no small part on being predictable. If the law can change all the time whenever a new judge comes along who does not like it, very soon we can find ourselves in a situation similar to having no laws at all. *Stare decisis* and judicial restraint protect the stability of the law, and judges who believe in them believe in protecting the legitimacy of the law by maintaining the law's stability. When Chief Justice John G. Roberts faced the Senate Judiciary Committee in his 2005 confirmation hearings, he agreed that *Roe v. Wade* is "settled law." As a Catholic himself, we know that Roberts does not agree with *Roe*. But the principle of *stare decisis* and interpreting the law according to judicial restraint demand that Roberts (who believes in those principles, too) give deference to the law once its meaning has become settled. He, like Sandra Day O'Connor, stands by what has been decided.

In the case of abortion, judicial restraint creates an interesting problem for judges who have a generally conservative temperament. *Roe* has been law for quite a while, and the longer it remains law the more some conservative judges are inclined by their commitment to *stare decisis* to leave *Roe* in place. That was essentially the argument Justice O'Connor made in *Webster*. Another generally conservative justice, Antonin Scalia, disagreed with O'Connor's reasoning. In *Webster*, Scalia wrote that he would have preferred that the Court had "reexamined *Roe*" and, objecting at length to how *Webster*'s "indecisive decision" assured that the Court would be "retaining control, through *Roe*, of what I believe to be, and many of our citizens recognize to be, a political issue," Scalia accused O'Connor and the other justices of taking an important and divisive political issue out of the hands of the voters. In general, we may say Scalia was right to say that the Court had chosen to keep hold of the abortion issue, to place abortion in a category of constitutional rights that the people of the United States are not permitted to give or take away through the political process. Scalia also was right to observe that, by seeking to avoid directly the questions raised by viability and the assumptions that the Supreme Court had made in *Roe*, the Supreme Court only kicked the can down the road with its *Webster* decision. The Court would revisit abortion again just three years later in *Planned Parenthood v. Casey* (1992).

The *Casey* decision concerned the Pennsylvania Abortion Control Act of 1982, which had created a number of requirements surrounding the obtaining of an abortion. Married women were required to verify they had notified husbands in cases where the husband was the father of the child, and minors were required to obtain either parental consent or the consent of a court. Pennsylvania established an informed consent requirement, which demanded that women seeking an abortion receive information about the procedure's risks and about the development of the fetus. The Supreme Court struck down the spousal notification, finding that it would give husbands a degree of control over a decision that belonged to the pregnant woman. The other requirements were not found to be so burdensome that they frustrated a constitutionally protected right to obtain an abortion. That right remained intact after *Casey*.

Justice O'Connor was one of three Reagan- and Bush-appointed justices who shaped the *Casey* ruling. The others were Anthony Kennedy and David Souter, and all three joined together to decide *Casey*, including the most important element of the decision. In *Casey*, those justices hinged their decision again on *stare decisis* when they wrote, "Liberty finds no refuge in a jurisprudence of doubt." Or, to put it differently, freedom will be difficult to protect when the law can be changed easily by judges. The most important part of the *Casey* ruling laid in its fundamental refusal to reverse *Roe*. *Casey* changed the rules of the road in abortion law. The *Casey* decision maintained those requirements to notify parents and to require informed consent about an abortion procedure. The *Casey* ruling also recognized how medical developments had changed the calculation of fetal viability, the point at which a child could live without the mother. But so far as the question of a constitutionally protected right to choose an abortion under certain circumstances was concerned, the three justices were adamant: "It must be stated at the outset and with clarity that Roe's essential holding . . . we reaffirm." A generation after *Roe*, *Casey* set *Roe*'s "essential holding" further into stone for judges who adhere to judicial restraint. The principle of *stare decisis* now even more guards that "essential holding" against change. Respect for precedent determined the course of the *Casey* decision and a quarter-century later has made *Roe* even more legally secure today.

Yet, holding the "essential" premise of *Roe*, the fundamental right to decide about an abortion, the Supreme Court in *Casey* did not determine that nothing in *Roe* could be changed. Where the *Roe* decision in 1973 had divided pregnancy into trimesters to determine viability, and where *Webster* in 1989 had placed viability somewhere between the twenty-fourth and twenty-eighth weeks of pregnancy, *Casey* now made a new determination that allowed states to require testing for viability before an abortion could be performed. If we recall the Court's original inspiration of *Roe*, to balance the interests of the pregnant woman and the unborn child, *Casey*'s ruling about fetal viability makes considerable sense. In 1983, Justice O'Connor observed that "the *Roe* framework, then, is clearly on a collision course with itself," because medical advancements were so rapidly changing the calculation of fetal viability and, with it, the balance between the mother's rights and the child's rights.[67] Medical science was rapidly beginning to make the constitutional right to an abortion something more like an abstract principle because, practically, the time before viability when an abortion could be performed was beginning to shrink rapidly. Permitting states to test for viability on a case-by-case basis, for as much as *Casey* affirmed the "essential" ruling of *Roe*, *Casey* also marked the point where O'Connor's prediction ("on a collision course") began to come true.

All of that should have come as good news for abortion's opponents throughout the pro-life movement and in the Catholic Church. Yet, somehow, the period after *Casey* witnessed an intensification of the polarization around abortion that surpassed principled debate to reach a point of harshness. Randall Terry of Operation Rescue told the *New York Times* that, failing to overturn *Roe* in *Casey*, "Three Reagan-Bush appointees stabbed the pro-life movement in the back," and the *Times* noted that *Casey* "would only intensify the pressure . . . to make sure that any future nominees are explicitly anti-abortion."[68] The president of the National Right to Life Committee called *Casey* "a loss for unborn children and a victory for pro abortion forces," and the bishops' conference adopted the attitude that "if one realizes the *Roe* decision was wrong, it is doubly wrong to keep imposing it on the country [with *Casey*]."[69]

The intensified polarization was not so surprising, really. After all, abortion brings considerations together that are proper to law, politics, ethics, and moral theology. These are different specializations, almost different languages that are spoken by different experts who do not understand one another's fields. Experts will disagree with one another often enough even if they are in the same field. Legal scholars disagree with other legal scholars, theologians disagree with one another, and so forth, all of which is appropriate to a good dialogue over important issues. All points of view need to be heard, and disagreements can be productive. We find ourselves in fruitful conversations when we test our beliefs against one another. But once we complicate those ordinary disagreements within one field of expertise by adding other fields, other experts, and multiplying disagreements, it is like wandering into a maze that cannot be escaped. Archbishops and judges both make important decisions about abortion, but they are coming at the problem from vastly different places and they are responding to different, often incompatible incentives and motivations. One serves the Gospel, the other serves the law. Not only are the Gospel and the law different, but they also approach problems differently. What we accept by faith is not the same as what we defend as precedent (*stare decisis*), and it is a mistake to try to collapse them into each other. Yet, while we preserve the distinctiveness of all the ways in which we approach and study abortion as a problem, we also invite some inevitable confusion. That confusion proliferated during the 1980s while abortion became a fixed feature of national politics and those many voices joined the public debate.

Unfortunately, the proliferation of that confusion during the 1980s came just at the moment when those new bishops appointed to the United States in the Laghi era pivoted away from engagement and dialogue with American culture toward confrontation. A debate that was growing more permanent and more confusing also became more entrenched and more aggressive because of that coincidence. In the years that that followed the 1980s, Cardinal Bernard Law of Boston would say, "Dialogue as a way to mediate between the truth and dissent is mutual deception." The Catholic engagement with the secular world outside the church, at least in the United States, would take that tone throughout the 1990s and sometimes was far worse. In 1994, a disturbed man shot several people in two abortion clinics, shouting at one victim, "You should pray the rosary!" before opening fire.[70] One exception to the darkening tone of those days was Cardinal O'Connor, who, in the last decade of his life, seemed to reject the more strident tone that abortion opposition had begun to take. At a 1992 march against abortion, he said, "We are not here to condemn anyone . . . but to pray," and, after the 1994 shootings, O'Connor pleaded, "If anyone is thinking about shooting an abortionist, let him shoot me first."[71] Violence remained the exception in the pro-life movement, an unusual event. But vituperation had become the norm. The lack of comity had two primary casualties, at least in terms of the public debate.

The first casualty was pro-life Democrats, as a group. As the 1990s dawned, the number of pro-life Democrats had shrunk to the point where Pennsylvania Governor Robert Casey was a notable exception in what was becoming a solidly pro-choice party. Casey attracted attention at the 1992 Democratic Convention, where he was denied a speaking spot. Whether the snub was because Casey was pro-life or, as James Carville insists, because Casey had not endorsed the Clinton-Gore ticket is not a question to settle here.[72] Rather, it was the controversy that was notable in a Democratic Party increasingly committed to women's issues. 1992 was the "Year of the Woman" in which five women won election to the US Senate, and the confirmation hearings that challenged Clarence Thomas with an accusation of sexual harassment before sending him to the US Supreme Court had occurred not quite a year earlier. In those days, the energy for candidates in the Democratic Party was not among pro-life Catholics, and a US Supreme Court decision that upheld the "essential holding" of *Roe* had only served to encourage Democratic support for *Roe* as the 1990s began. Since the 1970s, many US bishops had concluded, somewhat unfairly, that Catholics in the Democratic Party were ignoring their Catholic faith and pandering to women's groups. That analysis tended to overlook and oversimplify the abortion question from a political and legal perspective. As the 1990s began, the nation divided more clearly into a pro-life party and a pro-choice party.

The second casualty was the unity and forcefulness of the public voice coming from the bishops' conference. Since its organization in the early 1970s, the bishops' conference had been a remarkably effective megaphone for the Catholic perspective on national issues. Not all of the bishops agreed with one another, certainly. But as the 1980s began, those two pastoral letters on peace and economic justice showed the church at its best: coming together across disagreements, and forging compromises that spoke to important issues with the authentic voice of the Catholic social tradition. The bishops would be unable to repeat those successes after 1986. The next pastoral letter they planned was on the role of women, and it bogged down in debate within the conference. Perhaps it was not a coincidence, we should observe, that women's issues were the topic. The event marked the first time that the conference "failed to reach a two-thirds majority consensus on a proposed pastoral letter."[73] Even more troubling moments would lie ahead for the US bishops in the decades that followed, and the conference today has not yet regained the unity and the forcefulness it once had.

When Pope John Paul II sent Archbishop Laghi to the United States, he had several priorities in mind—"the effectiveness of the Church's evangelical mission, . . . the state of consecrated religious life in monasteries and convents, [and] the appointment of bishops."[74] Inevitably, "a different mode of engagement between the Church and American public life" would follow.[75] There would be, if nothing else, consistency.

Chapter 4

A Culture of Death

Father Fulton Sheen began his media ministry with a radio program, *The Catholic Hour,* in 1930. By the time Archbishop Fulton Sheen concluded his television ministry in 1968 he was among the most effective spokesmen for Catholicism in the United States, maybe the most effective who ever lived. Sheen's programs presented the most American face of immigrant Catholicism. Not only was there faith, but there was certainty. The certainty was defined by the rigors of the Catholic intellectual tradition. Anyone who ever had a good philosophy professor at a Catholic college or university in this period would recognize Sheen's style as he offered clear explanations about human life and difficult questions through the unwavering system of St. Thomas Aquinas's philosophy. Catholic faith never was in doubt, but neither was patriotism. In his familiar pose, clothed in a purple ferraiolo before his chalkboard, Sheen would expound on such ideas as, "We want to keep the United States a leader in the world and we believe that all God-believing people of the United States should unite to keep the country under Providence as the secondary cause for preservation of the liberties of the world."[1] At a time when immigrant Catholics were graduating slowly into the mainstream of American life by way of their fervent anti-communism, Fulton Sheen was a regular reminder of

Catholic patriotism who came into Catholic and non-Catholic homes for years.

Still, at the time when Sheen was broadcasting, "most evangelicals felt that Catholicism was sub-Christian at best, and many believed it was not Christian at all."[2] If we are thinking about it from the perspective of the years immediately following World War II, it does not seem at all obvious or self-evident that, one day, Roman Catholics and evangelical Christians would become firm partners. But that day was coming. Americans who were watching their televisions carefully would see it arrive. The Trinity Broadcasting Network (TBN) was founded by televangelists Paul and Jan Crouch in 1973, and it has become the most-watched network broadcasting Christian programming. Typically TBN's programming would be categorized as appealing to evangelicals. Even so, starting in the early 2000s, TBN began regular rebroadcasts of Fulton Sheen's *Life Is Worth Living*. It might seem jarring to find a Roman Catholic archbishop in his house cassock and purple cincture inscribing "J.M.J." on the chalkboard with each lesson on an evangelical Christian network that features Joel Osteen, John Hagee, and Kirk Cameron. But it was a sign of how much had changed for Catholics in American life and for American politics. Paul Crouch got some criticism from some fellow evangelicals for his close relationship with Rome. Still, by the earliest years of the twenty-first century, for most people, the alliance between Catholics and evangelicals seemed natural.

George W. Bush became president of the United States in 2001. Later that year, in an address to the General Assembly of the United Nations, Bush spoke against a "culture of death." The phrase gained prominence in Pope John Paul II's encyclical letter *Evangelium Vitae* (1995), in which the pope contrasted a "culture of life" that accepts and protects human life at every stage to a culture that accepts abortion, euthanasia, and other offenses against life. Bush was the first evangelical Christian to occupy the White House since Jimmy Carter's 1977–1981 administration. It could be tempting to see Bush's use of Pope John Paul II's phrase as a sign of the distance that had closed between evangelicals and Catholics. Of course, a lot of that distance had closed. That is part of the story. But the Bush administration came after the years of Reagan, George H.W. Bush, and Clinton, which had defined a polarization in American politics along lines determined by the abortion issue and at a time when the ending of the Cold War sent the polarized language of our politics searching for another division to describe.

As much as any other way to describe it, opposing a culture of life to a culture of death became a handy way to capture the two sides in American political life. As hopelessly divided as the worlds of the West and the East were during the decades before, the deeply entrenched battle over abortion and a range of other moral issues that divided Americans now would intensify to new levels. The conflict would reach its peak level in the years following the fall of the Berlin Wall and the publication of *Evangelium Vitae*. For Americans generally, and for Catholics in particular, this era brought a new sort of politics whose search for total moral clarity and stark divisions on issues ultimately only served to confuse and frustrate political discourse even further.

Evangelium Vitae

George Weigel records that "*Evangelium Vitae* actually began at the fourth plenary meeting of the College of Cardinals, held from April 4 to 7, 1991" in a "lecture by Cardinal Joseph Ratzinger."[3] The future Pope Benedict XVI told the cardinals that there was something new at work in the debate over human life: "it is no longer a question of a purely individual morality, but one of social morality, ever since states and even international organizations became guarantors of abortion and euthanasia, pass laws which authorize them, and provide the wherewithal to put them into practice."[4] This transformation of an individual moral question to a social question involving cultural morality became possible because of changes in how we live. Our relationship to one another and to technology has made it possible for us "to flee from the mystery of being."[5] Our sense of life's fragility, how in "birth and death" our own short lives force us to reflect on "the question of [our] own meaning and [our] own existence," has been replaced by the expectation that we can become the masters of reality, control the world and our own lives because we are free people who exercise individual rights over our own destinies and possess incredible technologies that lengthen our lives and permit us to do other wondrous things.[6] Cardinal Ratzinger suggested that those things that constrain us and bind us, such as pregnancy and our own suffering before death, become obstacles that frustrate our feelings of mastery and powerfulness. To regain a sense of the kind of control we expect to have over our own lives—the kind of control once thought to belong only to God—we turn to these "attacks on human life" that exercise the power of life and death in order to maintain our own illusion of control. Cardinal Ratzinger did not use the phrase "culture of death." But joining that sense of our mastery to the way in which moral attitudes had become social rather than individual, it makes sense to see how his address anticipated John Paul's encyclical. George Weigel records, "The cardinals, agreeing that a cultural turning point had been reached, adopted a closing declaration that asked the Pope" to write a new encyclical.[7] *Evangelium Vitae* was the result.

But the distance from Cardinal Ratzinger's lecture to the encyclical was not so short or so straightforward. Writing an encyclical letter, a teaching document that defines the Catholic faith, is never a quick project, and no pope ever undertakes it alone. Always, consultations are taken with bishops and theologians because, while the document is ultimately approved and signed by the pope, the teaching must be consistent with the tradition of Catholic faith. An encyclical reflects what a pope wants to teach, but, like anything else, it also will reflect the people who contributed to writing it. To understand something of how *Evangelium Vitae* came to oppose a "culture of life" to a "culture of death," it is necessary to know something about how it was written. Already we know that Cardinal Ratzinger was thinking in terms of a "logic of death" that was engaged in a "war on life" in 1991.[8] One of the earliest appearances of the phrase "culture of death" came in 1991, when Boston's Cardinal Bernard Law condemned Massachusetts Governor William Weld for promoting a "culture of death."[9] Pope John Paul used the phrase in his 1993 address at World Youth Day, urging a Denver audience to defend "the culture of life against all threats of death."[10] These iterations of the key phrase "culture of death" help us both to identify the involvement of people consulted in drafting *Evangelium Vitae* at the same time that they also chart a growing consensus to use the language of a "culture of life" and a "culture of death."

With that in mind, a statement we find published in the journal *First Things* a little less than a year before *Evangelium Vitae* begins to seem important. "Evangelicals & Catholics Together: The Christian Mission in the Third Millennium" brought together leaders in the evangelical and Catholic communities to express their broad agreement about the need to engage cultural issues in the United States through the lens of Christian faith. Those American Catholics and evangelicals lamented abortion as "the leading edge of an encroaching culture of death," and the hint of collaboration here between evangelical Christians in the United States and leading Catholics who were, at that time, being consulted about *Evangelium Vitae* seems too interesting to overlook.[11] George Weigel describes the "many evangelicals in the United States, who deeply admired *Evangelium Vitae* and were eagerly promoting it in their communities."[12] Something was happening in the meeting of American Catholics and American evangelical Protestants over the abortion issue. It is absurd to suggest that evangelical Christians in the United States were consulted in the writing of a papal encyclical. On the other hand, there is evidence in the public record to suggest that Catholic bishops and theologians who were consulted were building bridges to evangelicals who, as much as Catholics, had experienced the two decades since the *Roe v. Wade* decision and shared their frustration about their unsuccessful efforts to reverse *Roe*. The possibility of joint action in opposition to abortion had been present between Catholics and evangelical Christians in the United States since the 1976 election. Twenty years later, the possibility was becoming a reality and it reached beyond US law or American politics and into the moral teachings of the church.

Evangelium Vitae had its critics among Catholic theologians. One of them observed that *Evangelium Vitae*'s "thoroughgoing opposition" to abortion, framed "in terms of the struggle between the culture of life and the culture of death" like a "massive conflict between good and evil," proposes a way of approaching a moral problem that "has not been the typical Catholic approach" throughout the history of Catholic moral theology.[13] The Catholic tradition, unlike many varieties of Protestantism that "have seen the world primarily in terms of the opposition between grace and sin," does not approach moral problems in such generally apocalyptic terms.[14] We have seen George Weigel describe the worldview of a Cold War–era pope raised in Poland to see the world in apocalyptic terms, and we have watched polarization grow up during the Cold War in the United States, seep into the consciousness of all Americans, and, in a particular way, adapt itself to the increasing polarization around the abortion issue. But when we try to imagine how a strange, anomalous binary such as a "culture of death" opposed to a "culture of life" came to find a home in a papal encyclical, these circumstances begin to offer an explanation.

The allure of that binary may have had other explanations, too. Cardinal Bernardin had offered his Consistent Ethic of Life as a way of joining together the many threats facing human life so as to find some common principle that would defend human life in every case. That effort encountered opposition. Yet, a contemporary *New York Times* analysis of Pope John Paul's 1993 World Youth Day address makes the striking observation that the discussion of a "culture of death" sought "to advance a view of the challenges to human life beyond those like abortion that generally stir controversy."[15] While the *New York Times* may not always be the best source for analysis of Catholic moral theology, it is difficult to overlook how it seemed strikingly like Bernardin's Consistent Ethic when Pope John Paul gathered under the umbrella of the "culture of death" those things that threaten "children, the sick, the handicapped, the old, the poor and unemployed, the immigrant and Refugee."[16] There was a difference, of course. Pope John Paul's expression of this idea spoke in terms of "struggle," "onslaught," and "battle" that corresponded better to the divided, polarized expectations of his audience.[17] That language of struggle and its apocalyptic implications can also be found in the text of *Evangelium Vitae*. It is a characteristic of the approach that, in substance, said little that was different from what Cardinal Bernardin had said. It was just that Cardinal Bernardin had sought to engage the culture in a dialogue, while those who received *Evangelium Vitae* with enthusiasm had committed themselves to confrontation and struggle. In a strange way, that polarized outlook made it possible to look past the similarity between what Cardinal Bernardin and Pope John Paul sought, to see evangelical Protestants as allies and to see some Catholics as enemies.

It is necessary to step back and see that commitment to "struggle" not just against the backdrop of the American immigrant experience or the Cold War, but in the context of the most ambitious project of the John Paul II pontificate: the evangelization of culture. That ambition is there in the 1993 World Youth Day address, as it can be found throughout John Paul II's writings and remarks after the fall of the Berlin Wall. Pope John Paul discussed the evangelization of culture in greatest depth in his 1990 encyclical *Redemptoris Missio*, in which he considered the "urgency of missionary activity" (7) at a moment when the ending of the Cold War made clear an even greater crisis: the "de-Christianization of countries with ancient Christian traditions" (32) was at work, quietly eroding things long taken for granted. John Paul's apocalyptic language of "struggle" or "battle" resonated well with audiences who heard it throughout the 1990s because it satisfied their expectation for a polarized argument, and the Polish pope, shaped by experiences of Nazism and Stalinism, to some extent shared that expectation. But there is more at work than just a reflexive response to a desire to divide along clearly marked lines. The evaporation of the Soviet threat at the end of the 1980s did expose a spiritual crisis in the West, one observed by wide-ranging figures from the religious, academic, literary, and political worlds for decades before the fall of communism. Abortion and other issues emerging from the way Western societies were living at the close of the twentieth century disclosed how quickly the influence of religious traditions was vanishing from daily life. The emergence of those issues tracked with overall declines in church attendance and participation in religious life to draw a picture of what often is called a post-Christian society.

These developments certainly do raise a challenge for the church and for believers. That challenge must be met. Like many things, of course, the important question is: How? How to meet this challenge? If we view the challenge as a conflict between the present and the past with the future at stake, we will become tempted to build defenses against an attack. If we view the challenge as a struggle over values that are purely good and purely evil, we will choose a side. If we allow ourselves to see the world in terms of who agrees with us and who disagrees with us, we will quickly become divided and even polarized. But those are not the only options. Perhaps these developments, while not entirely good, are not entirely evil either. Although the taking of any born or unborn life always is evil, perhaps even the *Roe* decision can be a sign of how the political system and the legal system are taking the rights of women in particular and persons more generally ever more seriously amid what in general are tremendously complex political and legal circumstances in which the moral stakes cannot be higher.[18] We can decide to take *Roe* as an opportunity for division, to struggle in a battle against a foe, or we can choose to take *Roe* and everything else in modern life as an opportunity for dialogue, to find and build on what is good while we recognize where the voice of the Christian moral perspective still is needed.

Ultimately this is a question of faith. Do we believe in a possibility that the Gospel can become lost? Can the world, once entered by the Word made flesh, truly become post-Christian? It could be that the challenge of an apparently post-Christian age is not to recapture a lost past or to reenact whatever we think a Christian age was, but rather to imagine how the Christian revelation is found and experienced differently in a new time. We should not be naïve, certainly. From Diocletian in the ancient world to the Islamic State in contemporary headlines, Christians have suffered from terrible persecution. Dark things happen in a sinful world. But wherever that darkness takes hold, what always takes hold first is a division of an "us" from a "them," a worldly certainty that someone else is the problem. Polarizing divisions lead away from the radical message of the Gospel. Christianity has fallen prey to that temptation more than once over the centuries and, while such divisions never are good, they have never yet dimmed the light of the Christian message that eventually overcomes divisions and embraces the world with hope. Hope has not been the tone of recent decades in church history, but hope still is here with us.

Pope John Paul II embraced hope with his 1990 encyclical on the church's missionary mandate, and he embraced hope again when he published another encyclical just two months after *Evangelium Vitae*. With that second 1995 encyclical, *Ut Unum Sint*, and looking ahead to the year 2000, John Paul called Catholics to join in the search for unity with other Christians. In a strange sort of way, that hope found life in "Evangelicals & Catholics Together," a statement signed in 1994 by some leading evangelical and Catholic scholars, as American Catholics and evangelical Protestants found common cause together in their opposition to a culture of death.[19] In *Ut Unum Sint*, John Paul reflected on how "the theme of the family" is one of the issues that draws Christians of all types together over what is shared among them.[20] In particular, John Paul recalled an ecumenical meeting with American Protestants over that theme. The meeting took place in Columbia, South Carolina, a place where Catholics not long before had been "derided as 'mackerel snappers' and viewed with suspicion, if not disdain, because they worshipped in an alien language, Latin, and sought guidance from an alien power, the Vatican. To bigots, especially away from the coast, they were often lumped together with Jews and blacks for taunting and violence."[21] Catholics and evangelical Protestants had succeeded in hope to overcome a division. In overcoming their religious differences, however, they only had deepened other political and cultural differences with those they identified with a culture of death.

Judicial Philosophy

Just as Pope John Paul II embarked on ecumenical dialogue in the American Bible Belt, Judge Robert Bork was preparing for his confirmation hearings with the Senate Committee on the Judiciary after President Reagan had nominated him to the US Supreme Court. Antonin Scalia had been confirmed to the Court just one year earlier by a vote of 98-0, so it could be tempting to say that the political climate that followed *Roe* did not quickly change the dynamics of Supreme Court nominations. But Scalia took the seat of William Rehnquist, whom Reagan had elevated to Chief Justice and who was known to be a critic of the *Roe* decision. Bork was nominated to take the seat of Justice Lewis Powell, who had voted for the *Roe* decision in 1973. In the zero-sum politics of abortion, Scalia's nomination came with lower stakes because his presence on the Court did not change the abortion calculus. If Bork joined the Court, *Roe*'s supporters surmised, a vote would be flipped toward overturning the *Roe* decision. There was going to be a fight over Robert Bork.[22]

Bork himself held what was, at the time, an unusual position on constitutional issues. The twentieth century had been defined largely by the expansion of the Constitution's meaning to accommodate, among other things, vast economic and technological changes in American life as well as a growing consciousness of the importance of individual liberties and civil rights. Bork identified himself as an originalist, one who held that the meaning of the Constitution could not be expanded beyond the original understandings of the people who had chosen the Constitution's words and ratified them. In an interesting way, the originalist position coincided quite closely with the sorts of claims made by traditionalists in the Catholic Church who hold that the practices of the church do not and cannot change to accommodate a changing world. Perhaps for that reason, there has grown up a mutual admiration between legal originalists and Catholic traditionalists during the last three decades. The icon of those shared sympathies was Antonin Scalia, who preceded Bork's nomination and whose death touched off the uncertainty over the replacement of his successor that figured so prominently in the 2016 election. Scalia himself had a fondness for the Latin Mass and the practice of Catholic faith that prevailed before the Second Vatican Council.[23] Like many Catholics who prefer an originalist view of the Constitution, Scalia's faithful opposition to abortion found a corresponding legal perspective in the view that new rights cannot be found in the Constitution if they were not intended by those who ratified the Constitution.

The Bork confirmation hearings took place before the Senate Judiciary Committee between September 15 and 30, 1987, and they turned entirely on the nominee's judicial philosophy. Such a thing had never had happened before. Throughout the history of the United States, nominations to the Supreme Court generally have been supremely uncontroversial. Legal issues are technical by their nature, and the Supreme Court's work ranges across a daunting range of bafflingly complex questions. Judicial nominations at any level rarely had generated very much publicity, mostly because presidents almost always nominated well qualified candidates and because most members of the general public and journalists had not gone to law school. The public debate over Supreme Court nominations was one more thing that would change in the American experience following *Roe v. Wade*.

The idea that a Supreme Court nominee's judicial philosophy would become a topic of broad public debate was rather new. Beyond a general impression of whether a judge was conservative or liberal, most Americans did not and could not have had much opinion about debates between legal formalists and legal realists or any of the other technical distinctions that apply to the interpretation of law. The notion that the Senate should make a public examination of a judicial philosophy emerged from thorny political debates in which the Supreme Court found itself a player during the era of Chief Justice Earl Warren (1953–1969), when civil rights was chief among the preoccupying issues of the moment. When President Johnson nominated Abe Fortas to become Chief Justice in 1968, South Carolina Senator Strom Thurmond remarked, "it is my contention that the Supreme Court has assumed such a powerful role as a policymaker in the Government that the Senate must necessarily be concerned with the views of the prospective Justices or Chief Justices as they relate to broad issues confronting the American people, and the role of the Court in dealing with these issues."[24] The Fortas nomination was the first sign of the new era Supreme Court confirmation processes had entered.

The Fortas nomination had problems that had nothing to do with judicial philosophy. Fortas had acknowledged assisting President Johnson since joining the Court, including drafting the president's 1966 State of the Union message. In that way, Fortas was precariously close to breaching the constitutional separation of powers. On top of that, Johnson was an unpopular lame duck president who, just months earlier, had declined to seek another term in office. But the biggest problem was the shifting political mood in the United States that emboldened Senate Republicans—who were in the minority—to challenge and defeat Johnson's nomination. The Warren Court had issued a raft of landmark decisions since the first *Brown v. Board of Education* in 1954. On issues ranging from the rights of criminal defendants to free speech, the Warren Court had defined itself by its liberal decisions. But the tide was turning. Fortas had defended an experimental film, *Flaming Creatures*, on First Amendment grounds after it had run afoul of New York's obscenity laws. The *New York Times* reported how Senator Thurmond had screened the film for congressional colleagues, "to get across the ideas that the Supreme Court has been soft on hardcore pornography; that Justice Fortas is part of the Court; *ergo*, he should not be Chief Justice."[25] Senate Republicans determined to seize an opportunity to reverse the direction the Supreme Court had charted for nearly twenty years. The ethical rules for judges prevented nominees to the Court from commenting directly on cases or revealing how they would decide particular issues. Members of the Judiciary Committee were unable to probe Fortas's views about civil rights, the First Amendment, or the Supreme Court's 1965 discovery of a new right to privacy in its *Griswold v. Connecticut* decision (which anticipated the *Roe* decision).[26] Instead, senators probed Fortas's judicial views more generally, at a philosophical level, to reveal what he otherwise could not discuss. Senator Thurmond put Justice Fortas under "the most powerful magnifying glass ever used in such a hearing" with a kind of close interrogation no nominee for Chief Justice had ever been subjected to before.[27] The back-and-forth between Fortas and Thurmond reflected both men's agendas. Again and again, Fortas declined to offer answers to specific questions because of his obligation to maintain a public aura of neutrality. And again and again, Thurmond would press on with an insistence that his questions about Fortas's judicial philosophy were not "about any case that is coming before the Court," but about a case that "has already been completed."[28] At his bluntest, Thurmond told Fortas,

> every American today who is going to read the paper tomorrow is going to see that you refused today, that you failed today, to answer questions of vital importance to them, and they are going to get an impression, and maybe rightly so, that you are using this as a screen or an excuse not to go into these matters. The public wants these matters gone into. And a great many people feel that you are—that you are withholding your real true views, if you do not enter into the discussion of these matters as members of the Senate committee prefer to do.[29]

As a political matter, the senator seemed to say, the voters wanted to know—and were entitled to know—how a judge would rule before he has a chance to hear a case. Strom Thurmond was the ranking Republican on the Judiciary Committee nineteen years later when Judge Bork appeared, but in 1987 it would be the Democrats who wanted certainty about the nominee's answers to "questions of vital importance," such as *Roe*. Like so many things in this unfolding story of polarization in the life of the Catholic Church and in American politics, there are almost no clean hands anywhere. Both Republicans and Democrats have played their parts.

Bork had a prolific pen. His list of published works was impressive, and across four decades before President Reagan nominated him to the Supreme Court Bork had constructed his originalist perspective on the Constitution in the full light of day, for anyone to see. Bork's most influential book, *The Antitrust Paradox* (1978), dealt with a dense topic in economic regulation that most Americans never pause to think about. But the argument of *The Antitrust*

Paradox was built squarely on the foundations of originalism, lamenting that "the modern Supreme Court has reached out, usually through interpretations of the Constitution, to assume supervision of an ever-increasing span of activities," and asserting that building any analysis of law on the purposes intended by those who made it is "indispensable."[30] As much as Bork applied that analysis to economic regulation, he applied it to constitutional interpretation as well. Given how the Supreme Court had found a constitutional right to privacy in *Griswold*, and given how that right to privacy was the key to the *Roe* decision, the defenders of abortion rights had plain reasons to worry about what an originalist like Robert Bork would do if he were to sit on the US Supreme Court. Especially in light of the Fortas hearings, those considerations determined the course of the Bork confirmation.

The starkness of the confrontation was clear in the opening statement of the Judiciary Committee Chairman, Senator Joe Biden, who told Bork that "each generation has had as much to do to author our Constitution as those 39 men who affixed their signatures to it."[31] Biden was describing a Constitution whose meaning could be rediscovered and refashioned by new generations of Americans who were not bound by any original meaning from 1789. In his own opening statement, Bork addressed the elephant in the room by observing that "this is in large measure a discussion of judicial philosophy."[32] Bork went on to say that "the only legitimate way, in my opinion," for a judge to decide matters of law is to "attempt[] to discern what those who made the law intended."[33] Being so frank and forthright with the committee was a tribute to Bork's character and intellectual honesty. It did nothing to smooth his confirmation. Over five days of questioning, Bork was confronted by suggestions that he possessed a "peculiar constitutional philosophy," that "in Robert Bork's America, there is no room at the inn for blacks and no place in the Constitution for women," that his "views would take us back to the days when women were second-class citizens," and that "Mr. Bork is out of step with the Congress, out of step with the country, out of step with the Constitution and many of the most fundamental issues facing America."[34] Again and again, the topic returned to the central question of abortion (although other matters, such as affirmative action and presidential war powers, were also addressed). Given the extraordinary tone of the whole proceedings, there was little surprise when the Bork nomination failed by an extraordinary margin of 42-58.

The Bork hearings made undeniably clear how much the question of abortion now would dominate every nomination to the US Supreme Court. The fury of the onslaught against Bork was so extraordinary that his name—"Bork"—entered the vocabulary as a new verb, recognized by the *Oxford English Dictionary*: "To defame or vilify (a person) systematically, esp. in the mass media, usually with the aim of preventing his or her appointment to public office; to obstruct or thwart (a person) in this way."[35] A casualty of abortion politics, Robert Bork had lost a seat on the US Supreme Court but he had gained eternal renown in the English language, having become synonymous with what happened to him. Of course, future presidents resolved to find ways that would prevent their nominees from being Borked as Robert Bork had been.

The principal weakness of Robert Bork's nomination to the Court had been his vast public record, as well as the frankness and candor with which he defended it. In the polarizing politics of the late 1980s and early 1990s, the United States was entering a time when such clarity and forthrightness could not avoid controversy because of the centrality of abortion. When President George H. W. Bush nominated David Souter to fill Justice William Brennan's seat on the

Supreme Court, the harsh reality of abortion politics reached its strangest expression in Souter, who was described widely as a "stealth nominee." Like the new stealth fighter and stealth bomber being developed by the Pentagon in those days, the "stealth nominee" was one designed to conceal his approach. *Congressional Quarterly* described Souter as one who "had written little on major constitutional questions, and his ideology was difficult to define."[36] The *Wall Street Journal* praised Bush for his "artful selection" of a "judicial conservative with virtually no record on the abortion issue."[37] So long as Souter was able to keep silent about his specific views about abortion or any other controversial issue, citing judicial neutrality in just the way Fortas had done, there would be nothing for Democrats to seize on. In that effort, Souter succeeded fantastically. Senator Joe Biden pleaded, with unsuccessful frustration, that "to ask . . . what principles you would employ does not, in any way, tell me how you would rule on a specific" case.[38] Souter could not be drawn out, and he had defenders. Somewhat comically, in light of his questions to Justice Fortas, Senator Strom Thurmond cautioned his committee colleagues that "direct questioning about sensitive issues that may come before the court could impinge on the concept of an impartial, independent judiciary."[39] Saying practically nothing of substance about the controversial issues that preoccupied the senators and the divided American public, Souter was confirmed by a vote of 90-9. President Bush had happened on a successful formula to evade abortion politics with his first Supreme Court nomination. Along the way, we learned how much the law had become ensnared in the prevailing political divisions that surrounded abortion. It does bear saying that, while abortion was the most important feature of that political division, like so much else the roots of the Bork confirmation also laid in the Fortas confirmation, one event in a series that pitted Americans against one another in a cultural conflict. Abortion was a catalyst, a touchstone that sparked a deep division. But the division was not a sudden occurrence.

Neither, as time went on, was the division confined to abortion. As the next decade went on, the Supreme Court would take on an ever widening range of issues that broadened the argument over abortion into the culture wars. Those cases included, though certainly were not limited to:

- *Texas v. Johnson* (1990), which found that burning the American flag is protected by the First Amendment as symbolic speech
- *U.S. v. Virginia* (1996), which extended the protection against "separate but equal" treatment to prevent the use of separate, gender-specific training facilities for the military
- *Romer v. Evans* (1996), which held that the Fourteenth Amendment's guarantee of the equal protection of the laws prevented discrimination on the basis of sexual orientation
- *Reno v. ACLU* (1997), in which the Court ruled that Congress could not regulate obscenity on the Internet
- *Vacco v. Quill* (1997), which found that a ban on physician-assisted suicide was unconstitutional
- *Gonzales v. Carhart* (2007), which held that the practice known as partial-birth abortion could be banned by state law
- *Burwell v. Hobby Lobby* (2014), which found that a closely held, family-owned business could claim rights to the free exercise of religion under the Religious Freedom Restoration Act of 1993.

A division in American cultural and political life that had disturbed the certainty of Catholics who felt they had reached the mainstream of American life began on moral terms that Pope John Paul eventually captured with his description of a culture of death and was concerned originally with abortion and other so-called "life issues." As time went on, the division began to take on a broader cultural and political character. Old certainties about gender and sexuality were being challenged, and the feelings of patriotic attachment to their country that Catholics had developed were tested by a growing movement in constitutional law that challenged their ideas about what being American means, alienating many of them from the surrounding culture. Once again, perhaps this was why a preference for judicial conservatives or constitutional conservatives intersected with an energized movement among Catholics who also tended to be more conservative in their practice of faith.[40]

On no issue other than abortion was the division growing quite so quickly or in such a provocative way as on the question of the rights of gays and lesbians. As recently as 1986, in the year before the Robert Bork confirmation hearings, the Supreme Court had upheld state laws criminalizing sodomy in its *Bowers v. Hardwick* decision.[41] The Supreme Court has reversed landmark rulings before. It took the Court fifty-eight years for *Brown v. Board of Education* (1954) to reverse the *Plessy v. Ferguson* (1896) decision that gave constitutional protection to segregation. But the speed with which the Court acted to reverse *Bowers* was breathtaking. Only seventeen years later, in 2003, the Court ruled in *Lawrence v. Texas* (a case with nearly identical circumstances to *Bowers*) that state laws against sodomy intruded too deeply into the intimate lives of citizens without adequate justification. *Bowers* was completely reversed in just the way that the pro-life movement had been hoping to see *Roe* reversed since 1973. The Court found in *Lawrence* that the state had no interest in regulating sodomy that was as important as the privacy citizens should expect in their intimate lives. And, as quickly as the *Lawrence* decision was announced, the United States entered a national debate about whether same-sex couples ought to be permitted to marry legally. The speed with which that debate took off was dizzying. It is difficult to remember from where we are today, but some prominent Democrats were cautious to embrace same-sex marriages. Bill Clinton had signed the Defense of Marriage Act in 1996, which defined marriage only as between a man and a woman for purposes of federal tax filings and receiving federal benefits, saying, "I have long opposed governmental recognition of same-gender marriages."[42] Hillary Rodham Clinton said in 2000, "Marriage has got historic, religious, and moral content that goes back to the beginning of time, and I think a marriage is as a marriage always has been, between a man and a woman."[43] Barack Obama struck a similar tone as late as 2008: "I believe marriage is between a man and a woman. I am not in favor of gay marriage."[44] If Catholics found themselves a little disoriented and unsettled by the rapid changes taking place all around them, the evidence says it was not an absurd reaction.

While so many new challenges were raised against church teachings and the sensibilities of American Catholics, Pope John Paul addressed the role that Catholic public officials should play in a free system of government for the first time in an official teaching document. In *Evangelium Vitae*, Pope John Paul wrote, "From the very beginnings of the Church, the apostolic preaching reminded Christians of their duty to obey legitimately constituted public authorities (cf. Rom 13:1-7; 1 Pet 2:13-14), but at the same time it firmly warned that 'we must obey God rather than men' (Acts 5:29)."[45] In the most direct terms that the teaching of the Catholic Church ever had addressed the question of how Catholics in public life should approach their task when the prevailing political atmosphere pulled them away from church teaching, John Paul addressed himself directly to the argument that had been advanced by Mario Cuomo. Referring to "an elected official, whose absolute personal opposition to procured abortion was well known," *Evangelium Vitae* suggests that such Catholic public officials who seek only to limit abortions rather than eliminate them are, nevertheless, engaged in "a legitimate and proper attempt to limit its evil aspects."[46] In the same section, referring to the "grave obligation of conscience" that all Christians share "not to cooperate formally in practices which . . . are contrary to God's law," Pope John Paul writes of how some people may find themselves in situations in which "sacrifice of prestigious professional positions or relinquishing of reasonable hopes of career advancement" is required.[47] In this way, *Evangelium Vitae* comes rather close to sounding as though some Catholics should abandon their political careers if they believe their oaths as public officials to uphold the civil law require them not to act on the demands of their Catholic consciences. To put it a little differently, if Mario Cuomo felt he could not act on his Catholic conscience as an American public official, perhaps his conscience should have obliged him not to be a public official.

This reflects an expansive new understanding of how the public theology of the church interacts with the politics of nations like the United States, where the civil law conflicts with the moral teachings of the church because citizens possess different, conflicting moral beliefs. This standard never had been articulated so clearly before at the level of papal teaching. The suggestion that Catholics may need to withdraw from public responsibilities because of their conscientious positions on issues was new. Then again, viewed against how Cardinal Ratzinger had framed the problem in 1991, it was not surprising. As he surveyed "the modern age," Ratzinger concluded that "Christian values" placed a sort of a limit on freedom "in service of a social order and of a liberty guaranteed to all."[48] Legally protected abortion and other threats to human life had become possible because that limit, the reference to Christian values in public life, had vanished. The result became plain in the title of the address given by Cardinal Ratzinger in 1991, "Threats to Human Life." Those threats, Cardinal Ratzinger said, emerged from our political ideas and how we define freedom in the contemporary world. This problem created a new phenomenon, "the striking characteristic" of contemporary political problems: the moral question had been removed from an individual level to a "social" level.[49] The problem now lay in what was made possible through the actions of those who "pass laws which authorize [threats to human life], and provide the wherewithal for those who put them into practice."[50] No longer did the church think it was sufficient to address these moral questions through its teachings to individual believers. It now seemed necessary for the church to act through the public roles played by Catholics in political life, to take on social and political authority in a way it had never claimed before in the modern world.

Cardinal Ratzinger had, in effect, told Mario Cuomo he was dead wrong. He could not claim a public role separate from his personal conscience. A public official could not claim a duty under an oath to uphold the laws or the Constitution of the United States if those laws in any way cooperated in practices contrary to God's law. Fundamental claims in nations that keep a separation of church and state to accommodate the different moral convictions of diverse groups of citizens were, in fact, subject to God's law as the Catholic Church understands it through the public service of Catholics in political life. The effects were felt quickly.

"Wafer Wars"[51]

Divisions within American politics had been blurring with divisions among Catholics for a long time before the presidential election of 2004. In the decades since *Roe* Catholics had played prominent roles in presidential elections that cast them into unfamiliar roles as kingmakers and posed difficult questions about how much a Catholic public official could yield to the preferences of non-Catholic voters or laws that the church could not approve. As the debates over abortion grew more polarizing and the range of issues caught in the orbit of the culture war increased, perhaps it was inevitable that the conflict would spill over into the sanctuary and the sacramental life of the church. Whether inevitable or not, it was not a cheerful development.

Massachusetts Senator John Kerry was the first Catholic nominated by a major party for the White House since John F. Kennedy, and the first Catholic on the national ticket since Geraldine Ferraro. A CNN report described Kerry as "a former altar boy who complains when his campaign staff does not leave time in his Sunday schedule for Mass," a divorced and remarried Catholic who had sought and received an annulment because he wanted to continue to participate in the sacramental life of the church.[52] But as the 2004 presidential season developed, Kerry followed the Kennedy and Cuomo line about the relationship of his Catholic faith to his role as a public official. On the question of abortion, Kerry supported the *Roe* decision and the line of jurisprudence the Supreme Court had followed from the decision in 1973. During the campaign, he voted in the Senate against a provision that would have extended legal rights to the unborn. John Kerry was charting a course during 2004 into direct conflict with Pope John Paul II, Cardinal Ratzinger, and several American bishops who had defined the threats to human life in social terms, finding an obligation for Catholics in public life to place their Catholic consciences above the laws they had taken oaths to uphold.

During the summer of 2003, Boston's Archbishop Seán O'Malley, OFMCap, said through a press release that "a

Catholic politician who holds a public, pro-choice position should not be receiving Communion. . . . The Church presumes that each person is receiving in good faith. It is not our policy to deny Communion. It is up to the individual." It was a curiously ambivalent statement that seemed to affirm what Pope John Paul had said in *Evangelium Vitae* while stepping back from a policy of enforcement. Pro-choice Catholic Democrats in the Archdiocese of Boston such as Ted Kennedy and John Kerry were left to sort out the problem in their own consciences, where the archbishop would not intrude. But that would not be the last word. Trouble began in February 2004, as Howard Dean's candidacy for the presidential nomination waned and Kerry became the Democratic frontrunner. St. Louis Archbishop Raymond Burke said on a local television program that, if John Kerry were campaigning in the Archdiocese of St. Louis, "I would have to admonish him not to present himself for Communion." When he had previously been bishop of LaCrosse, Wisconsin, Burke had instructed priests to refuse Communion to three lawmakers who had cast pro-abortion votes and, we should observe, Burke really was not the first American bishop to act on Cardinal Ratzinger's and Pope John Paul's understanding of the political problem in this way, and he would not be alone for long in his determination to go further than O'Malley in such a public way. By May Burke was joined by Colorado Springs Bishop Michael Sheridan, and in August the archbishop of Atlanta issued a joint pastoral letter with the bishops of Charleston and Charlotte insisting that "Catholics serving in public life espousing positions contrary to the teaching of the Church on the sanctity and inviolability of human life, especially those running for or elected to public office are not to be admitted to Holy Communion in any Catholic church within our jurisdictions."[53] Archbishop John J. Myers of Newark and Archbishop Charles Chaput, OFMCap, of

Denver also joined their voices to the chorus, even as Senator Kerry was unlikely to be a regular communicant in any of those places.[54] The episode recalled how Mario Cuomo watched with his family while the archbishop of New York publicly speculated about his excommunication on the evening news.

The 2004 election unleashed an unprecedented level of political involvement for American Catholic bishops. Even 1976 did not so deeply implicate them in the process of selecting a president. Headlines like the one in the October 12 *New York Times* ("Group of Bishops Using Influence to Oppose Kerry") told only a part of the story that, by itself, went farther than the bishops had gone in 1976. The extraordinary claim that Catholics in public life have a "responsibility to exemplify in their public service the teaching of the Church" was a standard never enforced, for example, on the Catholic monarchs of Europe throughout many centuries.[55] Even more problematic was the notion that what Catholic Democrats like John Kerry or Mario Cuomo were doing somehow espoused "positions contrary to the teaching of the Church on the sanctity and inviolability of human life."[56] No Catholic in public life is on record anywhere encouraging pregnant women to obtain abortions, or praising abortion as something good or morally acceptable. The publicly available evidence does not confirm any more than that those politicians believe the US Supreme Court interpreted the civil law correctly in its jurisprudence, a secular competency, which is not the same thing as endorsing abortion. The subtle distinctions that disentangle two different things—support for abortion from support for *Roe v. Wade*—had gotten lost while a new "responsibility" for Catholics in public life had been created, one that had never existed before. Together with its new muscular presence in American politics, the Catholic Church had adopted an all-or-nothing position that overlooked these important distinctions that laid in the way of ending abortion.

Thirty years after the *Roe* decision, it was not difficult to guess why. The answer lay very close to why an evangelical president of the United States, George W. Bush, would quote so faithfully from the teachings of a pope.[57] Bush's political operation, particularly Karl Rove, understood well the frustration that had grown up among pro-life activists across three decades. For that reason, the Bush administration moved quickly in 2001 to prevent taxpayer funds from supporting fetal stem cell research and restored the Mexico City policy that prevented federal taxpayer dollars from funding organizations that promote abortion outside the United States. The Bush 2004 campaign embarked on an ambitious plan to widen the range of issues beyond abortion, taking advantage of the growing tumult over a practice known as partial-birth abortion. At their most ambitious, Bush strategists developed a plan to splinter African American voters, luring churchgoers to the Republican Party because their religious convictions opposed gay marriage. African Americans had supported Democrats by solid majorities since the Civil Rights era much in the same way Catholics once had been loyal to Democrats until Republicans succeeded in splintering the Catholic vote with abortion and other cultural issues.[58]

The goal of these efforts was uncomplicated. After a historically close 2000 election, the Bush campaign in 2004 made bold plans to redesign the political map through the use of moral issues and cultural issues. Bringing religious voters together over politics, regardless of their religious differences, was the key. "America's founders," George W. Bush said in 2002, believed "that religious faith is the moral anchor of American life" and not in "separating religious faith from political life."[59] Bush continued, "You and I share common commitments. We believe in fostering a culture of life and that marriage and family are sacred institutions that should be preserved and strengthened. We believe that a life is a creation, not a commodity, and that our children are gifts to be loved and protected, not products to be designed and manufactured by human cloning."[60] Not only did the tone of those remarks sound so much like the claims of Catholic bishops who laid down guidelines for public officials that it moved even centrist Republicans to raise alarms about "theocracy," but it also borrowed the language of Pope John Paul II in speaking of a "culture of life."[61] The only more remarkable fact was that Bush was not speaking to Catholics at all. His audience was the Southern Baptist Convention. By 2004, evangelical Protestant voters and Catholics had coalesced around a secular agenda that bore every hallmark of a carefully crafted lobbying campaign, and oftentimes they were using the same language to define that agenda even as they were coming from opposite theological beginnings.

At the heart of those efforts among Catholics was a new initiative at the Republican National Committee ("Catholic outreach") under the leadership of a onetime Baptist and convert to Catholicism, Deal Hudson.[62] Hudson was the officiant at a marriage between American Catholics and evangelical Protestants. He spoke in a language that combined the intellectual rigor of a scholar who had long studied St. Thomas Aquinas with the emotional expressiveness of one who never lost the yearning for "the full-throated hymn-singing of a Baptist congregation."[63] In 1997, a few years before Bush sought the White House, Hudson was speaking to a group of Catholic scholars and lamented the ineffectiveness of "the so-called 'Catholic vote'" which was "really not distinguishable from the general voting block [*sic*]." Hudson added, "If you wonder why Dole and the Republican Party never responded to 'pro-life' Catholic pressure, it was because they had good reason to believe there was no great advantage."[64] The key, Hudson and others realized, was to create an advantage. An alliance with evangelical Protestants would offer real prospects for success. Hudson was able to demonstrate a latent possibility, the meeting of those evangelicals with conservative Roman Catholics on the grounds of their mutual dissatisfaction with and alienation from American political life since *Roe* and, really, since the 1960s. Feeling marginalized and ignored for a long time despite their relatively large numbers, those two groups were thwarted only by the fact that they were working separately. Coming together over a political agenda, evangelicals and conservative Catholics might just be able to make progress on that agenda.[65] The only actual trouble was that a political agenda was all that held them together. As the power of their working together became clearer, the political agenda that made it possible became more important.

All of this was aimed at the US Supreme Court and the hope of at least maintaining the number of justices who would vote to overturn *Roe* if not building on that number to hasten the day when *Roe* could be overturned. Over time, other cultural and moral issues joined abortion. The prospect of a Court that would continue to let *Roe* stand or unsettle further the traditional moral beliefs of churchgoers could bring together enough pro-life voters between Catholics and evangelicals to form a stable coalition. In the 2000 election, Bush "carefully avoided saying he would appoint only Supreme Court justices who would vote against the constitutional right to abortion."[66] But that election was historically close, and the Bush administration understood clearly that there would be no margin for error in the 2004 election, especially with the controversial Iraq war growing less popular by the day. To galvanize support, Bush campaign officials turned to what they described as a "base strategy." In an election that was anticipated once again to be close, where the number of persuadable independent voters seemed to be historically low, the effort was to maximize turnout among Republican voters. In turn, that meant bringing the focus to issues that would energize conservatives. Creating that advantage for the Bush campaign, bringing evangelical and conservative Catholic voters together and bringing them to the polls, also demanded that some disadvantage be created for John Kerry.

George W. Bush was in Europe for a G-8 summit with American allies in June 2004—five months before the presidential election. During his time in Europe, Bush met with Pope John Paul II, presenting the ailing pontiff (who would die only ten months later) with the Presidential Medal of Freedom. Meetings with the pope and other officials of the Holy See, like most high-level talks among governments, were attended by countless aides. Precisely whatever is said in meetings like these is always confidential, between heads of state. But the presence of others in such meetings always opens the possibility that details of those discussions will leak out. In the case of a meeting between Bush and the Vatican Secretary of State, Cardinal Angelo Sodano, it was reported that Bush complained, " 'Not all the American bishops are with me' on the cultural issues. The implication was that he hoped the Vatican would nudge them toward more explicit activism."[67] These conversations, reported in multiple news outlets, took place after Archbishop Burke admonished Kerry not to present himself for Communion, but before bishops from Atlanta, Charleston, and Charlotte put themselves on the record. Bush made his Vatican appeal while several Catholic bishops already were putting Kerry at a very public disadvantage, seeking to increase the pressure at the highest levels of the church. No record is available to confirm whether Bush's effort at the Vatican was successful, or that it was a part of a strategy that had begun long before a meeting in Rome.[68] But from what has been reported and from what is available, it seems clear that the 2004 Bush campaign had embarked on a plan to maximize its prospects for victory by drawing the starkest possible contrasts between Democrats and Republicans on moral issues. That plan hinged on drawing evangelicals and conservative Catholics together over their shared outrage at abortion, the acceptance of gay relationships, fetal stem cell research, and partial-birth abortion. In explicit terms, the Bush campaign opposed a culture of life to a culture of death.

American politics would change after the 2004 election. A bubble in the US housing market began to contract in the summer of 2007. By the fall of 2008, more than $30 trillion vanished from the global economy in the worst economic crisis seen since the Great Depression. US unemployment would crest at 10 percent, though some American communities would see unemployment soar past 20 percent. American families would take years to recover; many still have not. While social and moral issues did not disappear, they did fade from prominence after the economic crisis. Those issues receded from the place they held in national political debates as the household issues that affected people's survival gained a stronger grip on public attention. But the alienation and dissatisfaction that had fueled arguments over social and religious issues for decades remained even after the issues themselves retreated from the front lines of political conflicts. That remnant of cultural alienation intersected with a different sort of alienation that was unleashed by the financial crisis of 2008. Globalization had been under way for decades, slowly eroding the manufacturing base of the American economy and hollowing out communities that depended on factory labor, textile mills, or other means of industrial production. Those communities were suffering already before 2008, but the financial crisis brought home the reality that many people no longer had the sort of security they had grown to expect as Americans. In many cases, the people most affected were already disposed by the ongoing culture wars not to trust elites who had, as far as they knew, undermined the moral, social, political, and religious foundations of their country. For those alienated people hurt by unemployment and hopelessness, it was not a stretch to blame elites also for how globalization had hurt their workplaces, communities, and families.

The American political conversation that opened with *Roe v. Wade* and stretched forward to encompass John Kerry's presidential campaign and the arguments over fetal stem cell research and gay marriage had been a long preparation in binary thinking. In mathematics, binaries are numerical systems that utilize only two digits: every binary number contains only a 0 or a 1. There are no other choices. American politics had become the same way. People were conservatives or liberals—no other choices made sense to most people, even after conservatives stopped looking and sounding like William F. Buckley, Jr., and after liberals embraced Wall Street. You are either with my side, or you are against us. But the church had played a role. There was only one correct position on abortion as a political issue, regardless of how the fine points of law, public policy, and moral theology reveal how infinitely more complex the abortion debate is. The bishops and the Vatican know what that position is, and if a politician or a churchgoer in the pews agrees that abortion is morally evil but cannot quite agree (for reasons of law, public policy, or moral theology) with the only correct political position, it may even be necessary to deny access to the sacraments. There is a culture of life and a culture of death. Everyone must choose a side. And that binary language was so effective and compelling that it would not remain exclusively Catholic for long. That language opened a way for Catholics and evangelicals to collaborate, and their collaboration grew powerful after thirty years. That collaboration would encounter the global economic crisis of 2008 and grow virulent.

Had the strong focus on social and moral issues persisted in the foreground of American political life, Pennsylvania Republican Senator Rick Santorum should have been the perfect candidate to capitalize on the meeting of evangelical and Republican sympathies. Santorum is a prominent Catholic whose activist positions on issues like abortion and gay marriage won him confidence from evangelicals as much as from conservative Catholics. In a particular way, when Santorum and his wife were told that their eighth child would suffer physical and intellectual disabilities, Santorum became a champion for pro-life causes as one who had resisted the pressure to procure a therapeutic abortion.

Yet, Santorum failed to excite any significant attention in 2012 or 2016. In 2012, Santorum bested other Republicans in six states. By 2016, he won barely more than 16,000 votes in total across the nation. In both cases, Republican voters turned to experienced businessmen—Mitt Romney and Donald Trump. Voters had softened their focus on the issues that once motivated them in 2004. But they kept the angry disaffection those issues had nurtured.

Chapter 5

Negotiating the Nonnegotiables

A November 1996 symposium in *First Things*, a journal of conservative Catholic opinion, asked "whether we have reached or are reaching the point where conscientious citizens can no longer give moral assent to the existing regime" in the United States.[1] The contributors were not extremists. They were writers from the generally Catholic or conservative mainstream: Hadley Arkes, Robert Bork, Charles Colson, Robert George, and Russell Hittinger. *First Things* was and is very far from more extreme Catholic publications like *Crisis* and *The Wanderer*. For a discussion that suggested that the American political system had become illegitimate even to appear in *First Things* signaled a significant change of tone and emphasis in American politics. Especially when we contrast that *First Things* symposium with the unapologetic patriotism of Fulton Sheen in earlier decades, it seems clear that something had broken.

Eight years later, in the months before the 2004 presidential election, an organization called Catholic Answers sent out a fundraising appeal that, in most ways, was not particularly unusual. Anyone with a mailbox in the United States is accustomed to the way nonprofit organizations sell mailing lists to one another, and pleas for donations come in every day's mail. Catholic Answers is one of those nonprofits and organizations that dates its origins to a Sunday morning in 1979 when "a Fundamentalist church in San

Diego, California, decided to leaflet the cars at a local parish during Mass," filling windshields with attacks on the Eucharist and other elements of Catholic faith.[2] One of that morning's congregants, Karl Keating, "placed his rebuttal on the windshields of cars in the Fundamentalist church's lot." Keating opened a post office box, eventually began a nonprofit organization, and has become a prominent apologist for Catholicism. In general, Keating and his organization have confined themselves to dogmatic and doctrinal matters, defending Catholic faith against critics. But in 2004, Keating turned his attention elsewhere.

"Catholics make up 26 percent of the electorate," he wrote in a fundraising appeal, but "Catholics are more likely to vote for 'liberal' candidates." Keating wanted to prepare a voting guide for Catholics that would help to bring about the day when America's 65 million Catholics will vote "in harmony with church teaching" to "change the face of American politics."[3] Keating's rallying cry was what he called "nonnegotiable" moral issues. The list is unsurprising: abortion, euthanasia, embryonic stem cell research, human cloning, and gay marriage. The implication, if these five are "nonnegotiable," seemed to be that everything else (capital punishment, nuclear war, torture, and so forth) is negotiable.

When we put the question raised by *First Things* together with the five nonnegotiable moral issues we begin to understand what became broken in American political life after the mid-1990s. The range of political options on every question had narrowed to two, and the lines between the two sides had become entirely nonnegotiable: compromise was out of the question. Yet, as we have surveyed the movements of American political and legal history, as well as those in Catholic theology and history, that have brought us to where we are, the specific and most recent contributions of the US Catholic bishops require some close attention.

Catholic Answers

The Boston Globe's headline of January 6, 2002, brought a watershed: "Church allowed abuse by priest for years."

During the previous two years scandal had engulfed the Archdiocese of Boston and its leader, Cardinal Bernard Law, as it gradually became clearer that the archdiocese had known how priest-abusers engaged in patterns of abusive behavior, then reassigned them to new parishes after allegations came to light. In one way, it bears saying that the news out of Boston in 2002 was not a total surprise. Catholics who had been fortunate not to encounter any abusive priest certainly heard whispers about them, and—of course—it would eventually become clear that there were thousands of victims who knew what was happening, and their families did too. As the 2015 film *Spotlight* described the conspiracy of silence that surrounded the sexual abuse of minors for decades, "If it takes a village to raise a child, it takes a village to abuse them." Still, after *The Boston Globe* mounted an intensive investigation that put a sense of the problem's scale on the public record, it became impossible to ignore the crisis any longer. By the end of 2002, Cardinal Law had resigned and the Catholic Church in the United States had entered a winter from which it has not yet fully recovered.

Every Roman Catholic diocese and archdiocese in the United States eventually became the focus of scrutiny. Dozens paid out large claims to abuse survivors, and those claims just in the period from 2007 to 2012 may have cost the church more than $1 billion, according to some estimates. Eight dioceses sought and received bankruptcy protections from the courts. More than the immediate financial cost, the damage to the reputation of the church was incalculable and, perhaps, irreparable. But on any understanding of what is important, the most grievous wound the scandal inflicted on the church was measured by the number of people who left. The church in the United States continued to grow after the scandal was headline news in 2002. But even faster between 2000 and 2015 grew the number of people in the United States described as "former Catholic adults." The overall Catholic population grew from 59.9 million to 67.7 million (13 percent), but former Catholic adults increased from 17.9 million to 30.1 million (68 percent). The church was hurting, and it still is hurting, because of the ways in which it cooperated in concealing sexual abuse for decades.

Against that backdrop, some of the choices made by the church's leaders in the United States during that time seemed peculiar. In 2004, while headlines swirled over the first archdiocesan bankruptcy in American Catholic history (Portland) and a John Jay College of Criminal Justice study that found 10,667 complaints of abuse against 4,392 priests and deacons since 1950, several US bishops issued their statements instructing Senator John Kerry not to present himself for Communion. In that same year, the bishops reiterated how "a well-formed Christian conscience does not permit one to vote for a political program or an individual law that contradicts the fundamental contents of faith and morals." The bishops also ranked "the defense of human life" and the protection of marriage "as a lifelong commitment between a man and a woman" prominently among a range of important issues, thereby leaving the unmistakable impression that only a pro-life candidate, almost certainly a Republican, was acceptable.[4] In 2005, the bishops' conference debated whether lay ecclesial ministers (such as religious educators and music ministers) should be called "ministers" at all, with Newark Archbishop John J. Myers preferring that "the word 'minister' be used as little as possible except when [referring] to the ordained." In 2007, Archbishop Burke in St. Louis held a press conference to announce that Sheryl Crow's pro-choice activism disqualified her from performing at a fundraiser for a Catholic children's hospital. In 2008, some US bishops instigated an apostolic visitation—an investigation—of the Leadership Council of Women Religious to scrutinize "serious theological, even doctrinal errors" among American women's religious communities. By 2010, the bishops' national conference experienced a sort of revolution itself when—defying its own unwritten rules—the sitting vice president of the conference was not elected president, in what John Allen described as "a broad conservative shift within the conference."[5] Even where the bishops did act to address the crisis—with the adoption of nationwide rules for the protection of minors in 2005—bishops in Kansas City and Philadelphia did not observe the new norms when accusations were made. Instead, they continued the pattern of concealing abusers. As Blase Cupich, then Bishop of Spokane, told the *New York Times*, "It's not the charter that's the problem. It seems to me to be whether or not the people are using the charter as a reference point appropriately."[6] By "the people," of course, he could only have meant Catholic bishops.

The bishops' overall response to the crisis engulfing the church at the beginning of the new century seemed less to be about taking stock internally and asking what had gone wrong inside the church than turning the focus outward, asking what in the world around the church needed to be fixed while building a higher rampart between the church and the world. To some degree, that tendency to look outward could be seen in the response to the sex abuse crisis itself. As scandal took hold, defenders of the church quickly turned their attention elsewhere, away from the pattern of concealing abuse and reassigning abusers to new parishes. The Catholic League for Religious and Civil Rights concluded that "the issue is homosexuality, not pedophilia."[7] In 2005, the Vatican's Congregation for Catholic Education released its "Instruction Concerning the Criteria for the Discernment of Vocations with regard to Persons with Homosexual Tendencies in view of their Admission to the

Seminary and to Holy Orders," which instructed that "the Church, while profoundly respecting the persons in question, cannot admit to the seminary or to holy orders those who practice homosexuality [or] present deep-seated homosexual tendencies" because, the Congregation said, gay men are hindered "from relating correctly to men and women." That document had been "demanded" by "bishops from all over the world" who had encountered "scandals" after ordaining gay men who had resumed "homosexual practice" because their "immaturity" made it nearly inevitable, according to a consultor to the Pontifical Council for the Family who wrote to defend the document.[8] The implication appeared to be that gay priests were the problem, and all of them were potential abusers.

Yet, even apart from defending itself against scandal, the church intensified its efforts to change the secular world during the years after the abuse crisis dawned. These were years during which the political involvement of the national bishops' conference and individual dioceses reached a new level of sophistication and professionalism. Around the time when the national conference of bishops modernized its statutes after the Second Vatican Council, groups of individual bishops in each state began to form Catholic conferences. According to the National Association of State Catholic Conference Directors, "A state Catholic conference is a church agency representing the dioceses within a state in order to provide for the coordination of the public policy concerns of the church." While not in the strictest sense lobbying organizations, these state Catholic conferences certainly do lobby state governments. Very much like Father McHugh's National Right to Life Committee (which we encountered in chapter 2) and the national conference of bishops, it bears saying that most of that work has been uncontroversially good. The work of the state Catholic conferences, like the national bishops' conference, is to offer "a moral framework, an ethical criteria" for lawmakers when they are thinking about issues such as abortion, healthcare, education, and poverty.[9] No Catholic should object to any of that. Yet, it also bears noting that the level of activity in state Catholic conferences ticked upward as the culture wars crested in the last decade, around the time of the 2004 election. Whether by coincidence or as an indication of their frustration with their situation, these changes also came at a time when bishops were dealing with the abuse scandal.

During the 2000s, some state Catholic conferences began to hold "policy days," described as "an annual day of public policy advocacy, workshops and prayer" when bishops and lay Catholics gather in state capitals to learn about issues and lobby their legislators. In a 2011 homily, New York's Cardinal Timothy Dolan told Catholics gathered for a policy day, "Nowhere is it more evident that you are Catholics than today," characterizing their gathering also as one of "loyal Americans" in a way that certainly resonated with the striving of generations of Catholic immigrants to be accepted in the United States. Yet, and even as it was only one part of a longer homily, Dolan seemed to offer a window into how he regarded political activity. Catholics never seemed more Catholic than when they were lobbying for positions on a list of issues the New York Catholic Conference had identified: against abortion and the redefinition of marriage, and for a conscience exception for Catholic healthcare providers, for Catholic schools, and for the poor. Policy day events are carefully orchestrated affairs that leverage the voting power of this nation's millions of Catholics in a way that is meant to show policymakers the muscles that bishops can flex in the public square. One lobbyist said, "Very few religions have the type of lobby machine in the United States" that the Catholic bishops can access through their weekly bulletins or these sorts of coordinated campaigns.[10] State Catholic conferences, and the professionals hired to work for them, exist to make that fact clear.

Yet, the actions of organizations internal to the church, such as the national bishops' conference and the state Catholic conferences, were only one part of this escalating lobbying effort. The bishops also encouraged other organizations to intensify their lobbying activities in recent years. Those organizations are Catholic in the sense that they are composed of Catholics (whether members of religious communities or laypeople) and they identify as Catholic, and quite a few have been very active. Some, like NETWORK Lobby, founded by women religious after Vatican II, have been at work lobbying in American politics for many years. But others, like Catholic Charities, were somewhat new to lobbying before recent times. Catholic Charities had embarked previously on modest acts of political persuasion, spending only $70,000 in all of 2007. By 2010, that amount had increased almost tenfold ($660,000), and Catholic Charities had hired professional lobbyists. As a provider of adoption services, Catholic Charities was encouraged by the bishops' conference to resist requirements to place children in nontraditional families. At that time, the bishops were embarking on a new campaign for religious liberty, and the evidence was seen in the increasing lobbying and activism of Catholic organizations.

Nowhere was the effect more evident than with the Knights of Columbus. The Knights were founded as a charitable organization in 1882. The Knights of Columbus was, and it remains, a fraternal society for Catholic men, and though it has become an international organization its primary focus remains here in the United States, where it continues to have a self-conscious identification with the immigrant past of American Catholicism. From Tootsie Roll Drives to Friday fish fries, the Knights are a widely recognized and admired part of Catholic life in the United States.

They have funded hospitals, scholarships, and food pantries. But the Knights have also taken on a new identity in the last two decades.

Carl A. Anderson was elected to be Supreme Knight in 2000. Anderson's predecessors were philanthropist businessmen like Virgil Dechant or career public servants like Judge John E. Swift. Prior to taking over the Knights, Anderson began his career as a legislative assistant in the office of North Carolina Senator Jesse Helms. There he helped to create the American Family Institute, of which he became director. The American Family Institute was one of a network of institutes funded through Helms's office. Others included the Institute of American Relations and the Institute on Money and Inflation. Ostensibly, these institutes existed "to provide him [Helms] timely research for Senate debates against the liberals."[11] In practice, these institutes raised considerable sums of tax-free money and, while Anderson's institute funded a US tour for Mother Teresa to speak against abortion, questions were raised about other uses of the money.[12] Once his work at the institute concluded, Anderson went to work in the Reagan administration for the White House Office of Public Liaison, which, despite its bland name, in fact was the White House political operation for coordinating activities with like-minded interest groups. When he left the White House, he became one of the founders of the Pontifical John Paul II Institute for Studies on Marriage and the Family, where he remains a vice president and professor of family law since his election as Supreme Knight in 2000. Under Anderson, for the first time in its history, the Knights of Columbus is led by a political operative, an activist with deep roots in interest group politics. The Knights always have engaged in political advocacy. They lobbied to add the words "under God" to the Pledge of Allegiance in the 1950s, and they won approval for Columbus Day to become a holiday. Their new public policy focus with American bishops that followed Anderson's election as Supreme Knight was something new altogether.

In 2006, the *New York Times* reported that "the Catholic bishops and many other religious leaders . . . have pledged to distribute postcards to their congregants to send to their senators," in a campaign orchestrated by the Knights, who had printed ten million postcards for distribution. In 2013, the *Times* reported that the Knights had given a two-million-dollar donation to launch the National Organization for Marriage, an institute much like those Anderson had begun while he was working for Jesse Helms. The National Organization for Marriage has collaborated with the bishops' conference in recent years to sponsor an annual March for Marriage. Over the course of several years, the Knights spent over a million dollars to pay for Catholic bishops to attend conferences on medical ethics. As benign as that sounds, in fact those conferences are sponsored by the National Catholic Bioethics Center (also supported by the Knights), which addresses itself to a wide range of issues that include premarital cohabitation and whether homosexuality is "intrinsically disordered." The Knights have been a regular sponsor of the annual March for Life, also supported by the bishops' conference, and they have been direct and indirect supporters of the conference itself. In 2015, the Knights donated over one million dollars directly to the conference. The Knights also have been generous to bishops individually and their dioceses, which, in turn, are the primary financial supporters of the conference. The Knights of Columbus have been particularly integral to the most prominent public campaign taken up by the bishops' conference in the last decade, the promotion of religious liberty. To promote that campaign, the Knights have supported the Susan B. Anthony Foundation, the Becket Fund for Religious Liberty, the Little Sisters of the Poor (whose religious liberty case went to the US Supreme Court), and the Ethics and Public Policy Center.[13]

The years after the sex abuse scandal brought all of these new expressions of the Catholic voice into the public square and, while something like the selection of Carl Anderson as Supreme Knight preceded the scandal and could not have come in reply to the new lens of scrutiny focused on the church in the United States, it certainly is true that church leaders continued to press down the avenue of issues advocacy, building the political profile of the church in the US in ways undreamed of by the US bishops at the time when Jimmy Carter and Gerald Ford struggled to win their endorsements.[14] After the scandal, political involvement appeared to become a substitute for substantial interior reform. Perhaps political action even was a mask for avoiding reform inside the church after the scandal. Whatever the case, the bishops spent those years following the scandal in Boston, as that scandal broke across the United States and around the world, deepening their commitment to the culture war and the divisions it affirms in American social and political life.

In 2008 Charles J. Chaput, OFMCap, then Archbishop of Denver, wrote a book in which he acknowledged the "indifference, institutionalism, and lack of courage among some bishops that led to the 2002 national sex-abuse crisis," but his acknowledgment is tempered by its presence in a chapter more focused on political action and the firm insistence that "American Catholics need to be *more* Catholic, not less; and not simply 'more Catholic,' but more *authentically* Catholic" in our "political choices."[15] In eleven pages Chaput moves from acknowledging the damage of the sex abuse crisis through a swift change of subject to a political program, much as the US bishops did on a broader scale in the last decade.

That *First Things* symposium in 1996, as the last century closed, asked whether the American regime had lost legitimacy because of abortion and other culture war issues. As the new century opened, the church lost a considerable amount of its own legitimacy to scandal. With the global economic crisis, an era was opening that would see confidence shaken in every established human institution. Perhaps in that era, confidence would be so difficult to win back for the bishops that only bad choices were available to them. Whether other good choices were available or not, one thing is demonstrated by a survey of history: the bishops chose to continue the culture war, and many Catholics followed them. Divisions would deepen.

Smaller and Purer

In 2016, Archbishop Chaput told an audience at the University of Notre Dame that "we should never be afraid of a smaller, lighter church if her members are also more faithful, more zealous, more missionary and more committed to holiness. . . . Losing people who are members of the church in name only is an imaginary loss," and "it may in fact be more honest for those who leave and healthier for those who stay." Archbishop Chaput's welcoming attitude toward a church that is smaller was not as shocking as it might seem. The discussion has been under way for a long time. Talk of a smaller and purer church seemed to have begun in arguments over whether Catholic politicians were Catholic enough to receive the Eucharist and to have been ignited by the election of Pope Benedict XVI. In fact, such talk had been around much longer, but, in any case, it reached a climax around 2010.

Eight years before his election, Cardinal Joseph Ratzinger wondered whether "we are facing a new and different kind of epoch . . . where Christianity will again be characterized more by the mustard seed." Observers of the 2005 papal conclave, such as the conservative Catholic commentator and biographer of John Paul II, George Weigel, wondered whether Pope Benedict's name hinted at shrinking the church, suggesting perhaps it was meant to echo one of the mottoes of the Order of Saint Benedict—*Succisa virescit*, or, "Pruned, it grows again." Weigel's speculation followed the work of Scottish philosopher Alasdair MacIntyre, who suggested in 1984 that the world was entering a new dark age and needed a new Saint Benedict, whose monasteries had been islands of civilization in the dark age that followed the fall of Rome. As the new millennium began, many Catholics found that thought appealing and a 2003 interview seemed to confirm that Cardinal Ratzinger was with them. He said, "The essential things in history begin always with the small, more convinced communities. . . . So [just as] the Church begins with the twelve Apostles . . . from these small numbers we will have a radiation of joy to the world." That radiation of joy from smaller communities will be waiting once the world tires of secularism and materialism, Ratzinger said, "and they will discover the little community of believers as something quite new . . . as a hope that is there for them, as the answer they have always been looking for."

The idea that the church has entered a new and difficult period with an unknown future is not a new one, and it certainly is not the exclusive property of conservative Catholics in the United States. Throughout World War II and into the first years of the Cold War, many astute observers knew that the church was not ready for the challenges of the modern world. In no small part, that is why the Second Vatican Council happened. Those were the kinds of conclusions that Joseph Ratzinger formed in the earliest years of his life and spoke about in the 1960s, when he predicted that "from the crisis of today the Church of tomorrow will emerge—a Church that has lost much. She will become small and will have to start afresh more or less from the beginning." As years went by, he merely repeated that uncontroversial idea that, from some perspectives, was quite liberal (in 1969, Father Ratzinger talked about how this new church would need new forms of ordained ministry). But when that talk of a church that needed to return to fundamentals and perhaps might emerge smaller from a trying period collided with the height of the culture wars during the 2005 election of Ratzinger to become Pope Benedict, a certain amount of confusion was inevitable. The critics of Ratzinger and his most ardent supporters both were guilty of the confusion—both assumed that a smaller church filled with more "authentically Catholic" believers seemed desirable. Indeed, for some people it seemed as though a smaller, more devoted church was more desirable, even if Pope Benedict may not have been one of them.

Some widely misquoted remarks made by Chicago's Cardinal Francis George, OMI, that were misunderstood by people on both sides of that question offer a good example. George proposed a hypothetical situation to an audience in 2010, saying that he expected "to die in bed," and "my successor will die in prison and his successor will die a martyr in the public square." That remark drew massive public attention, forcing George later to clarify that he was trying to "force people to think outside of the usual categories that limit and sometimes poison both private and public discourse." Cardinal George was being provocative, much like any philosophy professor might be in his classroom. When he offered his clarification, George added that the last part of his remarks was never quoted so widely. He had concluded in front of that 2010 audience with "a final phrase . . . about the bishop who follows a possibly martyred bishop: 'His successor will pick up the shards of a ruined society and slowly help rebuild civilization, as the church has done so often in human history.'" Cycles of decline and renewal take place in civilization and institutions as much as they take place in human life, and the cycle that Cardinal George described in provocative terms was the same one

Father Ratzinger described at work in the church forty years earlier. It never was a question of whether the church is in a difficult period. On the other hand, there was more than one way to approach the problem.

Having lived through the culture wars and the role in the culture wars played by the church in the United States, many Catholics do believe that a purification is under way in the church. Some even seem to take comfort from the idea of a smaller church. A bumper sticker emerged after Pope Benedict's election, one that played on the common description of liberal Catholics as cafeteria Catholics who only take what they like: the bumper sticker said, "The Cafeteria Is Closed." The suggestion seemed to be that liberal Catholics should go away and leave, as Archbishop Chaput suggested, a more "honest" church filled with more authentic believers. Indeed, there grew out of the culture wars a preoccupation with authenticity not just inside the Catholic Church but also in the political debate outside the church. These were years in which Republicans increasingly hurled against one another the charge that someone was a "Republican In Name Only" (or RINO), while campaign commercials brimmed with reassurances that a candidate was a "consistent conservative" or an "authentic conservative" or a "true conservative." American politics and American Catholicism had met in a strange preoccupation with authenticity and purity.

The academic literature on political theory and social anthropology becomes interesting at this point. Both agree, broadly, that cultural identity and nationhood are closely related concepts, and both agree that those concepts are historically artificial.[16] We construct the idea of a culture or a nation from those elements of history to which we choose to assign importance, but the particular claims that cultural or national relationships make on us do not particularly arise from nature and, if history could be repeated and different choices could be made, our national and cultural identities might be quite different.[17] To put it very simply—cultural identity, group identity, and national identity all are agreements that we have made silently with one another over time about how to understand ourselves. They are understandings we have, not definitive characteristics like height or shape. Those conceptual understandings tend to work well for us as long as they are easy to agree about. When those understandings come under pressure because something is challenging them, making it harder for everyone to agree about an identity, there are certain predictable reactions that will take place.

When cultural identity, group identity, or national identity is threatened in some way, a preoccupation with purity, authenticity, and consistency tends to follow. When the identity we have depended on begins to seem uncertain to us, or when those around us seem to be questioning that identity, it becomes natural to begin raising questions about who belongs and who does not. In good times, when agreement about an identity is strong and widely shared, identity is about distinguishing one group from another group and celebrating our ability to coexist even with our differences. In bad times, when agreement about an identity is challenged and feels shaky, groups tend to turn their focus inward, policing their own members for signs of disloyalty, disunity, or even uncertainty. Among many people in the United States whose lives were disrupted by the economic crisis of 2008, or who have felt apprehensive about the changing demographics of the US, anxiety about no longer being the country we once were was a reaction that was easy to predict. The reactions against immigrants and Muslims on one side of the political divide, the reactions against the so-called one-percenters and Wall Street on the other side, were not surprising when we view the problem this way.

Among American Catholics, the problem runs even deeper. Catholics came as immigrants to the United States, spending generations seeking acceptance only to gain acceptance at the moment when agreements about the nature of American culture were challenged in the 1960s and 1970s, culminating in *Roe v. Wade*. Many American Catholics felt that the rug had been pulled out from under them, and as the years went by their feelings of cultural alienation intensified. Those Catholics were not spared the economic jolt that struck the rest of the United States in 2008. And throughout the period from *Roe* to the 2016 election, American Catholics were led by bishops who themselves were having the same experiences and struggling in real time to understand what was happening in the once-familiar America around them while they also tried to figure out how to respond. Quite often, from the 1976 election and the disastrous meetings with Jimmy Carter and Gerald Ford down to the more recent and more direct entries the bishops have made into lobbying and political action, the responses of the Catholic leadership in the United States have not escaped from the orbit of cultural or group identity. Having spent so long inside a "Catholic ghetto," the sensibilities of most American Catholics remain shaped by a fixed perception of being outsiders who have to struggle to find their way in. The decades since *Roe* have tended to reinforce the lure of the ghetto mentality. Quite often those Catholics who have been accepting of the changes happening around them in the church and in the United States have become the objects of suspicion and the targets of questions about authenticity and sincerity. The discussion of a church that might have to become smaller through trials shifted from where it began, a conversation about adapting to the realities of the modern world, to someplace new with the suggestion that serious Catholics should remain while all others open to change probably should leave. Quite often, the battle lines of that argument were drawn inside the sanctuary.

The increasing popularity of the traditional Latin Mass and the so-called "liturgy wars" that have gotten under way across the last three decades have been another indicator of the forces driving Catholics into separate corners, one camp embracing change and accommodating the worship of the church to the cultural expectations of the people present at the Mass, and another camp ever more certain that the bastions have been stormed and the "authentic" or "faithful" Catholics grow fewer and fewer.[18] In fact, these conflicts over the liturgy were emerging even before the so-called "wafer wars," at a time when the culture war was building to its apex. Conflicts over the liturgy were the original inspiration behind Cardinal Joseph Bernardin's Catholic Common Ground Initiative, announced in 1996 to address "an increasing polarization within the Church," that pitted an

> informal or "horizontal" liturgy, demystified and stressing the participation of the congregation . . . against a solemn or "vertical" liturgy, unchangeable and focused on the sacerdotal action of the priest. The former is rightly feared as unable to carry the weight of the transcendent, and as opening the liturgy to the trivializing currents of the culture. The latter is rightly feared as becoming a concert, a show, or a spiritless exercise in rubrics, closed to the particular needs and gifts of the community.[19]

The Catholic Common Ground Initiative got under way when the National Pastoral Life Center and Bernardin joined forces to combat how those polarizations were infecting and dividing individual parish communities. As the name of Bernardin's initiative suggests, common ground was the goal: neither side was wholly right nor wholly wrong, and dialogue between them was the only way to be a church together. Of course, that gesture toward dialogue foundered quickly. Cardinal Bernard Law remarked after the initiative was announced, "Dialogue as a way to mediate between truth and dissent is mutual deception."

For too many Catholics, the boundaries of identity are not negotiable. There is no room for discussion and nothing to discuss. Indeed, from that point of view the real problem is not how to overcome conflict but, rather, how dissenters inside the church, with whom dialogue can offer no path toward reconciliation, might be corrected and turned right or, presumably, urged to leave behind a "lighter," "more honest" church for those who hold to the "truth." Under pressure within the church, across American life, the group identity of American Catholics has fallen into the gravitational pull of that outsider immigrant history. The lure of the old Catholic ghetto, the sureness about who is outside and who is inside, is powerful in the American Catholic imagination.

Pope John Paul II took up these themes in an unusual papal book, *Memory and Identity: Conversations at the Dawn of a Millennium* (Rizzoli, 2005). As a young man, Karol Wojtyła had lived through the consequences of German nationalism during World War II, and from the time he was Father Wojtyła to the time he was Cardinal Wojtyła he lived through the effects of Soviet nationalism on his Polish homeland. His experience of Polish nationhood in the light of those events is important for understanding how John Paul thought. His own treatment of memory and identity takes its bearings from the way "nations are endowed with historical memory" to sketch out how Poland's identity is intertwined with its "baptism" as a Christian nation.[20] Perhaps because of how the deep faith of Poland's history fueled its resistance against Soviet domination, John Paul had a stronger, more fixed concept of identity that was less capable of accommodating historical change than the way we have seen political theorists and social anthropologists describe identity in other contexts. Pope John Paul advanced an idea of cultural identity and national identity that treats nations and cultures as more permanent and fixed.[21] Most important, John Paul also conceived of the church as possessing a fixed identity. And when the fixed identity of a nation or a culture encounters the fixed identity of the church, John Paul had a clear understanding of which should prevail. That preference was visible even in the gestures of mercy that John Paul made toward schismatic, traditional Catholics. While respectful of "the feelings of all those who are attached to the Latin liturgical tradition," they too had no choice but to accommodate themselves to the central, unifying identity of the church. In this way, John Paul was a global leader for the church whose own way of thinking was rather well suited to how the preoccupation with identity was roiling the church in the United States from national political debates down to the level of local parishes.

There were other things being done at the level of papal authority that emphasized the harmony between Pope John Paul and those American Catholics. In 1998, the US bishops' conference approved a new translation of the English language Mass. Parts of the 1973 translation that followed the Second Vatican Council had not worn well, and some expressions were a little clunky even as the 1973 translators had consulted scholars and poets to try to craft the most beautiful English translation that would reflect the underlying meaning and speak to men and women of the twentieth century. It was widely agreed that an update was in order. Yet, the Vatican vetoed the 1998 translation at least in part because it used gender-inclusive language. That 1998 language was actually not any more drastic than "Glory to God in the highest, and peace to God's people on earth," and it had the same directness and simplicity found in the 1973 translation. When Pope John Paul set forth new principles for translation in 2001, he identified different priorities and set a new kind of emphasis on culture.[22] Where the Second Vatican Council had been guided by a spirit of "adapting the liturgy to the culture and traditions of peoples," now the liturgy would seek to shape human culture.[23] The translated language of the Mass was now to avoid "words that lack such a sacral character," preferring instead to cultivate a way of using language unique to the church ("a sacral vernacular, characterized by a vocabulary, syntax and grammar that are proper to divine worship") that subtly drew a line between the church and the world as worshippers participate in the Mass. As English-speaking Catholics now mouth words like "consubstantial" and must follow a sixty-four-word sentence recited at Mass, these were the principles that motivated the translation of their liturgy. They were principles of translation that encourage a smaller, more serious, and more "authentic" conception of the church, proceeding from a rigid conception of the church's identity as it encounters human culture.

The American leader of that effort to replace the 1998 translation with a more "sacral vernacular," in fact, was Cardinal Francis George, who was the president of the bishops' conference at that time. A philosopher like Pope John Paul, George shared many of the pope's ideas about culture and identity. And sharing a sense that other cultures must be respected while they also must bend to the identity of the church and its mission, George also led the church in the United States down a strange path of defining and protecting its religious liberty.

The US bishops' campaign to protect religious liberty began with the debate over the Affordable Care Act of 2010 ("Obamacare"), but the roots of the debate lay much deeper. In many ways, that debate had been under preparation since the *Roe* decision, although it could be argued that it goes back even further to legal disputes about funding for parochial schools that stretch back through the twentieth century. Like most of those public policy arguments we have already reviewed here, a significant part of the problem is that they are multidimensional. A public policy quarrel over abortion involves constitutional considerations, other legal considerations, political considerations, ethical considerations, and—for religious believers—theological and moral considerations. While all of those factors coincide and meet over an issue like abortion or gay marriage, experts in different fields approach issues from different directions, draw from different wells of knowledge, speak different technical languages, and observe different priorities. That is why our debates over these issues are so difficult and unsolvable. But unlike such particular issues as fetal stem cell research or capital punishment that are always so difficult when Catholic moral theology encounters legal or political considerations in a nation in which not everyone is Catholic, religious liberty should have been rather easy. Historically, it always was.

Catholics always wanted to fit in as Americans, since the earliest generations of Catholic immigrants down to the 1950s as they stood on the threshold of mainstream acceptance. It generally was the case throughout those many years, therefore, that Catholics did not call attention to their differences by making any special demands from the legal and political establishments.[24] For that reason, Catholics offered few complaints that their religious liberty was being threatened throughout American history. But there is an additional, deeper, and more important explanation for why Catholics have generally been quite content about their freedoms in the United States, where the constitutional separation of church and state enabled the church to "'blossom like a rose," in the phrase of Cardinal James Gibbons, even in a predominantly Protestant nation. That deeper explanation is rooted in the Catholic understanding of social life.

There is a conflict between the American political tradition and Catholic social teaching, and it is an important one. The American tradition is individualist. Just as the Declaration of Independence indicates, most Americans tend to think of their rights as being their own. Rights are given to us, they are ours, and nothing encumbers individuals in the exercise of their individual rights. Catholics have a different perspective and, even in conflict with the prevailing individualism of the United States, that different perspective has helped Catholics think about their rights in a way that has helped them to live peacefully in America. Catholics believe that our social life is interconnected, that no one is isolated by their individualism from their obligations to other people. Pope John XXIII explained this best in 1963 when he wrote that "one man's natural right gives rise to a corresponding duty in other men."[25] When we think about it this way, it seems quite clear that my rights end where someone else's rights begin. Community and a sense of the common good is built from our recognition that we each have to recognize that all of our own rights at some point must give way to the needs of others. So many of the problems in the American political debate stem from the fact that too many people cannot imagine limiting themselves in the enjoyment of their own rights. For Catholics, seeing the world this way, it is far easier.

Or it was. As the culture wars crested in the years immediately following the 2004 election and the election of Pope Benedict, the Obama administration moved swiftly to implement healthcare reform and US bishops quickly became alarmed by the prospect of Catholic employers being required to offer health insurance that would cover contraceptives or other services that the church's moral theology could not embrace. At the same time, as the debate over marriage progressed, church leaders grew increasingly concerned that adoption services funded by Catholic Charities might be compelled to place children in homes where two men or two women would be the parents. Catholic bishops voiced their fear that the right to free exercise of religion was being reduced to a protection of worship only, and that the witness that Catholics or others might want to give to their faith in the public square was being curtailed. Of course, that is a reasonable thing to be worried about. But there are good reasons to wonder whether there ever has been much of a threat in the United States as we know it today.

Like so much else in their encounter with American politics and American social life throughout the culture wars, the Catholic bishops here were engaging in a polarized kind of thinking that did not see any shades of gray. Either the federal government will not mandate contraceptive services at all, or Catholics are losing their religious liberty. Either religious believers can assert their rights and opt out of anything that the social community might ask from them, or religious liberty is being reduced to only a right to worship. Several good theological arguments were made during the argument over Obamacare that suggested, in fact, that there is a significant difference between paying for insurance that covers contraceptives and the morally objectionable decision an employee might make on her own to use contraceptives.[26] The Obama administration granted many religious exemptions, acknowledging and attempting to accommodate the objections of Catholics and others whose religious faiths teach against artificial contraceptives.[27] A "war on religion" never was the point for the Obama administration, no matter how often that was asserted by Catholic bishops and other leaders. Rather, those who make public policy sought to make decisions for the whole people of the United States, Catholic and non-Catholic, that proceeded from law, from data, and from economic necessities to build the best system they could come up with. All along, the US bishops were singularly averse to seeing it in such benign terms, and sometimes they were startlingly rash in their condemnations.[28]

After decades of culture war, with all of the alienation and anomie that the culture wars had produced, and amid a firm and fixed conception of national and cultural identity, the US bishops had led the church in the United States toward a kind of conservatism of resistance against secularism, atheism, and liberalism. The intersection of these forces in the decade leading up to the 2016 election was the critical juncture along the long road that led so many Catholic voters to Donald Trump. But that is not the last word.

Amoris Laetitia

Pope Francis's apostolic exhortation The Joy of Love (*Amoris Laetitia*) was the product of a long process in which bishops gathered in Rome after having consulted with their people about several questions relating to family life. They included the difficult questions about how the church should regard gay and lesbian people as well as divorced and remarried Catholics. The process alone reflected an extraordinary change in direction for how the church deals with controversial subjects, including wide consultation down to the level of individual parishes in a debate that Catholics were able to track practically as it happened. That process could have come about only because of one man's leadership.

In 2013 Pope Benedict XVI offered the first papal resignation in seven centuries, and that was only the first of many surprises that would follow. In scarcely more than a day of voting, the cardinals selected Cardinal Jorge Mario Bergoglio, SJ, who became the first occupant of the papacy to take the name Francis. Not only was Bergoglio the first pope to come from the Southern or Western hemispheres, but he was also the first member of a religious order to be elected since 1831 and the first Jesuit ever. As St. Francis of Assisi had heard the words "Rebuild my church" and given away all that he owned, Pope Francis adopted a simple, direct style as pope and set about restoring the confidence lost in the church around the world due to the sexual abuse crisis and a growing financial scandal inside the Vatican. At least part of a program for restoring confidence was found in changing how the church does things. The rest laid in reaching out to those who felt abandoned by the church.

Amoris Laetitia was the product of a lengthy process that Pope Francis calls synodality. The Second Vatican Council had envisioned a mechanism for the bishops of the world to work with the pope, to consult with him about difficult problems. The meetings at which these consultations would take place were called synods. Synods of bishops have taken place in the Vatican since 1967, roughly every three years. The topics of the synods have been chosen by the popes, and since 1967 the synods have been controlled tightly by Vatican officials.[29] With the 2015 synod on the family, Pope Francis opened the process up. Questionnaires were distributed through national conferences of bishops to Catholics in their local parishes, and responses were reported back to the synod. In the document that the synod produced, the bishops attempted to resolve "The Experiences and Challenges of Families." Dealing with questions of sexual preference and gender identity as much as with the dissolution of marriages and the breakdown of the family, the bishops engaged a process that was messy and tumultuous but that disclosed an important reality about a global church—"what seems normal for a bishop on one continent is considered strange and almost scandalous for a bishop from another; what is considered a violation of a right in one society is an evident and inviolable rule in another; what for some is freedom of conscience is for others simply confusion."[30] In a global church, the synod became an opportunity to recognize that many different cultural voices are heard inside the church. Francis firmly reminded the bishops at the synod's end that the church cannot fall into relativism or otherwise give up the bond of unity that holds a global church together. But that was not enough for some bishops who, during and after the synod, expressed "different opinions" in "at times, unfortunately, not . . . entirely well-meaning ways." Voices inside and outside the synod's meeting hall were uncomfortable with the synod process and the messy, clamorous way it attempted to capture the diversity of perspectives inside the church. Many seemed to be uncomfortable with the possibility, itself, of that diversity in a church that increasingly had committed itself to a more fixed, rigid identity.

Even while the synod was under way, a group of bishops publicly opposed Pope Francis and the synod process. Halfway through the 2015 synod meeting, thirteen bishops presented Francis with a letter they also released publicly. The letter alleged that the open synod process had been rigged to produce a predetermined outcome. While the letter was signed by only one American (Cardinal Timothy Dolan of New York), it reflected an opposition not just to the synod but to Pope Francis that had grown up among bishops who identified their view of the church with Pope John Paul II and Pope Benedict XVI, and with a fixed vision of the church's identity in opposition to the modern world. Those bishops' objections found support among American Catholics already embroiled in the culture wars. For many American Catholics, decades of the culture wars' us-versus-them spirit had made it possible even to question the faithfulness of the pope. That letter found favorable coverage in the broadcasts of the Eternal Word Television Network (EWTN) when Raymond Arroyo, the host of *The World Over*, advanced the idea that the letter represented the views of "many more" bishops at the synod and where commentators Robert Royal and Reverend Gerald Murray questioned the process by which the synod was unfolding.[31]

Of course many different opinions were voiced in the synod hall, unlike every other more tightly managed synod that preceded it. Of course the process was disjointed and a little disorderly, since it was open to so many perspectives and because the bishops had never had a synod like this one before. It was not that the criticisms of the synod were wrong factually, but rather that the criticisms missed the point. The bishops who signed the letter to Pope Francis were unnerved not by the "new synodal procedures" or a process that "seems designed to facilitate predetermined results" so much as by the prospect that the procedures might lead to results they could not predict at all. Every preceding synod, in fact, had been so choreographed as to lead to foreknown outcomes. For those bishops who felt that the answers to the world's questions about the family were already known and answered, and the synod only was a process by which the church would restate those answers in the same way, the Synod on the Family appeared as something new and dangerous. For those like Pope Francis who hoped that an open and honest conversation among bishops about these difficult issues facing Catholics around the world might lead to new answers, new opportunities of mercy and grace, this was an exciting and invigorating opportunity. People's responses to the synod really were a measure of their own openness to the possibility of seeing the teachings of the church in a new light. The synod laid bare how everyone felt about the relationship between church teachings and the identity of Catholics as a group. After decades of culture war arguments, whether the 2015 synod discouraged someone or excited them disclosed whether they could imagine change in the church or whether they were determined to resist change.

As either a healthy sign of how open the church is becoming to a vigorous dialogue or an unhealthy sign of how much the church has been overtaken by a political argument, perhaps it was unsurprising when several groups sent representatives to Rome during the synod so that they could lobby the bishops in attendance. Much like the offices of lobbyists ring Capitol Hill in Washington, the spirit of political opposition and the tactics born from the culture wars were at work in the church. Yet, it is important not to see this only as a matter of crass or ugly politics intruding on the sacred precincts of the church. There is some danger that the spirit of opposition and the desire to win will overtake any debate, as quite often in the United States it has among Catholics. Yet, real dialogue, in fact, does demand that participants approach one another ready to engage one another in a way that is full-throated, honest, and sometimes boisterous. There is nothing wrong with that. In fact, the church needs it. Having a dialogue in a way that does not deteriorate into a winner-takes-all struggle to defeat the opponent is a way the church can serve the people of the world and their governments by offering a model for a different, better way to engage with one another. What is essential is that the dialogue in the church, in fact, be different and better than the debate that is had in politics outside the church. While the 2015 synod on the family represented real progress, it seems clear from that process that the culture wars have had their effect and that the rigid conception of the church's unchanging identity had become a problem for the global church, to say nothing of the church in the United States.

That problem, when all is said and done, was a question of whether dialogue is even possible any longer inside the church. Dialogue was the goal of Pope Francis's synodality as much as it had been the goal when Cardinal Joseph Bernardin unveiled the Catholic Common Ground Initiative in 1996. Bernardin had seen the culture wars unfolding in the church and in the United States when he wrote in 1996 about how we need to see dialogue "not just as a way to dampen conflict, but as a way to make our conflicts constructive and ultimately as a way to understand for ourselves and articulate for our world the meaning of discipleship of Jesus Christ."[32] In this sense, dialogue is something entirely different from an argument or a debate. The goal of a debate or an argument is to hold fast to an idea, to prove that it is true. When we recall the argument over cultural or group identity, we can see that people who adhere to a closed identity will be inclined to argue or debate. They believe that they possess the answer to an important question. For members of their group, that answer holds authority and it must be defended. We heard that when Boston's Cardinal Bernard Law replied to the Common Ground Initiative, "Dialogue as a way to mediate between truth and dissent is mutual deception."

Dialogue depends on a more open conception of identity. It is important to note that an open conception of identity presumes that there is identity. Openness does not mean that we do not know who we are. Still, an open conception of identity allows for the possibility that the truth is not fully known. From that beginning, dialogue is a way for people with different perspectives to discover the truth together. While the goal of a debate or an argument is winning, the goal of dialogue is truth. It misunderstands dialogue entirely to think about it as a process of bargaining or negotiating, whittling away at the truth until there is so little left on which two parties can agree. Dialogue is the opposite. Real dialogue requires two parties to abandon the confidence that they are completely right and to enter a conversation whose goal is to learn from one another's experiences until both recognize some truth in their discussion. Inevitably, both sides will yield some ground. Yet, the wonderful thing about truthfulness is that it is constant. If truth is what we seek, then it needs no defense. It will not yield or become what we want it to be. If we are people who identify ourselves by our desire for the truth, then our identity is reaffirmed by our openness to a dialogue in which we seek truth.

The ending of the twentieth century and the beginning of the twenty-first has not been a time when American Catholics, generally, have grown more open about their identity or more committed to dialogue. Despite the best wishes expressed by the Second Vatican Council that the church would meet and encounter the modern world in a sincere dialogue that seeks the truth through the meeting of different experiences (see *Gaudium et Spes* 28), the events of the last fifty years have discouraged American Catholics from seeking a dialogue. As we have seen, forces began to gather against dialogue even before Vatican II in the difficult experience that Catholic immigrants had when they came to the United States. Out of the tumult over Pope Paul's encyclical *Humanae Vitae* and the possibilities it raised for questioning longstanding church teachings, and out of the US Supreme Court's *Roe v. Wade* decision, a momentum began to gather against dialogue. A tendency to see the church under siege was unleashed, and with that perspective came the tendency to think of identity in a closed, rigid way that sought to win arguments by defending truth rather than to seek truth through open dialogue. While all that happened, Catholics grew in influence and political importance in American life. Finally accepted in the American mainstream, Catholics encountered and influenced the development of similar tendencies across the United States and particularly among other Christians. The culture wars unfolded and, slowly, while many Catholics and other Christians resisted the temptation to withdraw into a closed identity that fought a culture war, many others have come to the defense of a closed identity that sees threats in other experiences and perspectives. Among Catholics, that tendency is found chiefly among the descendants of nineteenth-century Catholic immigrants who have a memory of the long struggle for acceptance that came to fruition in the moments when so much uncertainty was unleashed as the 1960s ended and the 1970s began. Their confidence already shaken by those events in the church's ability to sustain its identity in a dialogue, many of these same people also saw their confidence in the American economy and American strength around the world shaken by the 2008 financial crisis.

Catholics whose perspectives were shaped in these ways over a period of fifty years found clear and appealing answers to their worries from a presidential candidate in 2016 who promised an unquestioning view of American power, the return to a rigid and simple patriotism, and a clear sense of American identity against new groups of immigrants who sought to enter the United States. It did not seem to matter that he did not personally share those Catholics' values in his long public life as much as that he offered the reassurances that they were so desperate to find after the decades of culture wars and the economic crisis that had left them so shaken and so worried about whether their country and their church would continue to seem familiar to them.

For those reasons, many Catholics voted for Donald Trump.

Chapter 6

The Church and the World

At the first session of the Second Vatican Council, Cardinal Giovanni Battista Montini rose to address the bishops whom Pope John XXIII called to Saint Peter's Basilica to "consider attentively the world of today." In less than a year, Montini would become Pope Paul VI. But on this morning of the first session, before he knew he would become the pope who would conclude the Council and implement its decrees, Montini challenged the bishops: "For the world wants to know what the church of Christ is in our time." As much as for Pope John, for Cardinal Montini the church's most important audience is the world. Not only Catholics or Christians, or just a select few, but the whole world has an expectation for the church of Christ. The world is the field of salvation that the church harvests every day. For that reason, the church must respond to the world's expectation and answer women and men of good will everywhere to give an account of how the church lives out the Gospel. The world is watching.

That expectation that the world is watching suggests to us how deep and how unavoidable is the church's relationship to the world. The church and the world are inevitably paired together until the end of time. That is what Catholics believe.[1] Yet, during the last few centuries the church has faced new challenges in its relationship with the world.

We must be careful to remember that the church's relationship to the world has been difficult since the beginning. We find that difficulty present in the encounter between Jesus and Pontius Pilate. Questioned by Pilate, Jesus claims a kingdom that does not exist in the present world while Pilate, a provincial governor loyal to an earthbound Roman Empire, cannot conceive of what Jesus is telling him. Pilate's misunderstanding about Jesus's otherworldly kingdom identified the problem at the heart of the relationship between the church and the world, one that grew only more difficult once the Roman Empire vanished and the church was left with the task of governing. The church of Christ, a kingdom of the next world, is uniquely unsuited to governing this world. But for one thousand years after the sack of Rome the church did attempt to govern the world. The results were not very pleasing. They included Crusades and other wars, and they found the church defending unsavory behaviors that included lying and the enslavement of conquered peoples. The church exists to sanctify us and to prepare us for salvation by spreading the Gospel. The church exists in the world, and the church performs those tasks in the world. But to be worldly forces the church into uncomfortable compromises with the world, and those compromises almost always come at the expense of the church's saving mission.

That was the claim of many Protestant reformers of the sixteenth century. The Reformation was a complex series of events in world history, and we should say that the Reformation was as much about the competition among worldly powers as it was about seeking a more direct relationship to God. Sometimes princes supported Protestant churches while others supported the Catholic Church only as a way to gain power or influence over one another, and an argument about theology often masked how the real argument was about power. But there was earnestness among many reforming theologians who worried that the difficult relationship between the church and the world had grown too close at the cost of the church's mission to bring the world to God. Unintentionally, those reformers helped to make the church's relationship to the world even more difficult.

Christianity had been divided since the Great Schism of 1054 separated the Eastern church from the Western church. After the Reformation, Western Christianity was fragmented even more into a kaleidoscopic confusion of competing sects. Increasingly over the centuries that followed, Christians who believed in Christianity very differently lived side by side with one another in the same kingdom, or the same state, or the same republic. Politically, it became a challenge to keep the peace among citizens who believed fervently that they were right and their understanding of Christianity was the only one that could achieve the most important thing in human life because, not uncommonly and paradoxically, feeling absolutely right about religious judgments in world history has emboldened people to commit horrendous violence. To accommodate these new circumstances, and in a way that mirrored how the church changed to accommodate the world after the end of the Roman Empire, the political world changed after the Reformation in response to this crisis within Christianity. Nations began to accommodate themselves to pluralism, the tendency of citizens to believe different things and possess often conflicting values, by partitioning religious preferences off from political decision-making. For the first time since the fall of Rome, the state abandoned a close relationship with the church. Secularism became an accepted political principle.

The emergence of secularism and the accompanying liberties of conscience that deny legal and political advantages to churches were particularly difficult for Catholics. The Catholic Church resisted what it called modernism and liberalism for decades, while the world all around it embraced principles such as Thomas Jefferson's separation of church and state. For centuries, the Catholic Church had wielded the power of the state. Now the church had been reduced to the status of being just one religious option among others. Of course, that is exactly what Christianity had been at the time when Paul traveled throughout the Roman world to spread the Gospel before the church ever had or aspired to any earthly political power. The early church never enjoyed the advantages or suffered the burden of worldly power in the way we see in later history and today. The church flourished in those early days because it offered the world an appealing account of what the church of Christ is. From that powerful beginning, Christians conquered Rome without violence and Christianity overtook much of the world. Secularism in our time, for all it cost the church in worldly power, had returned the church to that root experience of something more like being a powerless witness to the Gospel. Still, accepting that situation has not been easy.

The church's difficulty with accepting modern political arrangements perhaps explains some of the awkwardness Catholics have long felt in American social and political life, attempting at once to be Catholics and live their faith while living in a new circumstance where their faith has no worldly power to assert itself. Catholics are the largest religious denomination in the United States, but even seventy million Catholics cannot determine the meaning of the Constitution, which has its own separate tradition of interpretation and jurisprudence. The structures of American politics cannot and do not favor any religious, ethical, or moral argument. Rather, the Constitution opens a space in which different religious, ethical, and moral claims enter a dialogue aiming at public policy. The boundaries of that debate are not determined by any one group's convictions but, rather, by settled laws and court decisions based on a long-standing political tradition of church-state separation in a nation dominated, historically, not by Roman Catholics but by Protestants. Even if that were not so, the long history of the church and the complexity of our circumstances frustrate easy claims about finding the "Catholic" answer to public policy problems in the United States because, especially since they won acceptance in the US, disagreement and discord have crept up among Catholics. To say that there is a Catholic answer to a public policy problem at all now, today, raises new questions. Even the natural law, for as often as it is invoked, does not offer a clear answer.[2] Would the Catholic answer be an interpretation preferred by the US bishops? Would an answer from the majority of the bishops be acceptable, or would that answer need to be unanimous? Would it be an answer preferred by a majority of Catholics? Would we mean some outcome determined by a smaller number of more vocal Catholics who have organized themselves as a pressure group to lobby public officials? Even where the Catholic answer seems simple—such as "Abortion is morally evil"—the application of that principle in law is not so easy to work out. Is abortion always a criminal act, or does it become criminal at some point in a pregnancy? Who is to be punished—the mother, or the doctor? In what cases might there be exceptions? Or, if not exceptions, what circumstances might bring about a lesser penalty? These all are arguable points that have to be settled before any public policy can be made.

These are only some of the reasons why, during the last several decades, Catholics especially in the United States have found their encounter with the world to be a particularly challenging problem. The political process has become a source of incredible frustration while the moral issues facing us concern new and unnerving threats to human life. Not only the questions of abortion and euthanasia, but also new bioethical issues have brought new challenges with such incredible speed that they would be difficult to answer if agreements were easy to reach between Catholics and the rest of the world and among Catholics. In this climate where ready agreement seems impossible, those frustrations bring confusion about why the Catholic answer or the "right" answer is so difficult to enact. The world begins to look like a problem to be overcome, rather than a field in which believers spread the seed of the Gospel and harvest the fruits of salvation. Especially amid the unsettling social forces at work in American life today, there can be a powerful temptation to reject the world, to see the world as filled with enemies. In the earliest years of the twenty-first century, many American Catholics gave into that temptation.

Religious Liberty

The Affordable Care Act of 2010 ("Obamacare") gathered this complex history and all of the problems it brings along with it into one terrible, singular focus. More than reorganizing one-sixth of the domestic economy and providing access to affordable healthcare for tens of millions of people, the Affordable Care Act also raised difficult questions in the details, such as whether employer-sponsored health insurance would cover abortions or contraceptives. Further yet, the Affordable Care Act arrived at a moment when another ongoing cultural debate over gay marriage had matured into a public policy question for Catholic health and adoption service providers. Whom would Catholic social service organizations or employers be required to recognize as a spouse? Would the church be required to place children for adoption with gay couples? The healthcare law took the brunt of the outrage over these questions, prompting the US bishops' conference in those circumstances to mount a campaign for religious liberty in 2012 as an organized political response that sought to safeguard the church's ability to reject public policy outcomes that are incompatible with the church's teachings.

In every sense, the campaign for religious liberty represented the fullest fruit of the culture wars among Catholics. The culture wars had been framed for decades as a two-sided, apocalyptic, us-versus-them battle between good and evil over a familiar range of issues such as abortion, euthanasia, and marriage. In the campaign for religious liberty, not only were those culture war issues litigated in political debates and courtrooms as they had been for decades, but now a new argument took shape as Catholics and other Christian believers shifted their focus. Catholic political action was no longer focused mainly on a legal or a political battle to end abortion or to protect marriage. Those efforts continued, of course, but they were joined to a new effort to summon the First Amendment's religion protections to defend the believer's right to opt out of a public policy deemed sufficiently offensive that it violated her or his right to the free exercise of religion. In a new, climactic moment of the culture wars the Affordable Care Act shifted the ground away from effecting a policy outcome for the whole United States toward carving out protections for offended consciences that cut them off from the larger community. A new insularity overtook cultural conservatives, including many Catholics. In an important political and legal sense, many Catholics began to withdraw from the wider American culture back into a safe enclave that was not unlike the one from which their immigrant parents and grandparents had emerged. The significant difference was that now Catholics no longer feared being walled off in an enclave because it seemed contrary to American values. In fact, now they were defending American values. A ghetto mentality did not make Catholics strange. Rather, protected by the fundamental guarantees of religious liberty, the Catholic ghetto claimed the authority of the Constitution and the American political tradition while Catholics, somewhat nostalgically, tried to return to a narrow Catholic world remembered from the 1940s and the 1950s. Armed with the Constitution to protect their religious liberty, the bishops subtly had begun urging Catholics to give up on coexisting in a world shared with those who did not believe. That was not an intended outcome when the bishops' conference embarked on a campaign for religious liberty. But the evidence after more than forty years argues strongly that this was the effect after so much Catholic political history in the United States since *Roe*. The world simply had become so challenging that now many Catholics needed a way to reject it and opt out.

The campaign for religious liberty marked a point at which Catholics, rather expressly, abandoned Pope Paul's vision of the world as a vital audience for the church's concern and evangelization—sometimes threatening to withhold vital social services—in favor of wielding their political rights in the hope they could exert control over the world from behind the walls of their enclave. Chicago's Cardinal Francis George made the most explicit threats to close hospitals and cease placing children for adoption in order to protect Catholic consciences, but other bishops joined him.[3] If policy programs for public health questions could not pass the test of moral theology, Catholics seemed increasingly to feel obliged to favor protecting their constitutional rights over performing corporal works of mercy. If marriage were defined in some way other than as between a man and a woman, many Catholics seemed to feel it was less important to place orphaned children in stable homes if married, gay couples might live in those homes. If a non-Catholic employee of a Catholic institution chose to use artificial contraception to postpone children or to prevent disease, even a waiver to excuse the Catholic employer from paying for the coverages was not seen as adequate to protect Catholic consciences. It is not as though the Catholic conscience on matters of morality should count for nothing in the public square, of course. As many Catholic supporters of the religious liberty campaign asserted, the First Amendment's protection of the free exercise of religion must reach beyond the four walls of the local parish church to protect believers out in public spaces. That proposition is indisputably true. But for as many times as it has been asserted, it is also beside the point. Being in the world has demanded compromises from Christian believers since the early church. Catholics consciences have struggled for a long time with worldliness, and nowhere has the struggle been more difficult than where some public good conflicted with Catholic moral teaching. For a long time, Catholics in the United States made those compromises quite willingly. Like their Christian forebears in the early church, American Catholics once were confident they could change the world by converting women and men to the Gospel. But suddenly during the Obama administration, the willingness to struggle and to compromise was gone. Many American Catholics seemed to forget how taking up a rifle to defend their country, as so many generations of Catholics have done, is a compromise and the arguments that Catholic leaders like Cardinal Francis Spellman made against Catholic conscientious objectors once reflected a very generous spirit of compromise with what the world demands from us.[4] Somehow, by 2012, permitting other people to use contraceptives while Catholic employers could be exempted from paying directly for them became too great a compromise.

Not every compromise is worth making, of course. But some compromises are worth it. The spirit of compromise holds together a community of people who believe in different things. Without that spirit we cannot have the thing that the Catholic tradition prizes most in social life. We cannot appreciate "the full truth of [our] existence," how our personal existence is joined to our "community and social existence": after all, a human being is "a community being."[5] Deal Hudson's political strategy to unite conservative Catholics and evangelical Christians between 2000 and 2004 arrived at a time when it could precipitate a fatal collapse of the spirit of compromise that holds communities together. After decades of culture wars, the 2004 election brought conservative Catholics and evangelicals together just in time to meet the social upheavals accompanying the economic crisis of 2008. A new insularity emerged among Christians who long had perceived and now turned away from a hostile American culture as their outrage intensified about culture war issues to fuel the 2004 Bush victory, deepening the polarization that had been under way since the years of the Cold War. In a new moment after the 2008 global economic crisis, the tendency to polarize and to divide took a new direction. No longer seeking to win a war for the culture, which at least expressed an interest in the broader community, those groups instead began to separate from the culture. Catholics and evangelicals withdrew behind religious liberty, but their withdrawal in these recent years cannot be explained only by a commitment to religious affiliation. Other factors also were in play.

Robert P. Jones wrote about the transformation of Deal Hudson's 2004 "values voters" into Steve Bannon's 2016 "nostalgia voters" in his book *The End of White Christian America*.[6] Jones wrote about evangelical Christians and the improbable way in which they rallied to Donald Trump, a twice-divorced, publicly promiscuous, gaudily grandiose billionaire from New York City who, in a long public life, had never given any evidence of a substantial religious commitment. That transformation of "values voters" into "nostalgia voters" tracked not just a deep commitment to a particular vision of a Christian nation in the light of the specific histories of European immigrants to the United States, but it also corresponded to a growing insecurity that the history of European immigrants in the US was on the demographic road to being overtaken by the different histories of immigrants from Latin America and Asia. As the twenty-first century began, it became clear that the American complexion was changing. In many ways, through immigration and childbirth rates, America was becoming a more global, more diverse place. American Catholics felt those changes coming as much as evangelicals did, and they also responded. But Catholics followed their own path from their own distinct history in response to these developments. Catholics and evangelicals began from different places, but by 2016 they landed at the same political solution to the problems they perceived for largely similar reasons. Their sense of dominating the American narrative was slipping away. For evangelical Protestants that was a sense of dominance to which a long hegemony of American Protestantism gave them a long-established feeling of entitlement. For Catholics, that sense of dominance was more recently won after a long, discouraging fight of many decades. By 2016, large numbers from both groups found their way to Donald Trump, who soothed their cultural anxiety and promised a return to the greatness of the past when everything was clearer and more comfortably familiar.

Yet, Jones writes only about theological and demographic causes. Like a commitment to the principles of religious liberty, they have been important factors in the remarkable and complex events that have unfolded in American politics, especially among Catholics during the last few decades. But finally, we cannot understand everything that has happened without appreciating the ways in which economic anxiety mingled with religious commitment to prepare the way to where we are now. Catholics especially appear to have joined their cultural alienation to their economic anxiety. After decades of polarized thinking, a crafty manipulator of opinion was able to imagine a way to unite the alienation that came from so many years of polarization with the sureness that our economic anxieties must be blamed on recent immigrants and other "outsiders." That was the potent formula that would bring Catholics and evangelical Christians together in the Trump campaign.

A Surprising Ecumenism

Shortly after the 2016 Republican National Convention named him as their party's nominee for the White House, Donald Trump named the third manager of his tumultuous campaign. Steve Bannon had been an investment banker with Goldman Sachs before he became the head of Breitbart News in 2012. Breitbart had been founded by Andrew Breitbart to nurture the most extreme fringes of the conservative movement with a steady content stream that rewarded and reinforced what they already believed. Trafficking in wild conspiracy theories that painted a portrait of a radical government at war with its people, Breitbart catered to an audience long claimed by Rush Limbaugh on AM talk radio and so long a part of the Republican coalition that William F. Buckley, Jr., once lamented them as "kooks."[7] Changes of technology only partially explain the rise of Breitbart, InfoWars, and Alex Jones during the Obama administration. The economic dislocation of the global economic crisis exposed the vulnerability of non-college-educated, blue-collar, white workers. Combine that vulnerable feeling with an increasingly diverse American culture, the racial politics that attended the nation's first African American president, a decades-long polarizing culture war, and it does not seem so surprising that there should have been a burst of new political energy on the far side of the American right.

Bannon's peculiar genius was to recognize the potential in that energy and to find new ways to tap it. In his study of the Trump-Bannon partnership, *Devil's Bargain* (Penguin, 2017), Joshua Green describes how Bannon seized on the advantage that Hillary Rodham Clinton posed as an opponent, shrewdly using her long public record and the public's long-standing perceptions against her. Rather than fomenting conspiracies, Bannon carefully picked through the factual record to identify and highlight those vulnerabilities that would energize Trump supporters.[8] Trump's endless laments during the 2016 campaign about Benghazi or Clinton's e-mail server were meant to do what they did—remind Republican-leaning voters about their suspicions of Hillary and Bill Clinton. The 1990s had established the Clintons in the public imagination, but they also became polarizing figures who opened a new chapter in what Barack Obama called the "psychodrama of the Baby Boom generation—a tale rooted in old grudges and revenge plots hatched on a handful of college campuses long ago."[9] That psychodrama cast the Clintons on the side of radicals, hippies, and draft-dodging elites against the hardworking men and women of the East Coast ethnic neighborhoods and middle America. The new charges of the 2016 campaign functioned like a leitmotif, a reminder of something Americans already had seen earlier in the ongoing drama:

> "The Clintons don't feel the same way about America as you do."
>
> "The Clintons are dishonest."
>
> "The Clintons are elitist."
>
> "The Clintons are weak."

The deadly attack on the State Department facility at Benghazi happened. The allegations about the vulnerability of a private e-mail server were largely true. Trump did not need to connect the dots for his rally crowds. Decades of a polarized political argument had prepared them to receive a carefully selected message. Bannon understood the polarization around the Clintons well enough to leave it alone. There was no need to embroider it with new conspiracy theories while the old ones would metastasize all by themselves.

But there was more to Steve Bannon than his Goldman Sachs background or his clever political tactics. Bannon is also a Catholic, and he is said to be a devotee of the Extraordinary Form, also sometimes called the traditional Latin Mass. In the summer of 2014, as a representative of the Breitbart organization, Bannon was invited to give a presentation at a Vatican conference sponsored by the *Dignitatis Humanae* Institute. Bannon's teleconferenced presentation can be found widely on the internet, and it has been transcribed in several places, presumably in the hope that it could offer a key to unlock Bannon's strategy or his agenda. In fact, that Vatican talk is so incoherent we cannot say it really makes anything very clear about Bannon. So far as it describes Bannon's worldview, however, his presentation for the Vatican in 2014 tells us a lot about Catholics like Bannon—that is to say, broadly, conservative Catholics—and how they approach the issues and problems that faced them in the years running up to the 2016 election. To put it mildly, we find that Deal Hudson and the 2004 Bush campaign's Catholic outreach were remarkably successful not only for how they helped George W. Bush win reelection, but also for how they carried forward the culture war and the US bishops' efforts to imprint a way of seeing American politics on Catholic voters beyond 2004, toward the 2008 global financial crisis and a time when issues like abortion no longer were at the top of most Catholics' lists of vital political issues. The divisions sowed by four decades of cultural arguments about abortion and other moral issues did not go away, though. Steve Bannon offered a politics of division, by division, for division, and Donald Trump was its ideal spokesman. What it was that divided Americans no longer mattered so much that it needed to make sense. Division had become the purpose. Polarization was the point.

Bannon's analysis of our cultural situation hinged on what seemed at first like a somewhat peculiar set of assumptions. The "world and particularly the Judeo-Christian west, is in a crisis." Breitbart, Bannon informed his listeners in Rome, is "a platform to bring news and information to people" so they may understand the crisis better. So far, this is only a very broad claim that seems only to serve as a commercial for Breitbart news. Bannon continued. What is the crisis? It "is a crisis both of capitalism but [*sic*] really the underpinnings of the Judeo-Christian west in our beliefs." Those beliefs never are named by Bannon in his presentation at all, beyond their identification with capitalism, which appears, in his telling, to represent the summit of Judeo-Christian civilization. The significance of where capitalism sits in Bannon's hierarchy of being is not found in how it draws our attention to Bannon's Harvard Business School education or his background with Goldman Sachs, his apparent sympathy with a certain strain of Catholic social thought (Michael Novak, Robert Sirico) that sees market forces and capitalism as promoting human dignity, or his support for a billionaire presidential candidate. Rather, it is the way Bannon sees those Judeo-Christian values (capitalism) in conflict with Islam as a civilizational threat to our values—again, capitalism—by those who do not share them. Even comparing the threat posed by ISIS to the Soviet threat of the Cold War, Bannon continues the polarization he and his generation learned during those Cold War years, which was absorbed by the culture of American Catholicism and imprinted its polarization on the Catholic imagination through the decades of the culture wars.

It is not an exaggeration at all to say that Bannon's entire analysis is one of a crisis in capitalism that he calls a crisis of "Judeo-Christian belief." Bannon names two trends in contemporary capitalism as "very disturbing." They are, first, "state-sponsored capitalism . . . [such as] you see in China and Russia," and, second, neoliberalism, which he describes as a form of "enlightened capitalism . . . that really looks to make people commodities, and to objectify people, and to use them." Incredibly, Bannon seamlessly ties these developments to secularization to conclude that they all converge with "an outright war against jihadist Islamic fascism." There is populism here in Bannon's skepticism about neoliberal wealth, and he raises questions about whether there should be "a cap on wealth creation" that might be pleasing to the unemployed blue-collar workers who turned out for Trump rallies during the 2016 campaign. Yet, the apocalyptic vision that joins this economic argument about a "crisis of the underpinnings of capitalism" with "a global war against Islamic fascism" is a little too much like how Bannon understands the twentieth century as "a century of barbaric [warfare] . . . [that] will be looked at almost as a new Dark Age" for its climactic Cold War struggle with "a barbaric empire in the Far East." Forces of "darkness" gathered in those Cold War days against a "*Pax Americana*" that defended Judeo-Christian values identified with capitalism, and now in our time a "new barbarity" in ISIS begins that, if unchecked, "will completely eradicate everything we've been bequeathed over the last 2,000, 2,500 years."

That worldview has deep roots not just in recent American political history but also in the ancient history of Christianity. It employs "a Manichean language that divides reality between absolute Good and absolute Evil," and it was described recently in an important article published in the Italian Jesuit journal *La Civiltà Cattolica*.[10] In that article, Antonio Spadaro, SJ, and Marcelo Figueroa, a Presbyterian pastor, explore the roots of this worldview, which they trace to American evangelicalism that sees danger in "modernist spirits, the black civil rights movement, the hippy movement, communism, feminist movements, and so on."[11] Evangelicalism embarked on that worldview from beginnings different from where Catholics began, but their culture war preoccupations are the same as Catholics' and that coincidence was the premise for a potent political alliance that was brokered in the years from the *Roe* decision to the 2004 Bush campaign, one that Spadaro and Figueroa worry may also reflect a "strange form of ecumenism . . . between Evangelical fundamentalists and Catholic integralists brought together by the same desire for religious influence in the public sphere."[12] Spadaro and Figueroa recognize the familiar range of issues involved—"abortion, same-sex marriage, religious education in schools, and other matters generally considered moral or tied to values," and they call attention to how this evangelical-Catholic alliance serves a "temptation to project divinity on political power" rather than to bring faith, hope, and love to the world.[13] They worry that political power has become the point of religious belief for too many people who imagine that something like a dominating Roman power should be comfortable for Christians. This is the paradox of Catholic and evangelical support for Donald Trump and the Americans before them since *Roe* who fought a culture war. Like a favored people in a city on a hill, these Catholics and evangelicals feel themselves entitled to the worldly power needed to enact and enforce their political preferences. As much as the early church was seduced by this relationship to power after the time of Emperor Constantine, today this otherworldly certainty has captured Catholics and evangelicals and ensnared them in worldliness to an extent that they have allied themselves to the most worldly of all presidential hopefuls in 2016. No candidate has ever boasted so much about wealth and sexual conquest as the candidate supported by so many Catholic and evangelical voters, Donald Trump. Yet, their

worldly certainty about the rightness of their moral and political argument utterly blinded those Christians to who Trump is. It did not matter as much to them as winning this long-running cultural argument. Spadaro and Figueroa's analysis focuses on this problem, one at the heart of any Christian engagement with politics. Christianity must be present to the world, yet Christianity must not become captured by the world.

Yet, Steve Bannon has proven to be alert to an important dimension of this problem that Spadaro and Figueroa glide past. Spadaro and Figueroa have critiqued the prosperity gospel, which holds that "God desires his followers to be physically healthy, materially rich, and personally happy," rejecting its mingling of Christian belief with worldly success. But Spadaro and Figueroa have overlooked what Steve Bannon knows. Most people—certainly, most Americans—find their material circumstances difficult to disentangle from their relationship to God. Nearly every analyst agrees that the economic insecurity felt by many Americans who supported Donald Trump was the decisive factor in the 2016 election. Economic insecurity bred, as often it does, a renewed sense of nationalism and suspicion of anyone who might look like an outsider. That economic anxiety was felt all over the United States but to different degrees. Some places suffered far more than others and, in general, where the economic dislocation was greatest was where Donald Trump drew his greatest support. Among Catholics who voted for Trump, however, the key states of Pennsylvania, Michigan, and Wisconsin, where Trump's victory was secured and where large numbers of blue-collar Catholic voters live, offer our best opportunity to see the interaction of economic insecurity and Catholic religious participation at work. Each of these three states is home to a Roman Catholic archdiocese (Philadelphia, Detroit, and Milwaukee) and, more importantly, all three stretch across an arc

from the mid-Atlantic to the Great Lakes, where Catholic immigrant groups of the nineteenth and early twentieth centuries settled in large cities. Those cities drew earlier immigrant groups because they offered opportunities for factory labor, the sorts of industrial jobs that have vanished in recent decades. Many places offer a good place to examine the way Catholics came together to provide essential support for Donald Trump's election, but few places are so important as Michigan, Pennsylvania, and Wisconsin.[14]

We can construct a comparison to try to measure the effect economic anxiety had on Catholics affected by the long polarization of the culture wars. Looking closely at Michigan, Pennsylvania, and Wisconsin, we can focus on counties that were hit the hardest by the economic crisis of 2008 and where religious participation by Catholics is greater than average.[15] Pennsylvania offers the clearest demonstration of an effect. Comparing the 2016 election to the 2012 election, we find that Donald Trump outperformed Mitt Romney's 2012 campaign by a statewide average of 4.96 percent. However, when we zero in on four counties in which more than one-third of residents practice as Catholics and unemployment was highest (Carbon, Elk, Lawrence, and Schuylkill), we find that Trump outperformed Romney by 11.25 percent. In Michigan, again looking to the counties with the highest unemployment and the highest levels of religious participation among Catholics (Alpena, Delta, Huron, Menominee, and Presque Isle), we find that Trump outperformed Romney by 9.18 percent, while overall, statewide, Trump averaged only 5.81 percent better than Romney in all Michigan counties. Wisconsin proves the case in a slightly different way. In Wisconsin counties with the highest unemployment and high levels of Catholic religious participation (Brown, Grant, Kewaunee, Manitowoc, and Menominee) Trump outperformed Romney at almost exactly the same level (6.66 percent) as in all counties throughout the state (6.98 percent):

there is no significant difference.[16] But Wisconsin is different. While Wisconsin's unemployment was high by ordinary standards, very few Wisconsin counties experienced rates of unemployment above the national average during the worst of the crisis. Michigan and Pennsylvania suffered more than most other states, while Wisconsin did not suffer quite so much. In Wisconsin, where both factors (unemployment rates above the national average and high levels of Catholic religious participation) are not found, Catholic voters did not turn to Trump at a rate any greater than the rest of the state. This is not really surprising.

To reinforce the picture that is forming, we can look just a little beyond Wisconsin to Minnesota, a state generally regarded as a Democratic stronghold in presidential elections, where we can see this pattern again. Minnesota is also home to a Catholic archdiocese and, while it did not see quite so much Catholic immigration in the nineteenth and twentieth centuries, there was some, especially in eastern Minnesota. Like Wisconsin and Michigan, Minnesota has trended more and more toward Republicans in recent decades and, in 2016, Hillary Rodham Clinton won Minnesota by a scant 1.51 percent. Overall in Minnesota, averaging across all counties, Trump outperformed Romney's 2012 total by an average 7.03 percent. But, when we focus only on counties with the highest unemployment and highest levels of religious participation among Catholics (Le Sueur, Marshall, Morrison, and Red Lake), we find a significant difference again. Trump outperformed Romney by 11.44 percent. Rather consistently in these mid-Atlantic and Great Lakes areas where Catholics have lived for generations and where the economic crisis hit hardest, we find that Trump performed significantly better than the 2012 Republican nominee. The effect is not a result only of economic anxiety or only of Catholic religious faith alone. Both reinforced each other because, by 2016, both had become part of the

same cultural alienation. Children and grandchildren of American immigrants in these places turned to Donald Trump's economic nationalism for the answers their pocketbook anxieties craved, and their cultivated sense of polarization in American life made it easier to accept a candidate whose aggrieved message depended on defining an "us" against a "them."

We should add here that the effect was not unique to Catholics. We can perform a similar comparison among evangelical Christians in the same states. Among Pennsylvania counties where unemployment and evangelical religious participation was highest (Lawrence, Mercer, Northumberland, and Somerset), Trump outperformed Romney by an average 8.02 percent. In similar Michigan counties (Alger, Alpena, Huron, Presque Isle, and Saginaw), Trump surpassed Romney by 7.82 percent. In Wisconsin (Dodge, Green Lake, Lincoln, Shawano, Taylor, and Waupaca) we see a somewhat greater effect among evangelicals, where Trump outperformed Romney by 8.02 percent. In Minnesota (McLeod, Mille Lacs, Sibley, Wabasha, and Winona), Trump outperformed Romney by 6.93 percent. Allowing again that Wisconsin's unemployment was not as bad as the others, we find a fairly consistent effect in these Trump states. When high levels of unemployment combined with high levels of religious participation, Trump benefited. But the effect was more pronounced among Catholics than among evangelicals.

Evangelicals' support for Trump perhaps can be described simply as a spontaneous response to events unfolding around them in American life. After a generations-long period of polarization rooted in moral issues that motivated many religious voters, economic anxiety became imprinted with a polarization that originated in religious concern but then moved beyond it. It was much the same for Catholics, except in their case spontaneity alone cannot explain what happened. Perhaps that explains why, among Catholics, the

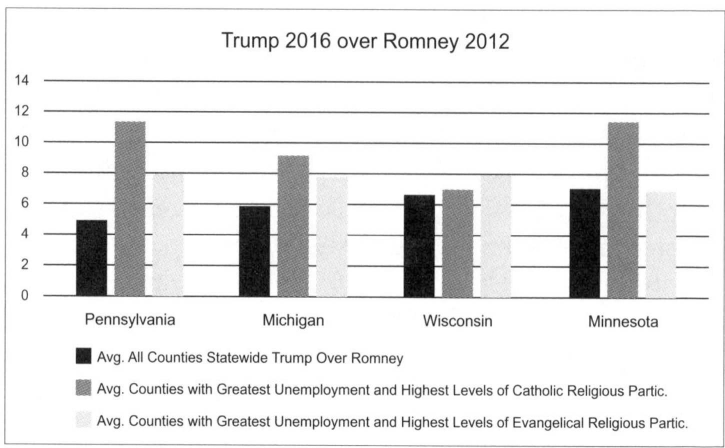
Trump 2016 over Romney 2012
14
12
10
8
6
4
2
0
Pennsylvania
Michigan
Wisconsin
Minnesota
Avg. All Counties Statewide Trump Over Romney
Avg. Counties with Greatest Unemployment and Highest Levels of Catholic Religious Partic.
Avg. Counties with Greatest Unemployment and Highest Levels of Evangelical Religious Partic.

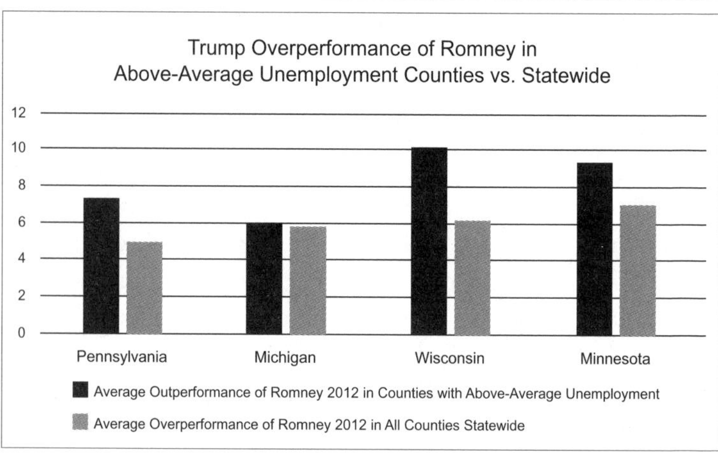
Trump Overperformance of Romney in
Above-Average Unemployment Counties vs. Statewide
12
10
8
6
4
2
0
Pennsylvania
Michigan
Wisconsin
Minnesota
Average Outperformance of Romney 2012 in Counties with Above-Average Unemployment
Average Overperformance of Romney 2012 in All Counties Statewide

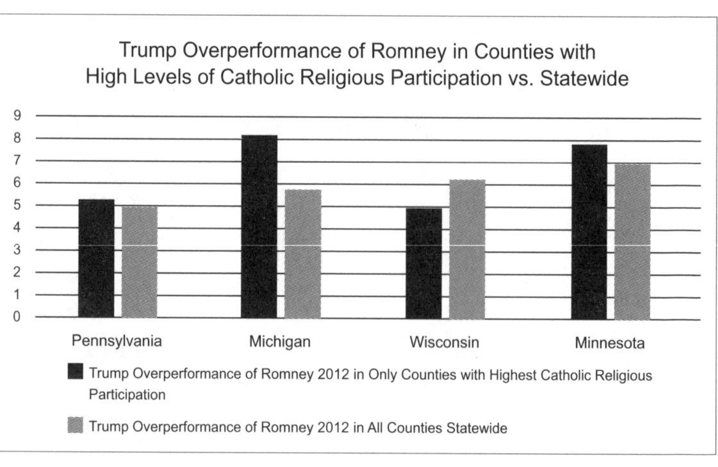
Trump Overperformance of Romney in Counties with
High Levels of Catholic Religious Participation vs. Statewide
9
8
7
6
5
4
3
2
1
0
Pennsylvania
Michigan
Wisconsin
Minnesota
Trump Overperformance of Romney 2012 in Only Counties with Highest Catholic Religious Participation
Trump Overperformance of Romney 2012 in All Counties Statewide

effects we see in 2016 voter behavior were not the same. The effect that church leaders can have on Catholic voters is different from other groups of religious voters. Protestantism exists in large part because of the sixteenth-century rejection of a formalized church structure that interprets Scripture and the world for believers. Evangelicalism emphasizes even more the individual's direct encounter with Scripture and with God. There is no United States Conference of Evangelical Leaders to mount a religious liberty campaign or embark on any other coordinated effort to lobby or to teach. That is not to say that evangelical Christians cannot coordinate their activity. Certainly, they have done that very effectively in American political life during the last four decades. The difference is that evangelical leaders do not possess the same organization of authority and obedience found among Catholic bishops, so their responsibility is more diffuse. There is no evangelical equivalent of a Catholic bishop, nor is there any overall bond of institutional unity that the bishops derive from their obedience to the tradition of the church and the pope as a first among equals who teach the faith. As the Catholic bishops of the United States have worked so steadily since *Roe* to effect change in American political life, the presence of a coordinating authority among bishops who dispense the sacraments and teach the faith to believers has given a different character to Catholic bishops' efforts to influence culture and politics. That was, after all, the essential meaning of the efforts to deny sacraments to John Kerry and other Democrats. The US Catholic bishops share a sort of responsibility for our nation's social and political condition that cannot be assigned to evangelical leaders for these structural reasons. It is not that the bishops were bad people who wanted to do bad things. What is worse is that they had only good intentions. They wanted to spread the Gospel and to protect the dignity of every human person. They simply made bad

decisions about how to do those things, then followed them with more bad decisions and grew captive to a deepening cycle of bad decision-making that has led American Catholics to where they are today. Today, Catholics find themselves in this "strange ecumenism" lamented by Spadaro and Figueroa that has united many Catholics with many evangelicals in a paradoxical worldliness.

The Dignity of Persons

Today's American Catholics sit at the end of a history that began with the Spanish explorations of *La Florida* and traveled through a long, immigrant experience of second-class citizenship. That history gave American bishops potent materials with which to work in the years since *Roe* as they sought to fashion a distinctly Catholic political approach that followed a different path from the one that had led American law and politics to *Roe* and beyond. That immigrant experience is the necessary background that distinguishes the Catholic experience of being "a people apart" from any way in which other Americans, including contemporary evangelicals, feel themselves to be a distinct and separate Christian community in the United States. For Catholics it is different because the immigrant groups whose experiences shaped Catholicism in the United States from the beginning until the very recent past shared a distinct cultural experience all their own as immigrant outsiders. The way American Catholics who descended from this long immigrant history embarked on the 2016 presidential election and the Trump era is different from other Americans. It played its role in the behavior of those Catholic voters.

Two scriptural examples tend to shape how Christians engage with politics, and both have left a deep imprint on the Catholic political imagination. One is the experience of the early Christian church under Roman domination that we find in the New Testament. The example of early Christians tends to promote a view that sees the Christian community as "the light of the world" (Matt 5:14), a community of believers in the world who are not "of this world" (John 18:36) but who obey civil authorities (Rom 13:1-7, 1 Pet. 2:13) and work within the structures of worldliness to bring about the reign of God in time while shining a beacon of light beyond the Christian community. Christians summon the world without overpowering it. This was the church of martyrs who did not abandon the faith, but it was also the church of compromises that understood that its task of changing the world could not be achieved by power or force. Early church leaders instructed Christians to pay taxes that contributed to Roman power in ways that might have offended their consciences. Those early Christians walked through marketplaces across the ancient world where human beings were trafficked and Saint Paul wrote uncritically about the fact of slavery (Gal 3:28). We should not think that early Christians supported human trafficking or cheered for how Roman legions armed themselves with the taxes they collected. Rather, we should see a way of being Christian that was not preoccupied with changing laws or customs so much as with changing hearts, one at a time. This was a way of being Christian that assumed no privileges came with the description.

The other scriptural example is found in the chosen people of the Old Testament. While this example of the ancient Israelite communities does not describe any people who ever exercised worldly power on the scale of the Roman exercise of power, the chosen people's most essential historical and literary characteristic we see described in Scripture is the remarkably close cohesiveness of their community. Internal division, conquest, exile, and diaspora cannot shake their remarkable faith that they are favored by God as Abraham's descendants, heirs to a covenant.

Throughout Christian history, this inheritance from Judaism has nurtured a powerful confidence about the role that Christians should play to shape the world. That model cannot fail to appeal to the immigrant descendants of American Catholics who inherited that scriptural legacy and who fought hard for generations to prove that they have a special role to play in a "Catholic public engagement [that] comes from the same religiously informed roots that gave life to the ideas and words of America's founders."[17] To focus exclusively on that model makes it possible to say something like, "As a bishop, I have a duty in charity to help Catholic officials understand and support church teaching on vital issues," without adding, "I also have an obligation to listen to Catholic officials who run for office, work in government, and represent all of the people to take seriously what they believe is and is not possible."[18] The people who feel themselves in a special relationship not just to God but also to their nation's founding are teachers with answers who help Catholic public officials understand vital issues. Their first instinct has not been a "profound social humility" that aims at "political dialogue and consensus building" because "the Church does not have solutions for every particular issue."[19] In fact, at least on the issues that matter most, they see the answers of the church's moral theology and they want them to be enacted as law or public policy.

The period since *Roe v. Wade* has been a time of considerable, confusing pressure for the generations of American Catholics whose ancestors came to the United States in the nineteenth and early twentieth centuries. That pressure slowly transformed a community that had been open to American influence and that sought for many years to demonstrate there was no conflict between American citizenship and Catholicism, just as early Christians lived within a Roman world, into a community at first actively seeking to reshape America and then, faced with the prospect of failure, one that would begin to turn away from America entirely, going so far as to question the legitimacy of its government. Along the way, not only would the church in the United States itself become polarized, but church teachings, along with the place of Catholics in American life, would become contested and Catholicism in the US itself would become somewhat distorted by these events. The same faith in chosenness that sustained Jewish communities for thousands of years and has given them a unique history among all the people of the earth has, among these American Catholics, become a temptation to make political claims and seek a sort of Roman power and influence over political and social life.

The combination of these two scriptural perspectives—the Old Testament's chosen people with a reading of the New Testament that looks beyond the small Christian community to the Roman power that dominated them—is not so new or unusual. Constantinianism, or Catholic integralism, has been around since the time of the early church. For a long time, Christian believers have been tempted by the idea that they should have a privileged voice in the political community, a union between spiritual power and worldly power. But to seek that union always quickly becomes treacherous. The otherworldly justification for joining worldly power to spiritual claims gives way to feelings of an entitlement to possess worldly power. It is a paradox, but often enough in history it has been true. The most otherworldly preoccupations can have a strange tendency to give way to the most earthly temptations to force our beliefs on others. Whatever else held conservative Catholics and evangelical Christians together as they approached the 2016 election, it seems that both had—from within their own traditions—found themselves at a point of wanting to reshape the world by any means necessary.

We should say that the US bishops' desire to craft an American Catholic engagement with political questions was not a foolish enterprise or a misguided one. The bishops were, in fact, responsive to the letter and the spirit of the Second Vatican Council that called on Catholics to "make [themselves] the neighbor of absolutely every person," "to play one's role in common endeavors," praising "those national procedures which allow the largest number of citizens to participate in public affairs."[20] The Second Vatican Council embraced the political systems of the United States and the developed democracies of Europe. There was a call for activism in the Council documents that Pope Paul VI and Pope John Paul II picked up and carried forward for the next several decades. In that perspective, nothing about the actions of the US bishops from their pro-life activism after *Roe* to their religious liberty campaign was wrong at all. To be Christian in the world of the twentieth and twenty-first centuries demands a close engagement with political and social questions. As religious leaders and teachers of the faith, Catholic bishops must exercise leadership when important questions arise. There is no question about that.

Not every exercise of leadership is prudent. Not every engagement with politics is constructive. Especially in the complex and fractious climate in which moral problems meet political realities, it can be easy to make mistakes. Even the best intentions can succumb to our all too human frailty in the heat of an argument. That is as true for a Catholic bishop or the people who work for a bishop as it is for anyone else in the world. That is a point about which we need to be extremely clear and precise. Catholic political action is necessary, and the Catholic faith teaches us that it is an important duty. Defending the dignity of each and every human person depends on it. Yet, politics is a realm of prudence. Especially in the circumstances of our time, with so many rapid advances in our technology that raise new, difficult issues so quickly, and amid a newly global world in which ideas can be communicated instantly across great distances, the experience of the last several decades in American Catholic life demonstrates that some greater thought and some better checks are needed in how Catholics generally, and Catholic bishops specifically, approach politics. The answers of moral theology and Christian ethics are not always appropriate to problems in politics and law. The realms of politics and law will not be shaped by justice and mercy if there is no place for Christian ethics and moral theology. We must find a way to have a politics that makes room for our deepest commitments of faith, but we also must practice a politics that is appropriate to a place in which our faith is not shared with everyone. But that only is the beginning of the challenge.

Almost fifty years of division since the *Roe* decision have played their part. So have the events that have occurred since *Roe* to intensify and reintensify that polarization in moments like the 1976 presidential campaign, the imbroglio over Mario Cuomo and Geraldine Ferraro, the Bork hearings, the outbreak of the 1990s culture wars, the 2004 Bush reelection campaign, and the 2008 global economic crisis. The accumulated historical, cultural, psychic, and spiritual weight of that polarization that has been so much a part of our individual and community lives for so long is another, separate problem that we must acknowledge. In other words, the problem of church and state has been with us for two thousand years, and it is irresolvable by itself. Yet, when we heap on top of that difficult problem the fractious, bitter polarization that has set into American Catholicism during the last several decades we face a church that quickly begins to seem unrecognizable. Descendants of Catholic immigrants raised in the communal theology of the church embrace nationalism and seek to close borders to migrants. Catholics embrace capitalism and embark on an alliance with evangelical Christians to hold fast to a nostalgic ideal of an America that once was great and no longer is. In 2016, the Center for Applied Research in the Apostolate at Georgetown University reported that only 14 percent of American Catholics have a favorable opinion about Muslims. Something has gone gravely wrong.

How can we recover from this condition?

This book is a history, and this is not the place to describe solutions to complex problems that have arisen across decades and centuries. No one book could do that, and certainly no book of this short length. Yet, acknowledging the way this polarization has become a part of our lives and has distorted how so many Catholics engage with social, economic, and political questions is a necessary first step. We must come to grips with this history, and we must admit to the way the taint of polarization has affected all of us. We all indulge a little too easily, whether in the church or in politics, the temptation to divide into two opposing camps and simply to assume the other side is always wrong. That is not our way; it is not what Catholic faith teaches us. The same church that teaches us that God has revealed things that are true among people who are not Christian cannot possibly be home to the belief that any group of people is always simply wrong.[21] The Christian understanding of the world is more complex than that. We must embrace that complexity, which always begins with the humble suspicion that there is something else for us to learn.

Only once we have acknowledged this new reflex we have learned from our polarization and divisions can we embark on the path that can offer the only way toward solutions. It is the path that Pope Francis and others have reminded us about so forcefully, the path of dialogue.

Conclusion

Father Frank Pavone is the national director of a pro-life organization, Priests for Life. Many Catholics would recognize him from his long-time direct mail appeals for financial support for his pro-life activities. Pavone began his priesthood in the Archdiocese of New York, where his service as a parish priest ended five years after his ordination. In 1993, Cardinal John O'Connor named him to his position at Priests for Life, and Pavone has been embroiled in national debate ever since. Pavone eventually fell out with Cardinal O'Connor and Cardinal Edward Egan, seeking transfer to the Diocese of Amarillo in Texas in 2005, where the bishop agreed to let him continue his work with Priests for Life in New York. In 2011, when the bishop of Amarillo suspended him from pro-life work amid questions about his organization's finances, Pavone appealed to the Congregation for Clergy in Rome. Even in 2017, Pavone continues to function as the national director of Priests for Life, where the webpage asserts that "the party of death is out to take down President Trump." Yet, Pavone peaked as an object of national political attention the day before the 2016 presidential election when, in a Facebook video, he laid an aborted child on an altar in an appeal to voters on behalf of Donald Trump.

Father Pavone's actions before the election capture the confusion that set into the way Catholics think about American politics during the decades after *Roe*. So certain about the rightness of his pro-life activities, Pavone quarreled with three of his bishops across more than a decade to keep his role at Priests for Life. Pavone's single-minded focus on abortion not only led him into those conflicts with bishops, but it also helped him to overlook serious deficiencies about Donald Trump as an individual and as a candidate. So blinded was Father Pavone by his determination to elect at any cost someone he thought would act to overturn *Roe*, as a blog post at the Archdiocese of New York website described it, "He used a dead aborted baby, laying naked and bloody on an altar, as a prop for his video. Yes, you read that correctly. A priest of the Catholic Church publicly displayed on a sacred altar a dead baby who was the victim of a terrible crime as part of a propaganda video in favor of a political candidate."[1] Apart from distastefulness and transgressing the appropriate boundaries for political activity, as well as the dignity of the dead human person whose body he had used for the video, Pavone had violated canon law, which says that the altar "is to be reserved for divine worship alone."[2] The Diocese of Amarillo launched an investigation, and the United States Conference of Catholic Bishops kept their distance from Pavone. Pavone struck back with a statement that laid blame with the Democratic Party, and sympathetic websites and social media accounts rushed to defend him.[3]

The Pavone episode illustrates several of the reasons that led to this book in the late days of 2016. Father Pavone's journey to that altar did not begin suddenly. It was a journey he had been on since 1993, amid a priesthood and an adult life shaped by the circumstances that grew out of the *Roe* decision—circumstances described in this book. Father Pavone's rigid certainty about his actions, and his seeming determination that practically anything is worth doing in order to reverse *Roe*, mark out his refusal to abandon his work with Priests for Life when his bishops asked him to do so as well as his rather strange actions shortly before the 2016 presidential election. But, finally, Father Pavone's attitude is indicative of a powerful trend among many Americans who have held to one side of the political and cultural divide supporting Donald Trump, no matter how otherwise inappropriate he may be as a candidate for pro-life or religiously committed voters.

Something happened to American politics that made the 2016 presidential election possible. The actions of Catholic voters alone do not explain what happened. There were many ingredients interacting with one another in complex ways. But Catholics find themselves in the Trump era bearing a distinct and unavoidable kind of responsibility for marshaling the forces that combined to lead the United States and the world to where we are. Those forces included the Catholic immigrant experience of the nineteenth and twentieth centuries, and the consciousness of being outsiders that experience nurtured among Bohemian, German, Irish, Italian, Polish, and other Catholic immigrants, their children, and their grandchildren. The ascent of Catholics into the mainstream of American life amid the bipolar paranoia of the Cold War brought those descendants of Catholic immigrants into American life still feeling that they had something to prove. Their anticommunist bona fides made Catholics good Americans in the 1950s and 1960s. Yet, as quickly as Catholics climbed into the American mainstream, the sudden tumult of the 1960s culminating in *Roe v. Wade* left Catholics feeling suddenly alienated from a mainstream that had only just accepted them. American life had changed suddenly and dramatically, and many Catholics felt left behind. Thus, Catholics entered the mainstream as the beneficiaries of a Cold War way of seeing the world as divided into two warring camps, becoming socially indistinguishable from their fellow citizens and with some of their fellow citizens embarking on a cultural argument to reclaim the

United States that accepted them and restore it to how they remembered it. Cultural conservatism was born in the years leading to the Reagan presidency, and it grew strong during those years. Many Catholics, especially bishops and other leaders, joined a culture war that took center stage in American politics after the end of the Cold War in the early 1990s. As the largest religious denomination in the United States, unified by the spiritual authority of the Catholic bishops and in step with a pope whose worldview was shaped by his experience of Soviet communism, Catholics spent the next decade building a coalition with evangelical Christians. That coalition culminated in the Catholic outreach of the Bush reelection campaign in 2004, and made Catholics and evangelical Christians a political bloc built on cultural resentments and their rejection of mainstream, elite opinions. That rejection was reinforced by the failures of elites that led to the 2008 global economic crisis. Especially where the crisis was felt worst, political instincts nurtured by long exposure to polarization and lost confidence in elites drew many Americans toward a bitter skepticism about the status quo that not only rejected Democrats, but left mainstream conservative Republicans on the outside. Throughout the Obama presidency and especially resulting from the campaign for religious liberty mounted by the US bishops to resist the mandates of the Affordable Care Act, the way was prepared for Catholic voters to find their way toward someone like Donald Trump. And, while others traveled this road with Catholics, the effect appears to have been measurably the greatest among Catholics who supported Trump. Finally, these voters were attracted not just to Trump or all that he came to represent, but the opportunity to cement a victory in the culture war by reshaping the federal judiciary.

The success of the Trump campaign and the Republican Party in 2016 almost certainly owes in considerable part to how skillfully they manipulated the vacancy of Antonin Scalia's seat on the US Supreme Court for a year leading up to the election. Barack Obama had nominated an eminently qualified and nearly universally respected senior jurist, Merrick Garland, for the seat. For most of a year, the Republican majority in the Senate simply refused to schedule a hearing. As wrongly as Judge Bork was treated in 1987, at least he had an opportunity to make his case in a public forum. As wrong as it was for subsequent judicial nominees after Bork to seek a stealthy path through their public hearings at the Senate, avoiding difficult questions about controversial issues, at least it was done in the light of day. The American people and their representatives had an opportunity to evaluate those candidates and the ways they presented themselves. Refusing even to schedule a hearing on Judge Garland's nomination was a disservice to the people and the Court, never mind how discourteous it was toward Judge Garland and President Obama. But it had a purpose.

To keep the vacant seat on the US Supreme Court open through the presidential election of 2016 made the election a referendum on the Supreme Court opening. Effectively, voters were posed not only with a choice for president but also with a choice for the nominee to the Court, since it can be imagined that Hillary Rodham Clinton and Donald Trump would have nominated for the seat starkly different sorts of candidates with markedly different views concerning *Roe*. Thus, the 2016 presidential election became perhaps the most direct conflict in the culture war that began, roughly, with the *Roe* decision, and, coincidentally or not, that conflict was joined by a Republican nominee who is more expert than any ordinary political figure at the sorts of incendiary tactics that excite voters to choose sides. We reached the apex of our polarization in the 2016 campaign season, and voters prepared by decades of cultural argument and increasing polarization were met by a choice that reinforced their instincts to divide and heightened the effects of the division. This path has brought us to where we are now.

We should be sure to note that it seems about half of all Catholic voters did not travel this path to Donald Trump. More recent immigrant groups, especially Latino Catholics, certainly did not support Trump in great numbers because their historical and cultural experiences of being Catholic in the United States are different. Not every Catholic who descends from one of those older immigrant groups supported Trump, either. But very close to half of Catholic voters did, and their choices have been worth exploring and trying to understand because of how obviously unfit Trump is to be the standard bearer for Catholic voters. By now it is unmistakable that Trump has winked at the racism of white nationalists and exploited their support to his advantage.[4] He called for the torture of suspected terrorists, he urged police to be "rough" with suspects, and he promised to "bomb the shit out of" ISIS.[5] Trump's opposition to abortion is at best recent, and there are reasons to wonder whether it is sincere or calculated.[6] He was heard boasting about seeking a sexual encounter with a married woman and suggesting he had assaulted other women in a recording heard widely several weeks before the election. The most senior Catholic in government as of this writing, House Speaker Paul Ryan, described himself as "sickened" by the *Access Hollywood* recording—and he should be. Paul Ryan's Catholic conscience was formed to understand any "forcible violation of the sexual intimacy of another person" as an "intrinsically evil act."[7] Of course Ryan—like many other Catholics who supported Trump—somehow ultimately found a way to overlook that revulsion just as they overlooked how he called for torture, how he ignored the principles of justice in warfare, and how he encouraged and abetted the ugliest racism that still lives in American culture. Something else seemed more important than all that to the Catholics who supported Trump.

In all of this, the US Conference of Catholic Bishops is not blameless. The bishops made many of the decisions that set American Catholics on this path. They had those disastrous meetings with the candidates in 1976, and they embarked on the path that significantly altered their public posture from spiritual leaders to lobbyists. They engaged in the quarrels with Catholic politicians from 1984 to 2008, and they embarked on a religious liberty campaign that set them against a law that extended healthcare to millions of Americans who previously had not had access. We have seen, as well, that though Catholics share with evangelicals the same frustrations about secular culture, there is evidence that the tendency to vote for Trump among Catholics most affected by the economic crisis was greater than the tendency among evangelicals. An obvious explanation for that must be the coordinating work done by a centralized leadership body, such as the US Conference, something unavailable among evangelicals. The road that Catholic voters have traveled from *Roe* to Trump has been an understandable one in light of their history in the United States, and that history is shared—of course—by the bishops who have led the church in the US. The polarization in which we all have found ourselves, the one that led Catholics to Donald Trump, has been sort of a quicksand trap. Catholics and their bishops found themselves in that trap along the way of a journey through American history they were already on. Once in the quicksand, making what seemed like natural movements only mired them more deeply in the trap. The trap becomes more and more restrictive of movements as the more deeply we find ourselves hopelessly ensnared. And in the end, no effort to struggle out of the trap can succeed. Unless someone outside the trap throws a lifeline, only making slow, deliberate, careful movements can lead to escape, calculating each motion to avoid making things worse.

There is little sign in the American political conversation today that many people are making slow, deliberate, careful movements at all. Most reactions are instant and instinctive. A reflexive default to polarization—the other side is wrong, my side is right—characterizes practically every discussion. Social media does not help very much and, to the degree that presidential tweets have grown to dominate the political discussion, it is fueling the ongoing division. This polarization, especially in the aftermath of the economic crisis of 2008, has transformed our politics into a culture war that divides us relentlessly, deeply, and destructively. There always have been divisions in American politics. In the early federal period Hamiltonian Federalists divided against Jeffersonian Anti-Federalists over the ratification and meaning of the Constitution. We had a Civil War, and we experienced the social tumult of the civil rights era, Vietnam, and Watergate. These divisions we are experiencing today are not worse than those older divisions. But somehow, they are different.

There used to be an expression in American public life—"Politics stops at the water's edge." Michigan Senator Arthur Vandenberg is said to have coined the phrase in the 1940s. A Republican, Vandenberg was the chairman of the Senate Foreign Relations Committee. Yet, he emerged as a supporter of President Harry Truman's containment policy against the expansionist ambitions of Stalin. Other Republicans did not mind saying in public that they disagreed with Truman. Many accused Truman of being "soft" on communism. Vandenberg made a more persuasive argument that endured throughout the Cold War years: there are some times (and, not even all the time) that Americans should put their disagreements aside, forget about defeating one another, and focus on solving some critical problem we all share. In 1962, while President Kennedy was still secretly putting strategic assets into position to surprise the Soviets that their missiles in Cuba had been discovered, the *New York Times* and the *Washington Post* learned about what was happening. The president asked those newspapers to wait to publish the story, let the US keep its advantage, and let the Soviets think their secret was safe. The newspapers agreed. Sometimes, we are Americans first. Before President Reagan was anesthetized for surgery to remove a gunman's bullet in 1981, he joked to the surgical staff, "I hope you're all Republicans." The surgeon replied, "Today we're all Republicans."[8] In the days and weeks after the September 11th attacks, Americans experienced a feeling of unity and common cause not felt since World War II. Of course, it did not last.

In 1999, a senior fellow at Stanford University's Hoover Institution actually wrote an essay, "Why Politics Should Not Stop at the Water's Edge."[9] Slowly during these last several decades, our ability to come together over our differences has worn away. Recent data from the Pew Research Center are illuminating. Over time, Pew has measured the percentage point gap between liberals and conservatives across ten key issues.[10] A dramatic expansion of the gap between liberals and conservatives only really began to widen during the years after the 2004 Bush reelection campaign, after the Deal Hudson Catholic outreach, after the culture-war marriage was brokered between Catholics and evangelicals, and after the 2008 economic crisis. We should observe that the coming of smartphones and social media platforms also coincides with this gap. But it is difficult to imagine that the economic crisis or the ways that technology changed how we gather information and communicate with one another could have had the effect they had without the polarization that grew so insidiously from the time of the

Roe decision. During those years, the idea that at some point we all are Americans together, or at some point our common faith as Catholics unites us, has suffered terribly. We now seem to identify more with a side that we are on than with a universal faith or with our shared, patriotic feeling of community. And while we have lived through rancorous divisions in the United States in the past, those earlier times at least saw us divided over *what it means* to be an American. Today's divisions make it seem very much like *being* an American or *being* a Catholic does not matter at all unless you also are *my kind* of American or *my kind* of Catholic. That division prepared us for the way that social media technologies and the economic crisis would widen that partisan gap over the last ten years, bringing us to where we are today. With their influence as the largest religious denomination in the United States, in a newfound position of social and political influence that made them bold, Catholics were leaders of that polarization. Catholics do not own all of the blame, certainly. But Catholics, for their commitment to a culture war during these decades, do own a significant share.

Our politics do not need to be this way, and Catholic faith also offers a more hopeful picture of what politics can be like. Pope Francis wrote about this in *Evangelii Gaudium*, reminding us that, "Politics, though often denigrated, remains a lofty vocation and one of the highest forms of charity, inasmuch as it seeks the common good" (205). In *Laudato Si'* he describes a bond of "civic and political" love we share that is rooted in the fact that "we need one another, that we have a shared responsibility for each other and the world" (231, 229). This is not airy, abstract talk. It is the most realistic, hardheaded way to think about politics that can be imagined. To live together in a community is natural for human beings—we are social creatures. We are stuck with each other, and there is no getting away. It has always been that way. Think of the United States, as we know it today: for all of our polarization and division for so many years, neither side has ever "won." There is no such thing as winning in politics because tomorrow always brings fresh challenges and new questions, another election always follows the last one. When we begin to think about politics this way, we quickly begin to see that we face a choice between, on one side, struggling with each other endlessly and futilely as we have for so many years and, on the other side, recognizing our natural and inevitable social connection in our community as a source of strength. Since we all have to be in this community together, let us act that way. This is just what Pope Francis meant when he called us to *parrhesia*, or "frank speech." Politics begins in being truthful with one another, joining in a dialogue with one another, and taking each other's concerns seriously. We do not seek to "win" something in politics, or to defeat an opponent. That would mean seeking something that never can be gotten. So, instead, politics aims at the common good of all. We should have robust, spirited debates about that. We do not always need to agree. But if we are guided sincerely by a desire to find the best solution to problems that everyone can live with, and if we embark on that search with a deep respect even for those with whom we disagree most, then we will sometimes persuade each other. Sometimes, through compromise, we can arrive at the common good. Discovering our unity as citizens and fellow believers, there can come times when our disagreements will seem less important to us than all that we share in common. Politics—and polarization—can end not just at the water's edge, but wherever the needs of our neighbors are found.

There are some glimmers of hope, and the US Catholic bishops are leading us toward that hope today. The Pavone episode illustrated the worst of our polarization as Catholics and Americans. At the same time, in the Pavone episode

we find at least some signs of encouragement. Pavone's bishop in Amarillo not only launched an investigation, but he also issued a statement that condemned Pavone's ugly stunt. Pavone got no help from any Catholic bishop or from the conference. The leadership structure of the whole Catholic Church in the United States seemed to recognize instantly, together, how Pavone simply had gone too far. A line had been crossed. And the bishops have been in a process of making recognitions like that for several years now. While outrageous things were said and a few outrageous things were done amid the resistance against the contraceptive mandate between 2010 and 2012, there was a discernible change of direction at the November 2013 meeting of the US bishops. As one writer put it, the bishops had begun to step off the limb they had walked out on.[11] The bishops began taking up a wider set of issues as the 2016 election drew nearer, several of them participating directly in action at the US border and undertaking a year-long study of the immigration question. Though the conference chose somewhat strangely to let an ad hoc committee on racial justice expire without renewal and at the same 2016 meeting at which they made the ad hoc committee on religious liberty permanent, the bishops have kept with migration issues and continue to engage that vital problem more and more closely. There are hopeful signs in the US Conference of Catholic Bishops that the poisonous, singular focus on abortion and a few similar divisive issues that feed the social and political polarization all around us is coming to a close. Some of that we must credit to Pope Francis and the new bishops he has appointed to join the conference. But perhaps, we can hope, some of that is the more natural instincts of American Catholics beginning to reassert themselves now that the polarization has reached its perverse peak in this political moment following the 2016 election. We can hope so.

But even if that most optimistic appraisal of our current situation turns out to be right, it remains the case that it has taken nearly a half-century to bring American politics, and the Catholic engagement with American politics, to this point. The problem will not go away overnight, and it will not go away without the determined action of Catholic women and men—everyone from cardinals to the people sitting next to us at our local parishes—to promote a better conversation about our problems and offer a better commitment to real dialogue that respects everyone who joins in a search for substantive solutions for serious problems. We will need to be careful about our movements for a long time. The movements that have felt natural have gotten us here, and continuing to make them has sunk us deeper into the mire. Slow, careful, deliberate movements will be needed, and so will be help from outside. We all have to participate less in shouting or correcting, and more in listening to what others can teach us. That will include fellow Catholics, but certainly it will include non-Catholics, too. The Catholic tradition contains remarkable resources that can assist us, but those resources all tell us the same thing—our commitment to truth or justice or mercy is a commitment to real, living human persons, all of whom have something to offer no matter who they are or where they come from. To overcome the polarization begins there. It must go on from there.

With only good intentions, American Catholics embarked on this road almost fifty years ago, and they have followed it ever since to where we are. The destination seems unappealing. And no matter how much American Catholics wanted the right things, they have not gotten any of them. *Roe* remains in place, and the cultural argument over it is as entrenched as ever, if not more so. Good intentions are never enough, which is a fine enough principle of moral theology familiar to anyone making a good confession. The

same must be true in our political and social lives. Until it is, the road that American Catholics are on can only continue to lead to strange places.

Notes

Introduction—pages xiii–xviii

1. Data drawn from the 2016 Cooperative Congressional Election Study, a joint project of the Harvard University Institute for Quantitative Social Science and MIT.

2. "The alternate domination of one faction over another, sharpened by the spirit of revenge, natural to party dissension, which in different ages and countries has perpetrated the most horrid enormities, is itself a frightful despotism. But this leads at length to a more formal and permanent despotism. The disorders and miseries which result gradually incline the minds of men to seek security and repose in the absolute power of an individual; and sooner or later the chief of some prevailing faction, more able or more fortunate than his competitors, turns this disposition to the purposes of his own elevation, on the ruins of public liberty."

3. "In short, upon closer examination of the work of the bishops Conference [*sic*] in its totality, you will find that the Consistent Ethic of Life approach has been present, and actively advanced, all along." In: Anthony R. Picarello, Jr., USCCB Associate General Secretary & General Counsel, to author (28 December 2016), 2.

Chapter 1—pages 1–28

1. The description, of course, is borrowed from David Vital's *A People Apart: The Jews in Europe, 1789–1939* (New York: Oxford University Press, 1999). To purloin the description in this way might suggest a too facile comparison between American Catholics and European Jews. Yet, while undertaking no effort to prove the point here, it seems not unreasonable to observe that religious traditions such as Judaism, Hinduism, and others like Catholicism that predate

modern constitutional states and the advent of secular culture share a similarly arms-length relationship to American life that does not trouble Protestantism, born amid the rise of the nation-state and the dawning of secularization. To cement the point, this book is not the first effort to purloin Vital's description. Peter Steinfels evoked a similar comparison just four years later with the publication of *A People Adrift: The Crisis of the Roman Catholic Church in America* (Simon & Schuster, 2003), in which Steinfels considered the church as an institution as it confronted a transitional moment among a Catholic "people" in the United States.

2. Judge John T. Noonan, Jr., advanced this claim most notably in *The Lustre of Our Country: The American Experience of Religious Freedom* (Berkeley, CA: The University of California Press, 1988), in which he argued for "the American mark upon the teaching of that church to which I adhere" (331), most specifically with respect to the debate over religious toleration that had raged for decades since the First Vatican Council, when American bishops led the effort to recognize religious liberty with *Dignitatis Humanae*, the Declaration on Religious Liberty. Charles R. Morris argued in *American Catholic: The Saints and Sinners Who Built America's Most Powerful Church* (New York: Times Books, 1997) that American Catholicism "has always been as much a culture as a religion, one defined by its prickly apartness from the broader, secular American culture—*in* America, usually enthusiastically *for* America, but never quite *of* America" (vii). The Pew Research Center found in a 2008 survey that the attitudes of American Catholics often are "a lot like other Americans," and there is general consensus that patterns of Catholic voting behavior have adhered to a greater inspiration from the American mainstream than to any sense of religious obligation (see especially: Matthew J. Streb and Brian Frederick, "The Myth of a Distinct Catholic Vote," in *Catholics and Politics: The Dynamic Tension between Faith and Power*, ed. Kristin E. Heyer, Mark J. Rozell, and Michael A. Genovese [Washington, DC: Georgetown University Press, 2008], 93–112.) It is the case, however, that research supports the idea that Catholics were "a unique political group" at least until the 1940s, perhaps as late as 1964, but since that time they "have not been immune to the broader changes that have occurred among the American electorate as a whole" (Streb and Frederick, 93). Even as it is the case that Catholics as a group have become indistinguishably American during the last two generations,

it remains the case that there is space in the history of American Catholicism prior to 1968 that argues for distinctly Catholic contributions and understandings that linger today.

3. The extent of Locke's exclusion of Catholics from toleration in his *Letter Concerning Toleration* (1688) is debated by scholars. In that text, Locke never specifically excludes Catholics even as he does exclude "That Church . . . that all those who enter into it, do thereby, *ipso facto* deliver themselves up to the Protection and Service of another Prince." In the understanding of the seventeenth century, "another Prince" would have included the pope, whose temporal claims to the Papal States numbered him among the monarchs of Europe. Less ambiguously, in the *Essay Concerning Toleration* (1667), Locke wrote, "Papists do not enjoy the benefit of toleration because where they have power they think themselves bound to deny it to others."

4. Remarkably, Thomas W. Spalding records that Carroll was "accounted the richest man in Revolutionary America," despite the tax, *The Encyclopedia of American Catholic History*, s.v. "Maryland, Catholic Church in."

5. "[E]ncamped at Cambridge in November, 1775 . . . [Washington] discovered that they once more [were] preparing to burn the pope in effigy and insult the Catholics in the annual celebration of Guy Fawkes Day. He put an end to the nonsense at once," John Tracy Ellis, *American Catholicism*, 2nd rev. ed. (Chicago: University of Chicago Press, 1969), 36.

6. See Thomas W. Spalding, *The Premier See: A History of the Archdiocese of Baltimore, 1789–1994* (Baltimore: The Johns Hopkins University Press, 1995), 13–14.

7. Roger Finke and Rodney Stark, *The Churching of America, 1776–1990: Winners and Losers in Our Religious Economy* (New Brunswick, NJ: Rutgers University Press, 1992), 110.

8. Roger Finke and Rodney Stark, "Turning Pews into People: Estimating 19th Century Church Membership," *Journal for the Scientific Study of Religion* 25, no. 2 (June 1986): 190. Finke and Starke estimated the rise from 4.6 percent of the US population in 1850 to 9.2 percent in 1870.

9. The 1910 census fixed the US population at a little more than 92 million people, of whom over 16 million were Catholic. By 1920, Catholics numbered nearly 20 million—19 percent. See James

Hennessey, SJ, *American Catholics: A History of the Roman Catholic Community in the United States* (New York: Oxford University Press, 1981), 207. At this writing, in 2017, Catholics make up 21 percent of the total US population.

10. The most infamous example, *Awful Disclosures of the Hôtel-Dieu Nunnery of Montreal* (1836), told the fictional tale of a convent and seminary joined by a secret tunnel in which the sisters were forced into liaisons with priests and seminarians. Unwilling sisters never were heard from again. According to the hoax, the babies who resulted from the unions were baptized, strangled, then dumped into a lime pit. A more outrageous tale would be difficult to imagine, but it is easy to imagine the effect it had on readers already willing to think the worst about Catholics.

11. John T. McGreevy, *Catholicism and American Freedom: A History* (New York: W.W. Norton & Company, 2003), 8.

12. Orestes Brownson, "Public and Parochial Schools," *Brownson's Quarterly Review* 21 (July 1859): 351.

13. O.A. Brownson, LL.D., *The American Republic: Its Constitution, Tendencies, and Destiny*, new ed. (New York: P. O'Shea, 1865), 392, 423.

14. "The Rambler," *Brownson's Quarterly Review* 13 (July 1856), 400–402. Also: Count de Montalembert to Orestes Brownson, November 1, 1855, I-3-l, cited at: John T. McGreevy, *Catholicism and American Freedom: A History* (New York: W.W. Norton & Company, Ltd., 2003), 48n27.

15. Isaac Hecker, "Notes in Rome," January 28, 1870, quoted in David J. O'Brien, "An Evangelical Imperative: Isaac Hecker, Catholicism, and Modern Society," in *Hecker Studies: Essays on the Thought of Isaac Hecker*, ed. John Farina (New York: Paulist Press, 1983), 123.

16. Reese's book, *A Flock of Shepherds: The National Conference of Catholic Bishops* (Kansas City: Sheed & Ward, 1992), offers so perfect a description of how we should imagine the US Catholic bishops that there can be no overlooking it—a flock of shepherds. At the same time, Reese credits generations of historians who agreed. He quotes James Hennessey, SJ, who described the early collaborations of American bishops and concluded, "No other nation, as far as I know, has such a record," James Hennessey, SJ, "Councils in America," in *A National Pastoral Council: Pro and Con* (Washington, DC: US Catholic Conference, 1971), 39. Hennessey, in turn, stood on the shoulders of Thomas T. McAvoy, CSC, who described those collaborations as an

expression of the unusual unity cultivated by the unusual circumstances of the fledgling American church, which was geographically enormous and, at the same time, drew its bishops together over shared problems of "the growth of the Catholic Church in the United States," the "size of the Catholic body," and "its growing importance in the affairs of the Church in general as well as in the national welfare," Thomas T. McAvoy, CSC, *The Great Crisis in American Catholic History: 1895–1900* (Chicago: Henry Regnery Company, 1957), 34.

17. Hennessey, "Councils in America," 39.

18. I have drawn these short definitions from: Albert J. Nevins, MM, ed., *The Maryknoll Catholic Dictionary* (New York: Grosset & Dunlap, 1965), s.v. "chapter, general," "synod, national," "council or synod, national," and "council, plenary."

19. Ellis, 121.

20. Margaret Reher, "Phantom Heresy: A Twice-Told Tale," *US Catholic Historian* 11, no. 3 (Summer 1993): 93–105.

21. Marvin R. O'Connell, *John Ireland and the American Catholic Church* (St. Paul, MN: Minnesota Historical Society Press, 1988), 462–465.

22. Reese, *A Flock of Shepherds*, 22. Reese records, "Although they lacked the authority to make binding decisions as a council would, at their first meeting in 1890 the archbishops did make recommendations to the Holy See on episcopal appointments, sought a broadening of faculties for granting matrimonial dispensations, and suggested revisions in the faculties granted to bishops by the Holy See" (22).

23. Ibid., 22–23. While it may seem strange viewed from our perspective today, Prohibition played an important role here. Prohibition was viewed at the time, in part, as a measure to control immigrants—Germans, Irish, Italians, and Poles—among others, who generally were laborers and perceived to be hard-drinking. They also were overwhelmingly Catholic. The Volstead Act and the Eighteenth Amendment were nearly approved at the time when the NCWC was formally organized, and the willingness of the bishops to hear Burke's proposal was motivated at least in part by the effectiveness of Protestant lobbying against Catholic immigrants.

24. Perhaps it is only a historical curiosity, but it was clear even before the Council produced *Lumen Gentium* that the bishops gathered for the Council saw the value of bishops' conferences and intended to put them to work. *Lumen Gentium* was published in

November, 1964, but already in the Constitution on the Sacred Liturgy (*Sacrosanctum Concilium*, 1963), one of the earliest documents produced by the Council, the task of translating the Mass into vernacular languages was assigned to "competent territorial bodies of bishops" (22), by which it was understood the Council meant national or regional conferences.

25. The issue of the conference's name, in fact, is even more confusing. In 1966, following the Council, the conference was organized as two entities under one control. The NCCB concerned itself with internal matters of the church, such as translation of the liturgy and rules concerning annulments. The United States Catholic Conference (USCC) was the lobbying arm that concerned itself with pressing the church's message about social and moral issues, not just to oppose things like abortion but also to encourage the care for the poor. Both the NCCB and USCC were governed under the same structure and statutes. The two were combined as the United States Conference of Catholic Bishops (USCCB) in 2001. Seeking as much simplicity as possible, this book refers to the bishops' conference only as "the conference" or "the bishops' conference" throughout, except where name changes must be mentioned to describe the development of the conference.

26. Ellis, 56–57.

27. Russell Shaw, *American Catholic: The Remarkable Rise, Meteoric Fall, and Uncertain Future of Catholicism in America* (San Francisco: Ignatius Press, 2013), 15.

28. Ibid., 16.

29. Ibid., 130.

30. Ibid., 139.

31. Ibid., 128.

32. Charles R. Morris, *American Catholic: The Saints and Sinners Who Built America's Most Powerful Church* (New York: Times Books, 1997), 281.

33. See Jay P. Dolan, *The American Catholic Experience: A History from Colonial Times to the Present* (Garden City, NY: Doubleday & Company, Inc., 1985), 203; John T. McGreevy, *Catholicism and American Freedom: A History* (New York: W.W. Norton & Company, 2003), 169, and Timothy B. Neary, *Crossing Parish Boundaries: Race, Sports, and Catholic Youth in Chicago 1914–1954* (Chicago: University of Chicago Press, 2016), 12.

34. Paul Blanshard, *American Freedom and Catholic Power* (Boston: The Beacon Press, 1949), 266–270ff.

35. One contemporary parallel will highlight the point. Rumana Ahmed was a member of the Obama administration National Security Council staff who wrote about the eight days she worked in the Trump administration before leaving. In 2015, after Franklin Graham alleged that Muslims had infiltrated the federal government, Ahmed described how another Muslim who worked in the White House had joked, "If only he knew they were in the halls of the West Wing and briefed the president of the United States multiple times!" The pride in that statement is as hard to miss as the pride in Ahmed's reply: *"Damn right I'm here, exactly where I belong, a proud American dedicated to protecting and serving my country."* Yet, the strange and "surreal" feeling never left her White House service, being an "American Muslim woman from Maryland who had been mocked and called names for covering my hair, working for the president of the United States." She left the White House after the Trump administration announced its travel ban in January 2017, and even as the contradictions between being Muslim and being a patriotic American grew unbearable in the Trump White House, Ahmed appears to be as much preoccupied by her Muslim and American identity as any Catholic today. See Rumana Ahmed, "I Was a Muslim in Trump's White House," *The Atlantic*, online at https://www.theatlantic.com/politics/archive/2017/02/rumana-ahmed/517521/.

36. John Courtney Murray, SJ, *We Hold These Truths: Catholic Reflections on the American Proposition* (New York: Sheed & Ward, 1960), 28–30.

37. "Perhaps most simply, Catholics as a whole have become like most Americans. Partisanship matters more than group affiliation. Mark M. Gray, Paul M. Perl, and Mary E. Bendyna certainly subscribe to this view: 'For Catholics, partisanship is substantially more important than religion now than it was in 1960,' they conclude in their recent study on Catholic voting behavior in presidential elections"; Matthew J. Streb and Brian Frederick, "The Myth of a Distinct Catholic Vote," *Catholics and Politics: The Dynamic Tension between Faith & Power*, ed. Kristin E. Heyer, Mark J. Rozell, and Michael A. Genovese (Washington, DC: Georgetown University Press, 2008), 97.

38. Pope John Paul II, *Memory and Identity: Conversations at the Dawn of a Millennium* (New York: Rizzoli, 2005), 64. See also p. 73.

39. Pope John Paul II, Encyclical Letter "*Redemptoris Missio*" (1990), 54, 10.

40. US Conference of Catholic Bishops (USCCB), *Faithful Citizenship: A Catholic Call to Political Responsibility* (September 2003), Introduction, 86, 12.

41. Ibid., 13.

42. Dan Herr, then the president of the Thomas More Association, wrote that, "Single-issue voting has become a nasty liberal shibboleth—many liberals being determined proponents of abortion. They find it easier and more effective to condemn single-issue voting than to become involved in discussing the question. I argue that single-issue voting is a perfectly acceptable and even laudable principle *provided* the issue involved is of paramount importance. Sometimes single-issue voting can be shameful, other times imperative. But when we disagree on its application, let's not condemn what has been and should continue to be an effective political reaction to a crucial, basic question,"; Dan Herr, "One-Issue Voting IS O.K.," *New York Times* (September 28, 1980): E21.

Chapter 2—pages 29–61

1. Joseph L. Bernardin, "The Archdiocese of Cincinnati, Office of the Archbishop, Statement Released by Archbishop Joseph L. Bernardin" (January 23, 1973), Joseph Cardinal Bernardin Collection, Speeches & Talks, Archdiocese of Chicago Joseph Cardinal Bernardin Archives and Records Center, Chicago, IL.

2. Later, in *Planned Parenthood v. Casey* (1992), the Supreme Court would abandon the trimester structure to consider fetal rights in terms of a viability standard that accommodated advancing medical technology. As the technology advanced that might permit an unborn child to live, viability could be construed earlier than the end of the first trimester. However, the Court upheld the essential position of *Roe* that saw abortion in terms of a balance between a pregnant woman's right and an unborn fetus's right, with viability as the tipping point.

3. President Nixon's Oval Office recordings for January 23, 1973 were released in 2009. They disclose his earliest thoughts about the *Roe* decision. He worried it would encourage sexual "permissiveness," and said that abortion "breaks the family." Yet, Nixon also

described how "there are times when an abortion is necessary. I know that. When you have a black and a white. Or a rape." See Charlie Savage, "On Nixon Tapes, Ambivalence Over Abortion, Not Watergate," *New York Times* (June 23, 2009). An even more recent appraisal put it this way: "President Nixon opposed abortion only when he had to, either to make policy or to play politics,"; Lawrence J. McAndrews, *What They Wished For: Catholics and American Presidents, 1960–2004* (Athens, GA: University of Georgia Press, 2014), 110.

4. Jeffrey W. Stempel and William D. Morris, "Electoral Folklore: An Empirical Examination of the Abortion Issue," *Yale Law & Policy Review* 1, no. 2 (Fall 1982): 19.

5. A 1984 study found that "Catholics had begun to move in the direction of political conservatism" in the 1950s, for reasons relating to their changing place in American life. Mostly, the shift reflected "the Church's vigorous anti-communism" and also "the rising affluence" of Catholics. In any event, it was before *Roe* in 1972 when Catholic voters first gave a majority to a Republican presidential candidate. See A. James Reichley, "Religion and Political Realignment," *Brookings Review* 3 (Fall 1984): 32. The picture is complicated whenever we attempt to quantify a Catholic vote. For many American Catholics, ethnic identity and religious identity are closely related even as they may "pull in politically divergent directions." See James M. Penning, "The Political Behavior of American Catholics: An Assessment of the Impact of Group Integration vs. Group Identification," *Western Political Quarterly* 41, no. 2 (June 1988): 306. The increasing identification of American Catholics with the Republican Party during the last two generations is a complex subject with several cross-cutting factors, of which abortion is only one. Abortion is a prominent factor, however, given the evident magnitude of the cultural shift with which we can identify it. Our focus here is not so much on explaining the pattern of Catholic voters' preference of Republicans (which was not a steady repetition after 1972—Catholics supported the Democratic presidential candidate in 2000, 2008, and 2012). Rather, this study seeks to explain the role of the bishops' teachings in the pattern of Catholic voting. Still, on the more general topic of the Catholic vote, we can at least say that Catholics who sought election to Congress and other offices were subject to the same political and social forces as those who did not seek office. It is only natural to chart a decline in the number of Catholic Democrats after 1972 under these assumptions.

6. Peter Steinfels, *A People Adrift: The Crisis of the Roman Catholic Church in America* (New York: Simon & Schuster, 2003), 91.

7. Committee on Constitutional Amendments of the Senate Committee on the Judiciary, *Abortion—Part I: Hearings on S.J. Res. 119 and S.J. Res. 130*, 93rd Cong., 2d sess., 1974, 212. The quoted text is in the conclusion of a statement inserted for the record on behalf of the US Catholic Conference during the March 8, 1974, testimony of Cardinal John Krol, Cardinal John Cody, Cardinal Humberto Madeiros, and Cardinal Timothy Manning.

8. "*How* a policy maker should go about striving to reduce the incidence of abortion in contemporary American culture . . . is an exceptionally complicated question. Good lawmaking is never simply a matter of directly transposing moral conclusions into rules of civil law," Gregory A. Kalscheur, SJ, "Catholics in Public Life: Judges, Legislators, and Voters," *Journal of Catholic Legal Studies* 46, no. 2 (2007): 225.

9. Much more could be said on this topic, which might exhaust a book longer than this one. Gregory A. Kalscheur, SJ, has written thoughtfully about the role that Catholic public officials play in the formation of policy about difficult issues like abortion, especially at Kalscheur, 2007. A distinctive feature of Kalscheur's treatment is the way he distinguishes the role of a Catholic judge from legislators and other policymakers. According to Kalscheur, the judge is constrained to use "the tools of legal analysis to interpret the Constitution and laws" (227) while the legislator has a greater freedom (and thus a greater accountability to Catholic moral teaching) to "promote the common good" as "conscientious prudential judgment" discloses it (226). Seen this way, a legislator faces a higher standard because the legislator *makes* the law, while the judge is constrained by how the law tells her or him the law may be interpreted. Kalscheur's analysis engages a thoughtful treatment of the moral theology at work in the distinctions among formal cooperation, proximate material cooperation, and remote material cooperation. Yet, distinguishing the role played by judges in this way overlooks a long and rich consideration of the role played by consent in politics and law. Writers since Roman times have asserted that a law can have no force if the people reject it, and this view enjoyed a wide popularity in the Middle Ages from St. Augustine to Nicholas of Cusa, who described law in terms of a complex interaction with the people who are to be governed by it. Even St. Thomas Aquinas (*ST*, I-II, Q.97, A.3) suggested that "the

greatest power of law comes from custom," suggesting that a lawmaker's range of choices is at least as constrained as a judge's range of choices under the law. M. Cathleen Kaveny offered a consideration that contrasted the perspectives of the "law as a teacher" with the "law as a police officer," in M. Cathleen Kaveny, *Law's Virtues: Fostering Autonomy and Solidarity in American Society* (Washington, DC: Georgetown University Press, 2012). In both of her models, Kaveny appears to regard the law paternally, much like Kalscheur, toward those who are governed by the law. While elements of our tradition have regarded positive law this paternalist way (Platonism, absolutism, and so forth), there are other strains of the tradition that see the law in terms that are based more on consent and seem to be more applicable to the republicanism of the American situation. In those ways, the choices of elected officials who are Catholics may be more constrained than Kalscheur, Kaveny, or the bishops have allowed.

10. Internal Revenue Code, §501(c)(3).

11. Most Reverend Joseph L. Bernardin to Most Reverend Thomas J. Grady (3 July 1969), American Catholic History Research Center, NCCB Collection, Box 35, Folder "Church: Church & State, 1967–1969." At the time, Bernardin was general secretary of the bishops' conference, and he was responding to an inquiry about the extent to which bishops could engage in political action.

12. Ibid.

13. Testimony in a federal lawsuit litigated in 1978 over whether the constitutional rights of religious groups such as the Catholic Church to influence legislation superseded protections in law against religious intrusion detailed how "'on several occasions' Mark Gallagher, lobbyist for the National Committee for a Human Life Amendment (which receives major financial support from the National Conference of Catholic Bishops), had 'leaned forward and slipped papers' to the legal counsel for Representative Daniel J. Flood, Democrat of Pennsylvania, chairman of the House conferees. . . . It looked as if Mr. Gallagher, Ms. Werner said, 'were saying something, or giving them information. . . .' Ms. Werner said, 'Even before I was told it was drafted at the direction of Mark Gallagher, I knew that it definitely had a theological bias in it,'"; Laurie Johnston, "Law and Religion Intermingled in Suit on Abortion Ban," *New York Times* (14 March 1978): 2d Section, 1. The US Supreme Court ultimately decided the case, *Harris v. McRae*, in 1980, finding that nothing in the Constitution prevents the church from lobbying. We would want,

however, to notice how quickly the bishops' conference set about to a very professional sort of lobbying effort, even as we should notice that the NRLC was only one group sponsored by the conference; the National Committee for a Human Life Amendment was another. Working on many fronts and through many organs, the bishops ended the 1970s as something they never had been before: sophisticated players of the American political game.

14. Russell Shaw to Rev. James Rausch (25 January 1973), American Catholic History Research Center, NCCB Collection, Box 62, Folder "NCCB Ad Hoc Committee, Pro-Life Activities, 1973, January–February."

15. "Report of the Ad Hoc Committee on Pro-Life Activities to the NCCB Administrative Committee Meeting," American Catholic History Research Center, NCCB Collection, Box 62, Folder "NCCB Pro-Life Activities, 1973, July–August," cited at McAndrews, 126.

16. "Constitutional Amendment on Abortion," attached to memorandum from Rev. James McHugh to Family Life Directors, Respect Life Coordinators, and State Catholic Conference Coordinators, 12 July 1973, American Catholic History Research Center, NCCB Collection, Box 62, Folder "NCCB Ad Hoc Committee, Pro-Life Activities, 1973, July–August," cited at McAndrews, 126.

17. "When the early meetings [of the theological commission], despite signs of wavering, supported the traditional teaching, Paul brought in additional theologians known for their liberal views, and finally introduced a number of lay experts on fertility and population studies, and even married couples. . . . At its final meeting, in 1966, the full commission voted 52–4 to drop the ban on artificial birth control in marriage. . . . [It] was therefore a profound shock when Paul, after a two-year delay, strongly reconfirmed the traditional doctrine in his 1968 encyclical, *Humanae Vitae* (Of Human Life)"; Charles R. Morris, *American Catholic: The Saints and Sinners Who Built America's Most Powerful Church* (New York: Random House, 1997), 360–361. John Paul II biographer Tad Szulc quotes "a Polish theologian who worked with Wojtyła," who verified that "'about sixty percent of our [Wojtyła's] draft is contained in the encyclical [*Humanae Vitae*],'"; Tad Szulc, *Pope John Paul II: The Biography* (New York: Pocket Books, 1995), 274.

18. A column published recently on the Catholic News Agency webpage asserts that "98 percent of Catholics and non-Catholics alike have used some form of birth control"; Jenn Giroux, "What Is the Big

Deal about Catholics Using Birth Control," online at http://www.catholicnewsagency.com/cw/post.php?id=638. The column repeats a claim made by Rep. Nancy Pelosi (D-CA) in 2012 that originated in a 2011 study funded by the Planned Parenthood–affiliated Guttmacher Institute. That claim proved so problematic that the Guttmacher Institute eventually withdrew it. See Glenn Kessler, "The claim that 98 percent of Catholic women use contraception: a media foul," *Washington Post* (17 February 2012), at https://www.washingtonpost.com/blogs/fact-checker/post/the-claim-that-98-percent-of-catholic-women-use-contraception-a-media-foul/2012/02/16/gIQAkPeqIR_blog.html. The Giroux column illustrates the difficulty of getting reliable data about an intimate matter, and how that difficulty compels even an official organ like the Catholic News Service to repeat claims that prove to be somewhat dubious. Still, there are more reliable data. A 1979 Department of Health, Education, and Welfare study reported data collected in 1973 that found that 66.3 percent of white, Catholic, married women 15–44 years old used artificial contraception, while 70.4 percent of African American women reported using birth control. Those results fell squarely in line with the range with white and black Protestant women (72 percent and 59.2 percent) and Jewish women (84.9 percent). See US Department of Health, Education, and Welfare, Public Health Service, Office of Health, Research, Statistics, and Technology, National Center for Health Statistics, *Contraceptive Utilization: United States*, Series 23, no. 2, DHEW Publication No. 79–1978, 8. Regrettably, subsequent iterations of the National Survey for Family Growth (NSFG) data did not capture religious affiliation, which makes it impossible to differentiate Catholics from other respondents. In order to capture a better sense of the contemporary picture, we can look to the annual "Values and Beliefs" survey conducted by the Gallup Organization. In 2014, Gallup reported that 90 percent of respondents approved of artificial contraception. In 2015, *New York Times* columnist Frank Bruni reported that he had requested from Gallup "a special breakdown of its 'Values and Beliefs' survey from last May," one that "looked at how the principles of people who identified themselves as Catholics diverged (or didn't) from those of Americans on the whole." As Bruni reports that Gallup data, "Catholics were only slightly less open to birth control, with 86 percent of them saying that it was 'morally acceptable' in comparison with 90 percent of all respondents"; Frank Bruni, "Be Fruitful, Not Bananas," *New York Times* (January 24, 2015), online at https://www.nytimes.com/2015/01/25/opinion/sunday/frank-bruni-pope-francis-birth-control-and-american-catholics.html. Naturally, even as we may be confident that the work done by the US Government and the Gallup Organization was methodologically sound, we should remain cautious when trying to be precise about how many Catholics have rejected the teaching about artificial contraception. Still, the consistency of the data over time seems to license us at least to say that a significant majority reject it.

19. Curran was returned to the faculty after a week-long demonstration in his support had shut the campus down. He would be dismissed from the university for good in 1986, once more in large part due to his writings about birth control, after the intervention of the Congregation for the Doctrine of the Faith under the direction of Cardinal Joseph Ratzinger.

20. McAndrews, 130.

21. Quoted in Patrick B. McGuigan and Dawn M. Weyrich, eds., *Ninth Justice: The Fight for Bork* (Lanham, MD: Rowan & Littlefield, 1993), 14.

22. Beyond the heavy emphasis on abortion in American politics, Lawrence J. McAndrews discusses another interesting way the bishops overplayed their hand in the years after *Roe*, even if the details are too complex to treat adequately in this book. "The bishops had managed to offend non-Catholics before they had even written their own [human life] amendment [to the Constitution]. As for the cardinals' appearance before Congress, 'If the purpose of the testimony—from the media point of view—was to make the point that this matter is something the Catholic Church takes seriously, the purpose was achieved,' the USCC's Russell Shaw concluded. 'If the purpose was to avoid linking the abortion issue with the Catholic Church, the purpose was not achieved—quite the opposite.'" The bishops embarked on a campaign of damage control after those early efforts had created a "rift" with Baptists, Jews, and other religious groups; McAndrews, 131.

23. Cardinal John Dearden, "The Church's Bicentennial Program: Potential for Coalition Building," American Catholic History Research Center, NCCB Collection, Box 119, Folder "Ad Hoc Bicentennial: 1976 Jan.–Jun.," 5.

24. Russell Shaw, *American Church: The Remarkable Rise, Meteoric Fall, and Uncertain Future of Catholicism in America* (San Francisco: Ignatius Press, 2013), 144.

25. Matthew J. Streb and Brian Frederick, "The Myth of a Distinct Catholic Vote," *Catholics and Politics: The Dynamic Tension between Faith & Power*, ed. Kristin E. Heyers, Mark J. Rozell, and Michael A. Genovese (Washington, DC: Georgetown University Press, 2008), 110.

26. Carter announced his support for the ERA to a group of girl scouts he encountered on the campaign trail. See Patrick Anderson, *Electing Jimmy Carter: The Campaign of 1976* (Baton Rouge, LA: Louisiana University Press, 1994), 10. The Girl Scout anecdote is charming, but it may explain why confidence in his position was not widespread. See also Eileen Shanahan, "Democratic Women to Discuss Role with Carter in an Attempt to Avoid a Convention Fight," *New York Times* (8 July 1976).

27. Charles Mohr, "Choice of Mondale Helps to Reconcile the Liberals," *New York Times* (16 July 1976).

28. David E. Rosenbaum, "Democrats Start Platform Draft," *New York Times* (12 June 1976).

29. Quoted in Timothy A. Byrnes, *Catholic Bishops in American Politics* (Princeton: Princeton University Press, 1991), 72.

30. Ibid., 72.

31. Carter gave the interview to Jim Castelli of the US bishops–sponsored Catholic News Service and the interview was distributed widely for publication in Catholic periodicals. See Jim Castelli, "Jimmy Carter and Catholics: Explanation," *The Anchor* 20, no. 34 (19 August 1976): 10.

32. In the midst of the controversy with the Catholic bishops, the Carter campaign was receiving letters from the National Abortion Rights Action League and other groups pressuring him to hold firm on the abortion plank. See especially Letter, Karen Mulhauser to Governor Jimmy Carter, September 8, 1976, Jimmy Carter Presidential Library, 1976 Campaign Committee to Elect Jimmy Carter Collection, Sterrett Subject Files, Box 77, Folder "Correspondence: Abortion." More letters and telexes pressuring Carter to remain firm can be found at Jimmy Carter Presidential Library, 1976 Campaign Committee to Elect Jimmy Carter Collection, 51.3 percent Committee, Box 294, Folder "Abortion."

33. Bishop Rausch Memorandum to The Files on "Developments Subsequent to the Andrew Young Breakfast" (9 August 1976), American Catholic History Research Center, NCCB Collection, Box

63, Folder "Ad Hoc Committee on Pro-Life Activities, Jul.–Sept., 1976," 6.

34. "A bishop's primary concern is the internal governance of his local church, but what happens in his local church can be affected by church institutions outside his diocese." See Thomas J. Reese, *Archbishop: Inside the Power Structure of the American Catholic Church* (New York: Harper & Row, 1989), 307.

35. "For the smaller and poorer dioceses, the expertise of the conference is very helpful. The staff at the conference can answer their question or refer them to an appropriate person or organization. In addition, the conference has run many workshops and conferences for diocesan personnel and provided speakers at others." See Reese, *A Flock of Shepherds*, 308–309. Larger archdioceses with greater resources may be able to advise their archbishops with staff who can provide perspective on legal and political issues, but those places are not the norm.

36. "The effect was that when the bill came before the Senate, it passed by a larger majority than it had at any time in the past. It went back to the House and the same thing happened there. I have on file a number of letters of appreciation from Members of both Houses of Congress, saying that we made a difference. We could make that difference because the support of our people is there"; Subcommittee on International Resources, Food, and Energy of the House Committee on International Relations, *The Right-to-Food Resolution—Hearings on H.Con.Res. 393*, 94th Cong., 2nd Sess., 1976, 138.

37. See Lewis Beale, "An Abortion That Shook Prime Time," *Los Angeles Times* (10 November 1992). See also Albin Krebs, "'Maude' Sponsorship Decline Laid to Abortion Foes," *New York Times* (10 August 1973).

38. Memorandum to The Files on "Developments Subsequent to the Andrew Young Breakfast" (9 August 1976), 6.

39. Memorandum on "Meeting with the Executive Committee National Conference of Catholic Bishops," Gerald R. Ford Presidential Library, James M. Cannon Files, Box 1, Folder "Abortion—Meeting with Catholic Bishops, September 9, 1976," Tab A, 1.

40. News Release: "Republican Pro-Life Plank Said 'Timely and Important,'" American Catholic History Research Center, NCCB Collection, Box 63, Folder "Ad Hoc Committee for Pro-Life Activities, Jul.–Sep. 1976," 2.

41. Shaw, 150.

42. "Report on the Meetings of the NCCB/USCC Executive Committees with the Democratic and Republican Presidential Candidates," American Catholic History Research Center, NCCB Collection, Box 63, Folder "Ad-Hoc Committee on Pro-Life Activities Jul.–Sep. 1976," 3. See also Timothy A. Byrnes, *Catholic Bishops in American Politics* (Princeton: Princeton University Press, 1991), 74–81. Also Shaw, 149–150.

43. Eugene Kennedy, *Bernardin: Life to the Full* (Chicago: Bonus Books, 1997), 160. Kennedy's biography is unsourced. There are no footnotes. However, Kennedy and Bernardin were friends for many years. It does not seem wrong in this case to credit Kennedy's report as reflecting Bernardin's own reaction.

44. Charles Mohr, "Abortion Stand by Carter Vexes Catholic Bishops," *New York Times* (1 September 1976): 10.

45. Ibid.

46. Robert G. Kaiser, "Labor, Kennedy Promise Carter Campaign Effort," *Washington Post* (1 September 1976): A1.

47. Jim Castelli, "Bishop Rausch Criticizes Media Coverage of Carter Meeting," NC News Service Release (September 7, 1976), Jimmy Carter Presidential Library, 1976 Campaign Committee to Elect Jimmy Carter Collection, Butler Subject Files, Box 202, Folder "Catholics."

48. Agenda for August 31, 1976 Meeting at Mayflower Hotel, Jimmy Carter Presidential Library, 1976 Campaign Committee to Elect Jimmy Carter Collection, Butler Subject Files, Mongiardo Subject Files, Box 247, Folder "Bishops' Meeting Statements."

49. A twelve-page background memorandum prepared for Carter ahead of the meeting suggested several topics that included Catholic schools, urban issues, threats to the family, and food policy as well as abortion. See Terry Sundy, Sr. and Victoria Mongiardo, "Memorandum to Governor Jimmy Carter" (no date), Jimmy Carter Presidential Library, 1976 Campaign Committee to Elect Jimmy Carter Collection, Mongiardo Subject Files, Box 247, Folder "Bishop's Meeting Statements," 6–12. Lawrence M. O'Roarke records in his biography of Geno Baroni that, "Carter opened the meeting. He said that he and the bishops agreed on a wide range of social issues. They shared a concern, Carter said, for the middle class and the working class as well as for the poor. Carter, casting his own and the Baroni agenda into his own words, said he believed in strong moral values,

and those values were respected by a nation that used its resources for shelter, medical care, education, and jobs"; Lawrence M. O'Roarke, *Geno: The Life and Mission of Geno Baroni* (New York: Paulist Press, 1991), 128. O'Roarke's Foreword describes the role Baroni played in writing the book, "open[ing] his records, undergo[ing] whatever interviews I needed, and he would urge his friends to cooperate fully" (2). For those reasons, we can take O'Roarke's account rather accurately to reflect Baroni's. Baroni was not at the August 31 meeting, but he was working closely with Stu Eizenstat and other Carter campaign officials to try to win the support of the bishops.

50. O'Roarke, 128.

51. Adam Walinsky, Memorandum to Stu Eizenstat, "The Northern Campaign and the Catholic Problem" (28 July 1976), Jimmy Carter Presidential Library, 1976 Campaign Committee to Elect Jimmy Carter Collection, Stuart Eizenstat Papers, Box 3, Folder "Catholics 8/23/76–10/76), 2. In 2016, Walinsky wrote a surprising piece for *Politico*, "I Was RFK's Speechwriter. Now I'm Voting for Trump. Here's Why" (September 21, 2016). Walinsky's rationale is more surprising than his title. He argues that the Democrats had become "the party of war," and Hillary Rodham Clinton "has pushed America into successive invasions, successive efforts at 'regime change.'" By Walinsky's lights, Donald Trump had emerged from the 2016 campaign as the "only . . . potential American president [who] has had the intelligence, the vision, the sheer sanity to see that America cannot fight the entire world at once." We should pass over the question here whether Walinsky made a good calculation, or whether President Trump (who described himself on the campaign trail as "the most militaristic person ever" and, in November 2015, promised that "I'm going to bomb the shit out of" ISIS) might not have fit the bill Walinsky had in mind. Walinsky's essay is notable at least because he describes a Catholic voter's case for Trump in terms of an interest in world peace, not abortion. Had Trump appeared that way to a greater number of Catholics, the election result might not have been different, even if this book would have. See http://www.politico.com/magazine/story/2016/09/rfk-trump-2016-democratic-party-speechwriter-214270.

52. See James M. Naughton, "Ford Hopes Linked to Catholic Vote," *New York Times* (September 5, 1976), 1, 26. On the same day, Donald M. Rothberg wrote for the Associated Press that "President Ford's campaign strategists think the dispute between Carter and Roman

Catholic bishops could be a decisive issue in several key states," and "at this point in the campaign, professional public opinion analysts say there is no way of knowing whether a single issue like abortion will swing a significant number of Catholic votes away from Carter"; Donald M. Rothberg, "Carter-Catholics," wire service early release, Jimmy Carter Presidential Library, 1976 Campaign Committee to Elect Jimmy Carter Collection, Stuart Eizenstat Papers, Box 1, Folder "Abortion 9/76," 1.

53. Memorandum from Michael Scanlon to Stuart Eizenstat (20 July 1976), Jimmy Carter Presidential Library, 1976 Campaign Committee to Elect Jimmy Carter Collection, Stuart Eizenstat Papers, Box 3, Folder "Catholics 5/76–8/20/76," 1. Also: Memorandum from Birch Bayh to Governor Carter (16 September 1976), Jimmy Carter Presidential Library, 1976 Campaign Committee to Elect Jimmy Carter Collection, Stuart Eizenstat Papers, Box 1, Folder "Abortion 9/76," 1.

54. Kenneth A. Briggs, "Catholic Bishops' Neutrality Pledge Quiets Dissension," *New York Times* (26 September 1976): 28. While the sourcing in the *Times* story is anonymous, Russell Shaw appears to confirm it in a confidential memo in which he wrote about "information from some bishop or bishops" that "depicts an NCCB/USCC torn by dissension among both bishops and top staff." Shaw concluded, "Not the least disturbing aspect of all this is the fact that the willingness of some persons to provide highly confidential information (along with highly subjective interpretations of events) to the *Times* is evidence in itself that such a picture of NCCB/USCC contains a measure of truth"; Memorandum from Russell Shaw to Most Rev. Joseph L. Bernardin (14 October 1976), American Catholic History Research Center, NCCB Collection, Box 63, Folder "Ad Hoc Committee on Pro-Life Activities, Oct.–Dec., 1976," 11.

55. Memorandum from J. Bryan Hehir to The Most Reverend Joseph L. Bernardin (5 September 1976), American Catholic History Research Center, NCCB Collection, Box 63, Folder "Ad Hoc Committee on Pro-Life Activities, Jul.–Sept. 1976."

56. In the meeting with Ford, Bernardin raised abortion, employment, food, immigration, and human rights in foreign policy. See "Report on the Meetings of the NCCB/USCC Executive Committees with the Democratic and Republican Presidential Candidates" (14 September 1976), American Catholic History Research Center, NCCB Collection, Box 63, Folder "Jul.–Sept. 1976."

57. Gerald R. Ford to The Most Reverend Joseph L. Bernardin (10 September 1976), Gerald R. Ford Presidential Library, James M. Cannon Files, Box 1, Folder "Abortion—Meeting with Catholic Bishops, September 9, 1976."

58. Eugene C. Harrington, "2 Words Hurt Church, Madison Bishop Says," *Milwaukee Journal* (2 October 1976), in Jimmy Carter Presidential Library, 1976 Campaign Committee to Elect Jimmy Carter Collection, Landon Butler Subject File, Box 202, Folder "Catholics." See also: "Homily by the Most Reverend Peter L. Geraty, Archbishop of Newark, St. Patrick's Cathedral, New York City" (8 September 1976), Jimmy Carter Presidential Library, 1976 Campaign Committee to Elect Jimmy Carter Collection, Vickie Mongiardo Subject File, Box 247, Folder "Catholics," 2.

59. For the documents and correspondence concerning the NCCB/USCC tax status in light of the 1976 abortion controversy, see T.C. Rademaker to Joseph L. Bernardin (2 August 1976), American Catholic History Research Center, NCCB Collection, Box 63, Folder "Pro-Life Activities, 1975–July, 1978." The memorandum from NCCB/USCC counsel and the requests from third-party candidates can be found in the same folder.

60. Daniel K. Williams, *Defenders of the Unborn: The Pro-Life Movement before* Roe v. Wade (New York: Oxford University Press, 2016), 4.

61. Ibid., 4. Also: Testimony of Cardinal John Cody, Committee on Constitutional Amendments of the Senate Committee on the Judiciary, *Abortion—Part I: Hearings on S.J. Res. 119 and S.J. Res. 130,* 93rd Cong., 2d sess., 1974, 226.

62. Southern states of the Confederacy came to be known in American political history as the "Solid South" when, from the time of Reconstruction (1876) to 1964, they almost invariably supported Democrats in presidential races. In 1968, Richard Nixon became the first Republican to win the South since the Civil War, and the South has tended to vote Republican since. The documents surrounding the August 31 meeting with the bishops in the Carter campaign's papers are filled with references to Catholic voters in northern cities and census counts of Catholics correlated to the electoral votes available in the states in which they lived.

63. With *Mapp v. Ohio*, the Supreme Court created the exclusionary rule, which requires a court to ignore evidence against a criminal defendant if it was obtained by the police in an illegal search. The effect might be for evidence of that defendant's guilt to be publicly

visible, even as the charges against that defendant might be dismissed. The *Miranda* decision, as most Americans know, established that the police must advise suspects of their rights prior to arrest or questioning. Failure to offer the *Miranda* warning, once again, may establish grounds on which charges against a defendant must be dismissed. Whether the reality of these Supreme Court decisions flooding the streets with criminals measured up to the perception did not finally matter. The effect of films, television shows, and newspaper accounts on popular imagination depicting the justice system as failing to punish the guilty was enough to fuel a widespread perception. The law and order message of the 1968 Nixon campaign capitalized on that already prevailing narrative, and that message clearly resonated with voters.

64. "Statement of Archbishop Bernardin" (23 June 1976), Jimmy Carter Presidential Library, 1976 Campaign Committee to Elect Jimmy Carter Collection, Landon Butler Subject File, Box 294, Folder "Abortion (1)."

65. In a representative example, Whittaker Chambers described communism as "the focus of the concentrated evil of our time"; Whittaker Chambers, *Witness* (New York: Random House, 1952), 8. Chambers certainly had some biases. Then again, Chambers held a young William F. Buckley, Jr., "in awe" as a "writer, as hero of the Hiss case"; Sam Tanenhaus, *Whittaker Chambers: A Biography* (New York: The Modern Library, 1998), 488–489. Buckley's *National Review* not only would coalesce the American conservative movement that united religious conservatives with economic conservatives in the Reagan campaign of 1980, but its editorial vision mirrored an "unspoken link between Catholicism and anticommunism" that defined Buckley's very influential view of the world; see John B. Judis, *William F. Buckley, Jr.: Patron Saint of the Conservatives* (New York: Simon & Schuster, 1998), 325. The continuity between Cold War absolutism and a conservative Catholic perspective on culture war issues is also borne out by Patrick J. Buchanan's 1992 address to the Republican National Convention: "There is a religious war going on in our country for the soul of America. It is a cultural war, as critical to the kind of nation we will one day be as the Cold War itself."

66. See Ira Shor, *Culture Wars: School and Society in the Conservative Restoration, 1969–1984* (New York: Routledge, 1988). Also George Weigel, *Catholicism and the Renewal of American Democracy* (Mahwah, NJ: Paulist Press, 1989), 5.

67. James Davison Hunter, *Culture Wars: The Struggle to Define America* (New York: Basic Books, 1991), 97.

68. James Davison Hunter, "The Enduring Culture War," in *Is There a Culture War? A Dialogue on Values and American Public Life*, ed. James Davison Hunter and Alan Wolfe (Washington, DC: Brookings Institution Press, 2006), 13.

69. Though these observations are somewhat off the larger point of this book, we should examine briefly how the language of the culture war argument generally and the pro-life movement specifically is often cast in terms very much like the language once used to describe the Cold War. For example, the bishops have frequently cast their opposition to *Roe* in terms of their better interpretation of the nation's founding documents and its constitutional tradition. Representatively, see the testimony of Cardinal Timothy Manning before the Senate Subcommittee on Constitutional Amendments in 1974: "When the Supreme Court speaks, it is presumed to be the authentic interpreter of the Constitution. But its interpretation can be mistaken. In the case of the abortion decisions the Court created constitutional doctrine out of opinions which appear arbitrary at best." The way the bishops make their pro-life argument appears to be rooted in John Courtney Murray's confidence that the principles embedded in the founding of the United States proceeded so directly from the medieval tradition of the natural law (a "close compatibility between Catholicism and American democracy"; Barry Hudock, *Struggle, Condemnation, Vindication: John Courtney Murray's Journey toward Vatican II* [Collegeville, MN: Liturgical Press, 2015], 103) that Catholics, from within their tradition, can claim a special set of insights into the American political tradition. This perspective persisted as recently as 2008, when Archbishop Charles Chaput wrote, "Evidence for the Christian role in founding and shaping the United States is so massive that denying it requires a peculiar kind of self-deception," and "Murray argued that the Catholic faith and American democracy are not merely compatible but congenial"; Charles J. Chaput, OFMCap, *Render Unto Caesar: Serving the Nation by Living Our Catholic Beliefs in Public Life* (New York: Doubleday, 2008), 28, 94. Arguments such as these, conflating the American tradition with the Catholic tradition, can lead to strange places. Among some Catholics, they have led to the determination that, in the words of Archbishop Fulton Sheen, "It is our solemn duty as Catholics . . . to be conscious of our duty to America, and to preserve its freedom by preserving its faith in God" (*The*

immigrants not just to fit into America but to be better Americans than their Protestant neighbors. The way the culture war argument over abortion rejects personal opposition to abortion and demands public proof of opposition recalls Cold War fears about disloyalty and hidden enemies. It also explains the intensifying, self-reinforcing nature of our political polarization that, even more than it is built on the opposition between liberals and conservatives, is driven by the fear that the disloyalty of friends is a greater danger than the errors of adversaries.

70. Charles Rice, "Can the Killing of Abortionists be Justified?" *The Wanderer* (1 September 1994): 6.

71. Address of Patrick J. Buchanan to the Republican National Convention, Houston, TX (17 August 1992).

72. See Joe Klein, "Patrick Buchanan Reveals Himself to Be the First Trumpist," review of *Nixon's White House Wars: The Battles that Made and Broke a President and Divided America Forever* for *New York Times* (8 May 2017). See also Patrick J. Buchanan, interview by Ira Glass and Zoe Chace, *This American Life*, American Public Media, 28 April 2017.

Chapter 3—pages 62–94

1. George Weigel, *Witness to Hope: The Biography of Pope John Paul II, 1920–2005* (New York: Perennial, 2005), 247–248. Weigel also records this recollection suggesting Wojtyła's premonition of what would follow: "Wojtyła began to describe what had happened to him the day the Pope died. He had been out on his parish visitation and a storm had exploded in the mountains during Mass. As he described the storm, he became unusually emotional. His friends listened in silence, not knowing what he was thinking. He then stopped, concerned that he had become too demonstrative. . . . As they left, Dziwisz said to Turowicz and Skwarnicki, 'Pray for Cardinal Wojtyła; pray for his return to Kraków' " (250).

2. See Peter Hebblethwaite, *Pope John Paul II and the Church* (Kansas City: Sheed & Ward, 1995), 262.

3. In 1984, the United States and the Holy See established formal diplomatic relations. For the brief purposes necessary for this study, the only effect was to change the title of the papal representative from apostolic delegate to its current form, apostolic nuncio, without any particular change to the duties mentioned.

4. Kenneth A. Briggs, "Pope's U.S. Delegate Takes Powerful Role," *New York Times* (27 February 1977): 26.

5. Ibid.

6. Kenneth A. Briggs, "Influential Papal Delegate to U.S. Is Named to a High Vatican Post," *New York Times* (28 June 1980): 2. Rev. Andrew Greeley recorded around the same time that officials in the Roman curia "don't so much push people as attack other people. They destroyed Cardinal Leo Josef Suenens of Belgium by saying he does peculiar things and the pope no longer approves of him. They are now working on Archbishop Jean Jadot. . . . They are pointing to Jadot's statements on the acceptability of 'altar girls' in liturgical functions as indications that he is frivolous and dangerous"; Andrew M. Greeley, *The Making of the Popes 1978: The Politics of Intrigue in the Vatican* (Kansas City: Andrew and McMeel, Inc., 1979), 20. Greeley obviously is describing gossip, but it corresponds to the record. The "appointment of bishops" was one of four concerns Pope John Paul named "about the Church in the United States to his new Washington representative," when Pio Laghi replaced Jadot in 1980; George Weigel, *Witness to Hope*, 379. Weigel has written elsewhere about John Paul's determination to "dismantle" an approach to appointing the sorts of bishops to the United States who had been advanced by Archbishop Joseph Bernardin's "relationship with Belgian archbishop, Jean Jadot"; George Weigel, "The End of the Bernardin Era," *First Things* (February 2011): 23, 20.

7. Thomas J. Reese, "The Laghi Legacy," *America* (23 June 1990), at http://www.americamagazine.org/issue/100/laghi-legacy. Also, "The bishops appointed during Jadot's tenure tended to be less enamored of the imperial trappings of the traditional hierarchy, and more attuned to the pastoral, collective style of the post–Vatican II church. And that style often found expression in the activities of the National Conference of Catholic Bishops"; Timothy A. Byrnes, *Catholic Bishops in American Politics* (Princeton: Princeton University Press, 1991), 51. Last, see the testimony of Russell Shaw: "There's substantial truth to conventional wisdom on the subject, namely that you have at least two distinct groups of bishops within the episcopal conference of the United States. . . . You have the Jadot bishops and the post-Jadot bishops, John Paul II bishops"; Reese, *A Flock of Shepherds*, 182.

8. Archbishop Bernard F. Law, Installation Homily, Cathedral of the Holy Cross, Boston, MA (24 March 1984). Also: Archbishop John

J. O'Connor, Installation Homily, St. Patrick's Cathedral, New York, NY (19 March 1984).

9. Weigel, *Witness to Hope*, 226.

10. Archbishop Bernard F. Law, Installation Homily, Cathedral of the Holy Cross, Boston, MA (24 March 1984).

11. See Steven P. Millies, *Joseph Bernardin: Seeking Common Ground* (Collegeville, MN: Liturgical Press, 2016), 52–55.

12. "It was his [Jadot's] displeasure with the way the top leadership of the hierarchy responded to the two major presidential candidates during the campaign, chiefly on the issue of abortion, that resulted in the leaders later declaring that they were politically neutral"; Kenneth A. Briggs, "Pope's U.S. Delegate Takes Powerful Role," *New York Times* (27 February 1977): 26.

13. "Resolution of the Administrative Committee, National Conference of Catholic Bishops, September 16, 1976," American Catholic History Research Center, NCCB Collection, Box 63, Folder "Ad-Hoc Committee on Pro-Life Activities, Jul.–Sept. 1976," 1–2.

14. On Bernardin's coming to Chicago and his relationship with Pope John Paul II, see Millies, *Joseph Bernardin*, 67–69, 94–95.

15. In *Sacrosanctum Concilium* the Council proclaimed that "the regulation of the liturgy within certain defined limits belongs also to various kinds of competent territorial bodies of bishops legitimately established" (SC 22). It is interesting to note that, since *SC* was among the first documents the Council produced and it came before any detailed treatment of national conferences, it can be said that "the ecclesiological development that led to the institution of episcopal conferences originated from the liturgical debate and the plan for the liturgical life of the Church after Vatican II"; Massimo Faggioli, *True Reform: Liturgy and Ecclesiology in* Sacrosanctum Concilium (Collegeville, MN: Liturgical Press, 2012), 61. The Council's vision of the church, from the Council's beginning, drove forward the development of bishops' conferences and centered its concern on liturgy. Chapter 3 of *Christus Dominus* sets forth the fullest thinking of the Council about conferences and establishes clearly that they exist to aid individual bishops as they "exercise their pastoral office by way of promoting that greater good which the Church offers mankind" (38). A key portion of this chapter ("Decisions of the episcopal conference, provided they have been made lawfully and by the choice of at least two-thirds of the prelates who have a deliberative vote in the conference, and have been reviewed by the Apostolic See, are to have

juridically binding force in those cases and in those only which are prescribed by common law or determined by special mandate of the Apostolic See") was limited in 1998 by Pope John Paul II in *Apostolos Suos*.

16. Bishop Anthony Pilla looked back on the way Catholics had struggled to gain acceptance throughout American history when he wrote, "Any reticence bred in the bishops by this anti-Catholicism which pervaded much of U.S. society was obliterated when the Supreme Court made 'abortion-on-demand' not only legal but a 'constitutional right.' Since that time the bishops have been outspoken. . . . The initial lonely public opposition to abortion gave an impetus to the conference's willingness to look critically at society and its attitudes" (2, 3). Pilla also pointed with particular emphasis to "the conference's consistency in the matter of abortion" (3). See Most Reverend Anthony M. Pilla, "Foreword," in *Pastoral Letters of the United States Catholic Bishops: 1989–1997*, vol. 6 (Washington, DC: USCCB, 1998).

17. Bishop Thomas Gumbleton, quoted in Jim Castelli, *The Bishops and the Bomb: Waging Peace in a Nuclear Age* (Garden City, NY: Image Books, 1983), 18. See pp. 13–18 for a full description of the decision to write the pastoral letter.

18. Joseph Cardinal Bernardin, "A Consistent Ethic of Life: An American-Catholic Dialogue," *Selected Works of Joseph Cardinal Bernardin*, Vol. 2, *Church and Society* (Collegeville, MN: Liturgical Press, 2000), 89. Bernardin's context was "using the follow-through for the pastoral letter" (89). Also, see the US bishops' *The Challenge of Peace*, 285: "No society can live in peace with itself, or with the world, without a full awareness of the worth and dignity of every human person, and of the sacredness of all human life (Jas 4:1-2). When we accept violence in any form as commonplace, our sensitivities become dulled. When we accept violence, war itself can be taken for granted. Violence has many faces: oppression of the poor, deprivation of basic human rights, economic exploitation, sexual exploitation and pornography, neglect or abuse of the aged and the helpless, and innumerable other acts of inhumanity. Abortion in particular blunts a sense of the sacredness of human life. In a society where the innocent unborn are killed wantonly, how can we expect people to feel righteous revulsion at the act or threat of killing noncombatants in war?"

19. See Castelli, *The Bishops and the Bomb*, 82. Also: Mary McGrory, "WAR," *Washington Post* (18 November 1982).

20. *Economic Justice for All*, 5.

21. David J. O'Brien and Thomas A. Shannon, eds., Introduction to "Part 5: The U.S. Bishops and Catholic Social Teaching," *Catholic Social Thought: The Documentary Heritage* (Maryknoll, NY: Orbis Books, 1992), 491.

22. In *The Bishops and the Bomb*, Jim Castelli describes Bernardin's determination that the pastoral letter should express a broad consensus view, for which reason Bernardin insisted that the committee include Bishop Thomas Gumbleton, a peace activist, and Bishop John O'Connor, who was the bishop for the military ordinariate and, as Chief of Chaplains for the US Navy, held the rank of rear admiral; Castelli, 19. Bernardin told Thomas J. Reese that, "unless we fight it out in the committee, unless we reach some consensus there, we will never get the consensus," the middle path that he wanted; Reese, *A Flock of Shepherds*, 120.

23. See Joseph Sobran, "Bishop in the Doghouse," *National Review* 38, no. 24 (19 December 1986): 29. The congressman was Bob Dornan of California, known throughout his career as "B-1 Bob" because of his vigorous support for defense build-up, most particularly the development of the B-1 bomber. Joe Biden was one of many Catholic Democrats to worry about whether to "impose" his faith through his public action as a member of Congress. See Bernard Weintraub, "Abortion Curbs Endorsed, 10–7, by Senate Panel," *New York Times* (11 March 1982): B9.

24. Bernardin, "A Consistent Ethic of Life," 84, 85.

25. Those characterizations of *Redemptor Hominis* are Bernardin's, in Bernardin, "A Consistent Ethic of Life," 86. John Paul II himself wrote: "The man of today seems ever to be under threat from what he produces" (15), and "The development of technology and the development of contemporary civilization, which is marked by the ascendancy of technology, demand a proportional development of morals and ethics. For the present, this last development seems unfortunately to be always left behind. Accordingly, in spite of the marvel of this progress, in which it is difficult not to see also authentic signs of man's greatness, signs that in their creative seeds were revealed to us in the pages of the Book of Genesis, as early as where it describes man's creation, this progress cannot fail to give rise to disquiet on many counts" (15).

26. Bernardin, "A Consistent Ethic of Life," 86.

27. Ibid.

28. Kenneth A. Briggs, "Bernardin Asks Catholics to Fight Both Nuclear Arms and Abortion," *New York Times* (7 December 1983): A1. Eugene Kennedy records that Bernardin used the phrase "seamless garment" "during the question period after the Fordham address"; Eugene Kennedy, *Bernardin: Life to the Full* (Chicago: Bonus Books, 1997), 251. Additionally, and importantly, Kennedy further holds, "Although he [Bernardin] never personally adopted these words ["seamless garment"] in any formal way, they were picked up popularly and have continued to be used, almost as a synonym, for the consistent ethic of life" (251). The record does not bear Kennedy out on this point, however. First, Bernardin incorporated "seamless garment" into his next address on the Consistent Ethic, the William Wade Lecture at St. Louis University on March 11, 1984: "That lecture [at Fordham University] has generated a substantial discussion both inside and outside the Church on the linkage of life issues which, I am convinced, constitute a 'seamless garment.'" The phrase appeared subsequently in two lectures on the Consistent Ethic Bernardin gave in 1985. Second, Bernardin had been using the phrase at least since 1976. In January 1976, Bernardin said, "Life before and after birth, from the moment of conception until death, is like a seamless garment. It all hangs together; one part cannot exist without the other. You cannot pick and choose. If we become insensitive to the beginning of life and condone abortion or if we become careless about the end of life and justify euthanasia, we have no reason to believe that there will be much respect for life in between. As a matter of fact, the evidence of history as well as the present moment leads us to the opposite conclusion"; Most Rev. Joseph L. Bernardin, "Homily for the Mass Commemorating Third Anniversary of the Supreme Court's Abortion Decision," Cincinnati, OH (22 January 1976), Joseph Louis Bernardin Collection, Archdiocese of Chicago Joseph Cardinal Bernardin Archives and Records Center, Addresses & Talks Collection.

29. Kennedy, *Bernardin: Life to the Full*, 251.

30. See Joseph Cardinal Bernardin, *Consistent Ethic of Life*, ed. Thomas G. Fuechtmann (Kansas City, MO: Sheed & Ward, 1988).

31. Richard A. McCormick, SJ, raised questions about whether the whole length of the Catholic tradition can support an ethic that is "consistent," and whether the Consistent Ethic's personalist focus is

so novel within the tradition that Bernardin's argument has a "soft underbelly"; ibid., 96–122. John Finnis identified several "bad side-effects" of the Consistent Ethic, such as the inevitable darkness of partisanship that will overshadow any statement coming from bishops about political questions; ibid., 140–181. Frans Jozef van Beeck, SJ, observed that Bernardin's argument depended on a foundation in natural rights, to which van Beeck objected as much as he agreed with McCormick that "there are real problems with the *application*, by the Church's magisterium, of the nature concept in individual, and especially in sexual, morality" (135). Van Beeck wondered if those problems would "preclude the possibility of any kind of *internally consistent* ethic of life" (135), Ibid., 123–139. James M. Gustafson zeroes in on the fact that "The theology is not developed in his [Bernardin's] work" (203). Nevertheless, none of these scholars wholly dismisses the Consistent Ethic. Indeed, the effect of their contributions is to propose further directions into which to chart its development.

32. "The idea of public order the Cardinal presents includes these three political values: public peace, essential protections of human rights, and the commonly accepted standards of moral behavior in a community of law. Further, he grants that not all moral imperatives are to be translated into prohibitive civil statutes and thinks it essential to the political and social order to protect human life and basic human rights. The denial of the right to abortion he hopes to justify on the basis of those three values. I don't assess his argument here, except to say it is clearly cast in the form of public reason. Whether it is itself reasonable or not, or more reasonable than arguments on the other side, is another matter. As with any form of reasoning in public reason, the reasoning may be fallacious or mistaken"; John Rawls, *Political Liberalism*, rev. ed. (New York: Columbia University Press, 2005), livn32.

33. United States Catholic Conference, "Political Responsibility: Reflections on an Election Year—A Statement of the Administrative Board of the United States Catholic Conference" (12 February 1976), Jimmy Carter Presidential Library, 1976 Campaign Committee to Elect Jimmy Carter Collection, Eizenstat Collection, Box 3, Folder "Catholics 5/76–8/20/76," 5, 6.

34. Ibid., 7.

35. "Resolution of the Administrative Committee, National Conference of Catholic Bishops, September 16, 1976," American Catholic

History Research Center, NCCB Collection, Box 63, Folder "Ad-Hoc Committee on Pro-Life Activities, Jul.–Sept. 1976," 2.

36. Marjorie Hyer, "Bernardin Views Prolife Issues as 'Seamless Garment,'" *Washington Post* (10 December 1983): B6.

37. Ibid., B6.

38. John F. Kennedy, "Address to the Greater Houston Ministerial Association," Houston, TX (12 September 1960).

39. A gathering of Protestant clergymen led by Norman Vincent Peale released a statement on September 7, 1960, allowing that while "no persons should engage in hate-mongering, bigotry, prejudice or unfounded charges" and "persons who are members of the Roman Catholic faith can be just as honest, patriotic and public-spirited as those of any other faith," nevertheless "the Roman Catholic Church is a political as well as a religious organization" and it claimed "control over its members in political and civic affairs." See "Protestant Groups' Statements," *New York Times* (8 September 1960): 25. Reporters pressed Peale about why his group had expressed no concern about Richard Nixon being a Quaker, to which Peale replied, "I don't know that he [Nixon] ever let it bother him"; Peter Braestrup, "Protestant Unit Wary on Kennedy," *New York Times* (8 September 1960): 25. The Kennedy campaign kept a thick file of literature and correspondence expressing anti-Catholic sentiments, including the notion that the "main scheme" of the Catholic Church was to nominate "a Roman Catholic in both tickets" so that "the American public will be left without any choice, but to elect a Roman Catholic" in 1960 ("The Pope and the President"), and that "a Catholic has no choice [*sic*] either he accepts Rome's doctrines without question, or he is excommunicated" ("I Was a Roman Priest"). Most interesting was the message of the Sovereign Grand Commander of the Supreme Council 33° Ancient & Accepted Scottish Rite of Freemasonry, Southern Jurisdiction of the United States of America, Luther A. Smith, who cast the matter in terms of suspecting immigrants who have not accepted "the New Order of religious freedom and independence" that Protestant churches gained by severing themselves from "their 'Mother' churches in Europe." Keeping their ties to Rome and the pope, on Smith's understanding, was what made Catholics suspect. For these and other examples from the Kennedy campaign files, see John F. Kennedy Presidential Library and Museum, Papers of John F. Kennedy, Pre-Presidential Papers, Presidential Campaign Files,

1960, Issues, Religious Issue Files, 1956–1959, Correspondence: Unanswered: September 1959–October 1959.

40. The historian Arthur M. Schlesinger, Sr. (father of Kennedy aide Arthur Schlesinger, Jr.) remarked to John Tracy Ellis, "I regard the prejudice against your Church as the deepest bias in the history of the American people," quoted in John Tracy Ellis, *American Catholicism*, 2nd rev. ed. (Chicago: University of Chicago Press, 1969), 151.

41. Mario Cuomo, "The Democratic Party and the 1984 Campaign," Address to the Institute of Politics, Harvard University, Cambridge, MA (5 July 1984).

42. Mario M. Cuomo, "Introduction," in *The Diaries of Mario M. Cuomo: The Campaign for Governor* (New York: Random House, 1984), 4.

43. Ibid., 4, 11.

44. Ibid., 16.

45. Mario Cuomo, "Religious Belief and Public Morality: A Catholic Governor's Perspective," University of Notre Dame, South Bend, IN (13 September 1984).

46. Ibid.

47. Ibid. St. Thomas Aquinas wrote over seven centuries ago, "The purpose of human law is to lead men to virtue, not suddenly but gradually. Wherefore it does not lay upon the multitude of imperfect men the burdens of those who are already virtuous. . . . Otherwise, these imperfect ones, being unable to bear such precepts, would break out into yet greater evils"; *ST* I-II, Q.96, A.2. To put it more plainly, a law that people (even when they are wrong about it) feel is beyond their reach is apt to cultivate disrespect for all laws in general.

48. Cuomo, "Religious Belief and Public Morality: A Catholic Governor's Perspective."

49. Since the earliest decades after Jesus's ministry, the church has taught, "Do not kill a fetus by abortion" (*Didache*, 2.2). It is true that the definition of abortion has shifted across the centuries, as the church's theology has struggled with the question of when life begins. This is evident even in John Paul II's *Evangelium Vitae* ("Throughout Christianity's two thousand year history, this same doctrine has been constantly taught by the Fathers of the Church and by her Pastors and Doctors. Even scientific and philosophical discussions about the precise moment of the infusion of the spiritual soul have never given rise to any hesitation about the moral condemnation of abortion,"

61). There has been a diversity of views about when life begins even in Christian history, and the church still is careful to observe that difficulty. But abortion itself always has been gravely sinful.

50. Cuomo, "Religious Belief and Public Morality: A Catholic Governor's Perspective."

51. As Bernardin clarified and deepened his Consistent Ethic, he made plain that abortion is unlike issues of poverty or the questions about the justness of wars ("The consistent ethic rejects collapsing all issues into one," at *Selected Works*, vol. 2, 111). At the same time, the Consistent Ethic was not concerned with linking issues together. Rather, it was concerned with developing a response to each of those issues "in a disciplined, systematic fashion" (115). This was a subtle distinction, but one that preserved the important differences between different moral issues.

52. Henry J. Hyde, "Keeping God in the Closet," Address to the Theodore J. White Center on Law and Government, University of Notre Dame Law School, South Bend, IN (24 September 1984).

53. Ibid. Hyde's criticism appears fair at first glance. On closer appraisal, it seems that Hyde makes an error that is the mirror image of Cuomo's error about the grave sinfulness of abortion. Where Cuomo overlooked a theological distinction, Hyde overlooked an important legal distinction. After all, nuclear disarmament is a strategic consideration respecting national defense that a president lawfully may or may not value. That is strictly a question of judgments an elected official may make. Abortion is in a different, much less optional category since the US Supreme Court defined access to abortion as a constitutionally protected right. No elected official in the United States may dismiss the civil liberties protections of the Constitution. A double standard is not possible when we speak of two incompatible things. Cuomo was as wrong to compare abortion with disarmament on grounds of moral theology as Hyde was wrong to compare them on grounds of constitutional law.

54. The Week, *National Review* (13 December 1985): 10.

55. The identification of Bernardin with Cuomo persists. Onetime *National Review* columnist Joseph Sobran wrote in 2005 how Bernardin "endeared himself to liberals, especially liberal Catholic politicians, by adopting the metaphor of life as a 'seamless garment,'" and, "Politicians like New York's Mario Cuomo felt they had been vindicated in their empty 'personal' opposition to abortion"; Joseph

Sobran, "The 'Seamless Garment' Revisited," *Sobran's Real News of the Month* (16 August 2005), at http://www.sobran.com/columns/2005/050816.shtml. While eulogizing Cardinal John O'Connor, Richard John Neuhaus described "Cuomo declaim[ing] on the 'seamless garment,' an image that suggests that abortion is one issue among others, such as opposing handguns, capital punishment, drunken driving, and unkindness to whales"; Richard John Neuhaus, "John Cardinal O'Connor, 1920–2000," *First Things* (https://www.firstthings.com/web-exclusives/2008/05/john-cardinal-oconnor). Michael W. Cuneo treated the "seamless garment" and Cuomo's argument that "one cannot enshrine religious values . . . into public law" together, in Michael W. Cuneo, "Life Battles: The Rise of Catholic Militancy within the American Pro-Life Movement," in *Being Right: Conservative Catholics in America*, ed. Mary Jo Weaver and R. Scott Appleby (Indianapolis: Indiana University Press, 1995), 291–293. James Hitchcock brought Cuomo and Bernardin together, writing that "it has been the obvious strategy of those Catholics rendered uncomfortable by the issue [abortion] to bury it amidst a number of other issues"; James Hitchcock, "Abortion and the Catholic Church," *Human Life Review* 12, no. 7 (Winter 1986): 64. Obviously, this enumeration is only a sample selected to highlight the consistency of the pattern across decades.

56. In October 1960, 166 prominent lay Catholics signed a statement supporting Kennedy's Houston address. The signers included academics (Paul R. Dean, dean of the Georgetown School of Law, and Jerome G. Kerwin, political theorist at the University of Chicago) and political officials (Gov. Michael DiSalle of Ohio and Sen. Thomas Dodd of Connecticut), as well as prominent Catholics Clare Boothe Luce and James B. Carey, president of the International Brotherhood of Electrical Workers. See John D. Morris, "Catholic Laymen Uphold Kennedy," *New York Times* (6 October 1960): 31. Theologian Gustave Weigel, SJ, offered a public lecture in which he observed that "an elected official has a 'double life,' worshipping as he pleases in his private life, but in his public role he is a man of the law which is framed for practical purposes and canonizes no philosophy or theology"; John W. Finney, "Jesuit Rules Out Church Control over President," *New York Times* (28 September 1960): 1. No Catholic bishop spoke out at the time, since they "had decided to be silent about the election, lest they fuel charges of meddling in politics," but Pittsburgh's Bishop (later Cardinal) John Wright and future New Orleans

archbishop Philip Hannan assisted Kennedy behind the scenes. See Msgr. Owen F. Campion, "JFK's Houston Speech," *OSV Newsweekly* (25 August 2010), at https://www.osv.com/OSVNewsweekly/ByIssue/Article/TabId/735/ArtMID/13636/ArticleID/6684/JFKs-Houston-speech.aspx.

57. Charles J. Chaput, OFMCap, *Render unto Caesar: Serving the Nation by Living Our Catholic Beliefs in Political Life* (New York: Doubleday, 2008), 136.

58. Ibid., 171.

59. Morris, *American Catholic*, 424–425. O'Connor had said in a television interview that "he did not see 'how a Catholic in good conscience can vote for a candidate who explicitly supports abortion" ("Catholics Urged to Press Views Held by Church," *New York Times* [10 August 1984]: 1), to which Cuomo replied, "You have the Archbishop of New York saying that no Catholic can vote for Ed Koch, no Catholic can vote for Jay Goldin, for Carol Bellamy, nor for Pat Moynihan or Mario Cuomo" ("Politicians and Religion: Discussion Signals Shift," *New York Times* [6 August 1984]: 14). Archbishop O'Connor subsequently insisted that "Cuomo had misinterpreted his words, and that it was not his [O'Connor's] responsibility or desire to give voters evaluations of public officials or candidates" ("Politicians and Religion: Discussion Signals Shift," 14).

60. Morris, *American Catholic*, 426.

61. Michael Oreskes, "Politicians and Religion: Discussion Signals Shift," *New York Times* (6 August 1984): 14.

62. Michael Oreskes, "Cuomo Questions O'Connor's Views," *New York Times* (11 September 1984): 27.

63. Fox Butterfield, "Archbishop of Boston Cites Abortion as 'Critical' Issue," *New York Times* (6 September 1984), Metropolitan Report Section, B13.

64. Ibid., B13.

65. *Roe v. Wade* had created the viability standard, the point at which the fetus could live on its own outside the mother's body. The medical science of the early 1970s placed viability between the twenty-fourth and twenty-eight weeks. The progress of medical science between 1973 and the late 1980s and early 1990s will figure importantly in the ongoing jurisprudence surrounding abortion.

66. *Black's Law Dictionary* defines judicial restraint either as "the principle that, when a court can resolve a case based on a particular issue, it should do so, without reaching unnecessary issues," or as

"a philosophy of judicial decision-making whereby judges avoid indulging their personal beliefs about the public good and instead try merely to interpret the law as legislated and according to precedent"; *Black's Law Dictionary*, 9th ed., s.v. "judicial restraint." I have conflated judicial restraint somewhat with *stare decisis* for simplicity here, a choice driven by the desire to explain these legal and other topics to general readers. The choice is defensible, however, so far as a judge stands by what is decided in legislation or precedent and avoids seeking larger issues that substitute "beliefs about the public good" beyond what the law and the legitimacy of the law demand.

67. *Akron v. Akron Center for Reproductive Health* (1983).

68. Robin Toner, "Ruling Eases a Worry for Bush, But Just Wait, His Critics Warn," *New York Times* (30 June 1992): A15.

69. Ibid. Also: United States Conference of Catholic Bishops, *Pro-Life Coordinator Handbook* (Washington, DC: United States Conference of Catholic Bishops, 2005), G-30.

70. Christopher B. Daly, "Salvi Convicted of Murder in Shootings," *Washington Post* (19 March 1996): A1.

71. Maria Newman, "O'Connor Leads March on Abortion," *New York Times* (14 June 1992): 41. Also: Frank Pavone, "Fearless Defender of Life," *First Things*, online https://www.firstthings.com/web-exclusives/2010/05/a-tribute-to-cardinal-john-oconnorndash2000.

72. Michael Crowley, "Casey Closed," *The New Republic* 215, no. 12/13 (16 September 1996): 12.

73. Peter Steinfels, "Catholic Bishops in US Reject Policy Letter on Role of Women," *New York Times* (19 November 1992): 1.

74. George Weigel, "The End of the Bernardin Era," *First Things* (February 2011): 23.

75. Ibid., 19.

Chapter 4—pages 95–127

1. Quoted in Irvin D.S. Winsboro and Michael Epple, "Religions, Culture, and the Cold War: Bishop Fulton J. Sheen and America's Anti-Communist Crusade of the 1950's," *The Historian* 71, no. 2 (Summer 2009): 226.

2. Grant Wacker, *America's Pastor: Billy Graham and the Shaping of a Nation* (Cambridge, MA: The Belknap Press of Harvard University, 2014), 189.

3. George Weigel, *Witness to Hope: The Biography of Pope John Paul II, 1920–2005* (New York: Perennial, 2005), 756.

4. Cardinal Joseph Ratzinger, "The Problem of Threats to Human Life," "address to the Extraordinary Consistory of Cardinals discussing the challenges faced by today's *war on life*, the reasons for the *logic of death* and some possible responses," in *L'Osservatore Romano* (8 April 1991).

5. Ibid.

6. Ibid.

7. Weigel, *Witness to Hope*, 756. The cardinals asked Pope John Paul to "give an authoritative voice and expression to the Church's Magisterium in regard to the dignity of human life" (756).

8. Ratzinger, "The Problem of Threats to Human Life."

9. Fox Butterfield, "Massachusetts Is Asked to Ease Abortion Laws," *New York Times* (21 September 1991): 6.

10. Message of the Holy Father Pope John Paul II for the VIII World Youth Day (15 August 1993), 5. A passage more specifically citing a culture of death ("In our own century, the 'culture of death' has assumed a social and institutional form of legality to justify the most horrible crimes against humanity: genocide, 'final solutions', 'ethnic cleansing' and the massive 'taking of human beings even before they are born or before they reach the natural point of death' ") appeared in the pope's prepared remarks, but was omitted from the speech he delivered. See Alan Cowell, "Pope Edits His Most Critical Language to End on a Positive Note," *New York Times* (16 August 1993): A12.

11. "Evangelicals & Catholics Together: The Christian Mission in the Third Millennium," *First Things* (May 1994), at https://www.firstthings.com/article/1994/05/evangelicals-catholics-together-the-christian-mission-in-the-third-millennium. The occurrence of that language, "culture of death," which would become such a prominent feature of John Paul's encyclical that opposed a "culture of life" to it, one year before the encyclical was published suggests to us how some of the signers of "Evangelicals & Catholics Together" may have been knowledgeable about the drafting. The term was not in wide use prior to the encyclical. We should observe first that George Weigel was a participant in drafting "Evangelicals & Catholics Together." We can go on to observe that Weigel strongly suggests that other bishops were consulted, and we get the impression that Weigel knows who they were ("John Paul also got counsel from bishops with long

public experience in pro-life activism, like New York's Cardinal John O'Connor," 756). A portion of Weigel's commentary on *Evangelium Vitae* in his biography of John Paul II is attributed to an "interview with Cardinal Joseph Ratzinger, September 20, 1997," while *Witness to Hope* identifies three additional occasions on which Weigel interviewed Cardinal Ratzinger. Weigel conducted many interviews for his book, and by themselves interviews with Cardinal Ratzinger suggest nothing irregular. For the second most influential man in the Vatican to have made time for Weigel interviews on at least four occasions, however, suggests an ongoing relationship, a willingness to commit substantial time. Cardinal Ratzinger and other church officials who were involved in the drafting of *Evangelium Vitae* between 1991 and 1995 were in dialogue with Weigel and other figures around the church who were engaged in an ongoing conversation about how to press the social message of the church in the late twentieth century. We know from Weigel's *Witness to Hope* that Cardinal John O'Connor was consulted in the drafting of *Evangelium Vitae*, and O'Connor went on to become an endorser of "Evangelicals & Catholics Together" (756). Cardinal Bernard Law did not participate in drafting "Evangelicals & Catholics Together" (though William Murphy, his diocesan chancellor and the future bishop of Rockville Centre, did). Bishop Francis George, OMI, whom Cardinal Law would advance as the next archbishop of Chicago and who later would join the College of Cardinals ("Many observers believe Law's sponsorship explains" George's rapid rise to Chicago, wrote John Allen, "Chicago Cardinal Francis George, the 'American Ratzinger,' Dies," *CRUX*, 17 April 2015), was also a participant in "Evangelicals & Catholics Together" together with evangelical figures like Charles Colson.

12. Weigel, *Witness to Hope*, 762.

13. Charles E. Curran, "*Evangelium Vitae* and Its Broader Context," in *John Paul II and Moral Theology*, ed. Charles E. Curran and Richard A. McCormick, SJ (Mahwah, NJ: Paulist Press, 1998), 123. We have dealt with Curran above, at p. 38, in the context of his dismissal from Catholic University over his theological dissent from church teaching on contraception. Curran is a controversial figure. However, his claim about the Catholic tradition as not seeing "sin as destroying the human and its basic goodness, but only infecting it" (123) and recognizing "the nuances and the different levels of certitude with regard to" (124) moral teaching is unquestionably valid. See the *Catechism of the Catholic Church*, 405, 1754.

14. Curran, "*Evangelium Vitae* and Its Broader Context," 123.

15. Alan Cowell, "Pope Edits His Most Critical Language to End on a Positive Note," *New York Times* (16 August 1993): A12.

16. Message of the Holy Father Pope John Paul II for the VIII World Youth Day (15 August 1993), 4. Margaret O'Brien Steinfels also recognized this, describing *Evangelium Vitae* as the Consistent Ethic's "Manichaean shadow"; Margaret O'Brien Steinfels, "Defenders of the Faith! A Personal Reflection on Recent History," *Commonweal* 137, no. 21 (3 December 2010): 14.

17. Message of the Holy Father Pope John Paul II for the VIII World Youth Day (15 August 1993), 4. Marc Ouellet, later archbishop of Quebec, a cardinal, and prefect of the Vatican's Congregation for Bishops, also wrote about the culture of life and the culture of death as "God's Battle" and a "great struggle," and quoted verse from Charles Péguy about those who "died in battle in the sight of God"; Marc Ouellet, "The Mystery of Easter and the Culture of Death," in *John Paul II and Moral Theology*, ed. Charles E. Curran and Richard A. McCormick, SJ (Mahwah, NJ: Paulist Press, 1998), 116, 117, 119n.

18. "If we look at today's world, we are struck by many negative factors that can lead to pessimism. But this feeling is unjustified: we have faith in God our Father and Lord, in his goodness and mercy. As the third millennium of the redemption draws near, God is preparing a great springtime for Christianity, and we can already see its first signs. In fact, both in the non-Christian world and in the traditionally Christian world, people are gradually drawing closer to gospel ideals and values, a development which the Church seeks to encourage. Today in fact there is a new consensus among peoples about these values: the rejection of violence and war; respect for the human person and for human rights; the desire for freedom, justice and brotherhood; the surmounting of different forms of racism and nationalism; the affirmation of the dignity and role of women. Christian hope sustains us in committing ourselves fully to the new evangelization and to the worldwide mission, and leads us to pray as Jesus taught us: 'Thy Kingdom come. Thy will be done, on earth as it is in heaven' (Mt 6:10)"; John Paul II, *Redemptoris Missio*, 86.

19. *First Things* (May 1994). "Evangelicals & Catholics Together" was self-consciously rooted in the opposition to *Roe* that dated to the 1970s and drew evangelicals and Catholics together even then. See above, n. 11.

20. John Paul II, *Ut Unum Sint*, 72.

21. Ari L. Goldman, "Visit to South Carolina Reflects Rise of Catholics in Bible Belt," *New York Times* (11 September 1987): A17.

22. While hardly important for the larger argument of this book, it should still be noted here that Bork came to the Judiciary Committee with unusual political baggage. On the night of October 20, 1973, in the depths of the Watergate scandal, President Nixon had ordered Attorney General Elliot Richardson to fire an independent prosecutor, Archibald Cox, who was investigating the president. Rather than obey the order, Richardson resigned. The responsibility fell next to the Deputy Attorney General, William Ruckelshaus, who also resigned. The next person in the Department of Justice leadership was the Solicitor General, Robert Bork, who fired Cox in an episode known as the "Saturday Night Massacre." Bork took more than a little criticism for firing an independent prosecutor and, in effect, abetting the president's desire to thwart an investigation into his own wrongdoing. Historians have been somewhat more forgiving. The point against the president had been made with two resignations, and someone in senior leadership needed to run the United States Department of Justice which, besides dealing with presidential scandals, did other important business of the people every day. In his memoir, Bork recalled that, after Ruckelshaus's resignation left the task to him, Bork told White House Chief of Staff Alexander Haig, "I had already decided I would fire Cox. 'The only question is whether I resign after I do it . . . .' I knew I could not resign, but still wished circumstances had allowed me to make the Massacre a murder-suicide," Robert H. Bork, *Saving Justice: Watergate, the Saturday Night Massacre, and Other Adventures of a Solicitor General* (New York: Encounter Books, 2013), 89.

23. "We have always traveled long distances to go to a church that we thought had a really reverent Mass, the kind of church that when you go in, it is quiet—not that kind of church where it is like a community hall and everybody is talking"; Michael O'Loughlin, "Scalia was a champion of traditional Catholicism," *CRUX* (14 February 2016), at http://www.cruxnow.com/faith/2016/02/14/scalia-was-a-champion-of-traditional-catholicism/.

24. Quoted in Norman Vieira and Leonard Gross, *Supreme Court Appointments: Judge Bork and the Politicization of Senate Confirmations* (Carbondale, IL: Southern Illinois University Press, 1998), 56.

25. Editorial, "The Fortas Nomination," *New York Times* (14 September 1968): 30. In 2017, Patrick J. Buchanan revealed how, "with

Nixon's knowledge, some of us on his staff . . . urged Senate conservatives to block Fortas. Foremost among these was Strom Thurmond, who needed little prodding, and who was provided with 'Flaming Creatures,' a graphic film of transvestite sex which Fortas, alone among the nine justices, had deemed acceptable for public viewing. Senators were invited to a closed room for a screening. Some walked out wobbly. And as I told friend Sim Fentress of *Time*, the 'Fortas Film Festival' was going to do in our new chief justice." See Patrick J. Buchanan, "Nixon, LBJ, & the First Shots in the Judges' War," at https://www.creators.com/read/pat-buchanan/04/17/nixon-lbj-the-first-shots-in-the-judges-war.

26. The *Griswold* case concerned a Connecticut law against contraceptive devices. The Court ruled that the decision to have a baby is among the most intimate decisions in human life, and government could not regulate it by forbidding contraceptives. To argue that conclusion, the Court determined that the protections of the First, Third, Fourth, and Fifth Amendments suggested the existence of a right to privacy, and the Ninth Amendment (which assures us that the people possess other rights not listed in the Bill of Rights) entitled the Court to discover it. From *Griswold*'s conclusion that medical decisions about whether to have children are private, the findings of the *Roe* decision are a very short next step.

27. Richard Dubin, "The 1968 Confirmation Hearings of Justice Abe Fortas," *Colonial Lawyer* 7, no. 1 (Spring 1977): 10.

28. "Excerpt from Transcript of Senate Committee's Hearing on Fortas Nomination," *New York Times* (19 July 1968): 16.

29. Ibid., 16.

30. Robert H. Bork, *The Antitrust Paradox: A Policy at War with Itself* (New York: Basic Books, 1978), 411, 57.

31. US Senate Committee on the Judiciary, *Nomination of Robert H. Bork to be Associate Justice of the Supreme Court of the United States*, 100th Cong., 1st sess., 1987, 146.

32. Ibid., 155.

33. Ibid.

34. Ibid., 201, 86, 212, 720.

35. *Oxford English Dictionary*, 3rd ed., s.v. "Bork."

36. Congressional Quarterly, Inc., *Historic Documents of 1990*, ed. Hoyt Gimlin (Washington, DC: Congressional Quarterly, Inc., 1991), 616. *Congressional Quarterly* also attributes the phrase "stealth nominee" to Senator Howell Heflin (R-AL).

37. Quoted in ibid., 616.

38. Ibid., 625.

39. Ibid., 619.

40. A symposium published in the November 1996 of the Catholic journal *First Things* took up the question of whether the courts had usurped so much authority in our constitutional system that the federal government had lost its legitimacy. Authors praised the "original understanding" of the Constitution (Robert H. Bork) and the principle of "judicial restraint" (Charles W. Colson). A more recent 2016 Pew Forum poll found that, while a plurality of Catholics prefer for the Constitution to be interpreted according to a meaning in light of "current times," 42 percent of Catholics would have the document read in light of what it "meant as originally written." The proportion of Catholic originalists is less than the proportion of the overall population (47 percent) who subscribe to originalism and far less than the proportion of evangelical Christians (79 percent). Those data, together with the *First Things* symposium, help us to chart a segment of Catholics in the United States who have identified evangelicals as allies in a perspective defined as much by moral convictions as constitutional values.

41. In a legal sense, sodomy refers to any nonprocreative sexual act. The *Bowers* case concerned a Georgia law that, strictly speaking, could have been enforced against heterosexual partners as easily as against homosexual partners. As a practical matter, the case turned on the question of whether the state could regulate sexual behavior in this way as a matter of its ordinary powers to make rules for the public welfare or whether, under the Fourteenth Amendment's guarantee of equal protection and the *Griswold* decision's protection of privacy, such laws subjected nonheterosexual partners to unequal treatment by intruding too far into their intimate lives. By a narrow 5–4 majority, the Court upheld the Georgia law.

42. *Public Papers of the Presidents of the United States: William J. Clinton, 1993–2001: 1996*, Book 2 (Washington, DC: GPO, 1998), 1635.

43. Adam Nagourney, "Mrs. Clinton Joins Battle over Running City's Schools," *New York Times* (11 January 2000): B8.

44. Chris Harris, "Barack Obama Answers Your Questions about Gay Marriage, Paying for College, More" (1 November 2008), at http://www.mtv.com/news/1598407/barack-obama-answers-your-questions-about-gay-marriage-paying-for-college-more/.

45. John Paul II, *Evangelium Vitae*, 73.

46. Ibid.

47. Ibid., 74.

48. Ratzinger, "The Problem of Threats to Human Life."

49. Ibid.

50. Ibid.

51. I agree with the evaluation of Reuters reporter Tom Heneghan, who wrote about the 2004 election: "Pundits dreamed up terrible catch phrases like 'wafer watch' and 'wafer war'" to describe the conflict between Catholic bishops and Senator John Kerry over receiving Communion. See Tom Heneghan, "Wafer Wars, Wedge Issues, and the Pope's Visit" (20 April 2008), at http://blogs.reuters.com/faithworld/2008/04/20/wafer-wars-wedge-issues-and-the-popes-visit/. The phrase is as indisputably irreverent as it was common at the time, appearing not just in Reuters but also in *Commonweal* and at Faith in Public Life. Catholics of deep and serious faith all will agree readily that calling the Eucharist a "wafer" is as lamentable as identifying the sacrament of unity with conflict ("war"). Then again, when the Eucharist has become the focal point of a political conflict there are very few good ways to describe the circumstance.

52. Karen Tumulty and Perry Bacon, Jr., "A Test of Kerry's Faith" (29 March 2004), at http://www.cnn.com/2004/ALLPOLITICS/03/29/kerry.faith.tm/.

53. Archbishop John F. Donoghue, Bishop Robert J. Baker, and Bishop Peter J. Jugis, "Worthy to Receive the Lamb: Catholics in Political Life and the Reception of Holy Communion" (4 August 2004).

54. David D. Kirkpatrick and Laurie Goodstein, "Group of Bishops Using Influence to Oppose Kerry," *New York Times* (12 October 2004).

55. Donoghue, Baker, and Jugis, 2004.

56. Ibid.

57. Bush is a practicing Methodist, but that does not exclude him from being described as evangelical. While Bush's mid-life conversion usually is attributed to Billy Graham, Stephen Mansfield gives the lion's share of credit to Arthur Blessitt, whose entry in Randall Herbert Balmer's *Encyclopedia of Evangelicalism* (Waco, TX: Baylor University Press, 2004) identifies him with the movement. For a description of Blessitt's influence on Bush's faith, see Stephen Mansfield, *The Faith of George W. Bush* (New York: Penguin, 2003), 61–69. See also an account reproduced in David Aikman, *A Man of Faith: The Spiritual Journey of George W. Bush* (Nashville: Thomas Nelson, 2004), 69–70.

58. Genevieve Wood, a representative from the Family Research Council, told an audience of African American evangelical ministers in 2004, " 'They are wrapping themselves in the flag of civil rights. I can make arguments against that. But not nearly like you all can." See Lynette Clemetson, "Both Sides Court Black Churches in the Battle over Gay Marriage," *New York Times* (1 March 2004). Those efforts failed overall, but they were not without successes. NBC News reported in 2004 how "in Chicago, the Rev. Gregory Daniels, senior pastor of the Greater Shiloh Missionary Baptist Church, went so far as to tell his congregation that 'if the KKK opposes gay marriage, I would ride with them' " at: John Murph, "Moral Values Push Bush to Victory," at http://www.nbcnews.com/id/6531772/ns/us_news-life/t/moral-values-push-bush-victory/#.WV9dbITyvIU.

59. George W. Bush, Satellite Remarks to the Southern Baptist Convention (11 June 2002).

60. Ibid.

61. See Kevin Phillips, *American Theocracy: The Peril and Politics of Radical Religion, Oil, and Borrowed Money in the 21st Century* (New York: Viking 2006). Also: *Evangelium Vitae*, 21, 28, 50, 77, 82, 86, 87, 92, 95, 98, 100.

62. Hudson's biography at avemariaradio.net tells us, "During 1999 and 2000 Dr. Hudson worked with Karl Rove in coordinating then Gov. Bush's outreach to Catholic voters, and four years later he coordinated the Catholic Outreach effort of the 2004 campaign. In December 2000, Rove asked Hudson to put together a Catholic working group to advise the White House on issues important to Catholics. During Bush's first term he led a weekly call with the White House of prominent Catholics who advised the administration on issues of mutual importance. President George W. Bush appointed Dr. Hudson to the President's Council on Service and Civic Participation in recognition of his leadership among lay Catholics in the United States."

63. Deal W. Hudson, *An American Conversion: One Man's Discovery of Beauty and Truth in Times of Crisis* (New York: The Crossroad Publishing Company, 2003), 148.

64. Deal W. Hudson, "Public Philosophy in the Recent Catholic Experience," in *Proceedings of the Fellowship of Catholic Scholars 20th Annual Convention: Is a Culture of Life Still Possible in the US?*, ed. Anthony Mastroeni (South Bend, IN: St. Augustine's Press, 1999), 3.

65. The *Washington Post* described "a mobilization of evangelical Protestants and conservative Roman Catholics" that drove Bush's

2004 victory; see Alan Cooperman and Thomas B. Edsall, "Evangelicals Say They Led Charge for the GOP," *Washington Post* (8 November 2004): A1. The *Post* reported on efforts to identify "friendly congregations" in battleground states, including both evangelical and Catholic churches, "urging Christian supporters to turn over their church directories" to build mailing lists and develop tools for voter mobilization that crossed lines between evangelicals and Catholics.

66. Robin Toner, "Both Sides on Abortion Issue Step Up Fight," *New York Times* (27 October 2000).

67. John L. Allen, "Bush in Meeting with Pope: 'Not All the Bishops Are with Me,'" blog posting at http://ncronline.org (10 June 2004). The account was framed somewhat differently in a June 14 CNN report: "Bush asked Sodano to 'push the bishops to become more actively involved' in promoting those issues that are part of his social agenda. The Vatican official said Sodano did not respond to Bush's request. The official said 'it was the Vatican's interpretation that [Bush] wanted [the bishops] to get involved in time for the campaign.'" See Suzanne Malveaux, "Vatican: Bush Wants Bishops to Back His Agenda," at http://www.cnn.com/2004/ALLPOLITICS/06/14/bush.vatican/index.html.

68. Records exist which may confirm how a strategy had been in motion long before the Rome meeting took place, and those records may substantially describe the shape of that strategy. A Freedom of Information Act request made by this author to the George W. Bush Presidential Library on July 12, 2017, sought corrspondence between the Executive Office of the President, the Domestic Policy Council, the Office of Faith Based and Community Initiatives, the Office of Political Affairs, the Speechwriting Office, and the Office of Strategic Initiatives and several Catholic leaders and groups such as the National Right to Life Committee, Priests for Life, and the USCCB Secretariat for Pro-Life Activities between January 20, 2001, and January 31, 2005. The review process for presidential materials is lengthy, and the records could not be delivered in time for publication of this book. Initial reviews for this FOIA request were suggestive by themselves, however. That review found 2,798 pages of relevant correspondance and 13,747 electronic files—an enormous amount of material that, even without having yet read what it contains, verifies close contact between the first Bush Administration's White House political offices and several pro-life groups and Catholic leaders. It is regrettable that the review process could not be completed in time

for this publication. At the same time, there are strong indications that an important story about the Catholic church's involvement in national politics can be found in the Bush Administration papers, and that story waits to be told.

Chapter 5—pages 128–59

1. Editorial Introduction, "The End of Democracy," *First Things* (November 1996), at http://www.firstthings.com/article/1996/11/001-the-end-of-democracy-and-the-judicial-usurpation-of-politics/.

2. See https://www.catholic.com/about.

3. Quoted in: Steven P. Millies, "A Catholic Response to Catholic Answers," *National Catholic Reporter* 41, no. 31 (5 November 2004): 19.

4. US Conference of Catholic Bishops, *Faithful Citizenship: A Catholic Call to Political Responsibility* (September 2003).

5. John L. Allen, "Three Keys to Reading the Dolan Win at USCCB," *National Catholic Reporter* (17 November 2010), at https://www.ncronline.org/blogs/ncr-today/three-keys-reading-dolan-win-usccb.

6. Laurie Goodstein, "Bishops Won't Focus on Abuse Policies," *New York Times* (14 June 2011).

7. See http://www.catholicleague.org/homosexuality-and-sexual-abuse/.

8. Msgr. Tony Anatrella, "Reflections on the Instruction on the Admittance of Homosexuals into Seminaries," *Catholic News Agency*, online at http://www.catholicnewsagency.com/resources/life-and-family/homosexuality/reflections-on-the-instruction-on-the-admittance-of-homosexuals-into-seminaries/.

9. Peter Overby, "Catholic Bishops' Lobby a Force on the Hill," *National Public Radio* (13 November 2009), at http://www.npr.org/templates/story/story.php?storyId=120399270. One study has noted how state Catholic conferences operate in a "complex environment in which they must be effective politically without being partisan—a situation that many conference directors have come to see as an advantage"; Maurice T. Cunningham, "A Christian Coalition for Catholics? The Massachusetts Model," *Review of Religious Research* 51, no. 1 (September, 2009): 56.

10. Overby.

11. Ernest B. Furgurson, *Hard Right: The Rise of Jesse Helms* (New York: W.W. Norton & Company, 1986), 198.

12. The institutes sponsored by Helms's Senate office were investigated by *Congressional Quarterly* in 1982 (see "The Helms Network," *Congressional Quarterly Special Report*, March 6, 1982, 499–505), in which several questions about the use of funds and possible ethics violations were raised. Anderson was never implicated in wrongdoing and a July 1, 1982 *New York Times* report ("Departing Senate Aide Leaves Trail of Questions") suggested that the institutes were shut down by Helms himself after growing concern "that several Senate rules might have been stretched or violated." The American Family Institute and Carl Anderson's involvement with it are not important here for any suggestion of wrongdoing on Anderson's part, since there is none. Rather, those institutes together comprised a network of fundraising and issues activism that included abortion, cutting taxes and promoting economic growth, and opposing communism in Latin America. The network not only stretched across the whole range of conservative political causes, but also brought Roman Catholics like Anderson and Southern Baptists like Jesse Helms together over common political interests. It built a fundraising network to support that partnership that laid groundwork for future collaborations.

13. About the Knights of Columbus, their issues advocacy, and their financial connections to the bishops' conference and these other organizations, see Sheryl Gay Stolberg, "Ready to Fight Gay Marriage at Court Door," *New York Times* (22 March 2013). Also: David D. Kirkpatrick, "A Religious Push Against Gay Unions," *New York Times* (24 June 2006). Finally, see Tom Roberts, "Knights of Columbus' financial forms show wealth, influence," *National Catholic Reporter* (15 May 2017). While the *National Catholic Reporter*, particularly, has an editorial voice in its coverage, the data compiled from tax filings and gathered in this report are plain facts organized indispensably by this article.

14. The *National Catholic Reporter* noted in its May 2017 report, "The Knights gave $50,000 each year, in 2014 and 2015, to the Federalist Society, described in a recent *New Yorker* article as 'a nationwide organization of conservative lawyers' whose executive vice president, Leonard Leo, 'served, in effect, as Trump's subcontractor on the selection of [Neil] Gorsuch' as nominee, eventually confirmed, for justice

to the Supreme Court. Aside from Leo's reputation as a devout Catholic, the society is thoroughly secular and largely an operation benefitting the Republican Party." While the overwhelming number of grantees listed on the Knights' 2015 disclosure forms plainly are religious or charitable organizations, there is a discernible political tilt among the activist causes supported by the Knights. Still, in fairness, we will note here a donation to the Connecticut State NAACP ($10,000).

15. Charles J. Chaput, OFMCap, *Render unto Caesar: Serving the Nation by Living Our Catholic Beliefs in Political Life* (New York: Doubleday, 2008), 208, 219–220.

16. Representatively, see the work of the German-born American political writer Eric Voegelin, who wrote that such notions of culture or nationhood generally depend on racial categories. Yet, even when they do not, the goal remains the same: "to integrate a community spiritually and politically" according to some agreed-upon definition of who belongs and who does not. See Eric Voegelin, "The Growth of the Race Idea," *The Review of Politics* 2, no. 3 (July 1940): 283. Such ideas thrive, Voegelin wrote, amid the pressure of secularization when people's intimate connection to a transcendent source of order has been obstructed or cut off. And while secularization is the root of the problem, the church is not immune to the effects. Even for the Catholic Church, "man becomes completely insignificant in comparison to his membership in an interest group"; Eric Voegelin, "Hitler and the Germans," in *Collected Works of Eric Voegelin*, Vol. 31, ed. and trans. Detlev Clemens and Brendan Purcell (Columbia, MO: University of Missouri Press, 1999), 188. In the literature of social anthropology, see the work of Thomas Hylland Erickson, who builds on the work of Ernest Gellner (*Thought and Change*, 1964, and *Nations and Nationalism*, 1983), writing that "a critical look at the historical sources of any nationalist project will quickly reveal that they are ambiguous" because nationalism collapses under the same pressure of historical analysis that Voegelin described (see Thomas Hylland Erickson, "The Nation as a Human Being—a Metaphor in a Mid-Life Crisis?" in *Siting Culture: The Shifting Anthropological Project*, ed. Kirsten Hastrup and Karen Fog Olwig [London: Routledge, 1997], 107). Voegelin described the inadequacy of the "symbol of blood relation" to expose the weakness of the body metaphor as a unifying social symbol when he observed that "even in this case [the family consisting of parents and children] the unit includes normally at least

two persons who are not blood relatives—I mean the parents. . . . As soon as the idea of the blood unit goes beyond one generation, including grand children and further descent, the function of the blood symbolism becomes more apparent because the departure from reality grows wider. The ancestors of any given individual go back in time indefinitely, increasing in number with every generation by powers of two. No simple principle of order can be derived from this pattern of reality"; Voegelin, "The Race Idea," 285.

17. To cite just one case, Erickson tells us that "the history—or histories—of the Nordic region may just as well be used to justify a Scandinavian or regional identity as a Norwegian one," Erickson, 107. The fact that a particular group of Scandinavians chose to distinguish themselves from Danes at a particular point in history rather than group themselves all together as Scandinavians was a historical choice incidental to all of the things that Scandinavians have in common with one another or that Norwegians do not share in common with each another.

18. The traditional Latin Mass—more properly called the Tridentine Mass—never really went away after the Second Vatican Council. It was preserved in the years immediately following the Council by dissenters who did not accept Vatican II. They were unwilling to embrace change, to make accommodations in the practice of the church to the world in which women and men lived. They saw the church as eternal, unchanging, even at an institutional level and at the level of church discipline. Outside of a very few permitted exceptions, the practitioners of the Tridentine Mass in those early days were followers of a variety of traditionalist Catholic movements. These movements centered chiefly on the figure of Archbishop Marcel Lefebvre, who, as the 1980s got under way, grew closer and closer to open schism with Rome as he became more and more convinced that he should ordain bishops who adhered to his traditionalist movement, lest it die out with his generation. Seemingly in a bid to placate Lefebvre and other traditionalists, in 1984 Pope John Paul II extended to diocesan bishops the power to grant exceptions for the celebration of the Tridentine Mass. Four years later, LeFebvre ordained four bishops anyway. John Paul excommunicated LeFebvre and those four bishops and at the same time released a letter urging that "respect must everywhere be shown for the feelings of all those who are attached to the Latin liturgical tradition," in the apparent hope that LeFebvre and his followers might return to the fold. When he was

the church's enforcer of doctrine, Cardinal Ratzinger had to follow the struggle with the traditionalists closely. Once he became Pope Benedict, he reached out again to try to heal the breach, first in 2007 when he allowed for the widespread use of the Tridentine Mass without any special permissions, then in 2009 when he reversed the excommunications. Still today, the traditionalists have not returned. They are sure they are right, and they are unwilling to make any concessions to the passing of time. The liturgy must remain the same. While those excommunications and the consecrations of illicit bishops were sketching out the boundaries of a struggle over church discipline and how much the church can embrace the reforms of Vatican II to change, the drama has often played out at the parish level.

19. Joseph Cardinal Bernardin, "Remarks: Catholic Common Ground News Conference, Chicago, Illinois, August 12, 1996," in *Selected Works of Joseph Cardinal Bernardin: Church and Society*, ed. Alphonse P. Spilly, CPPS (Collegeville, MN: Liturgical Press, 2000), 311. See also Cardinal Joseph Bernardin, "Called to Be Catholic: Church in a Time of Peril," Inaugural Statement of the Catholic Common Ground Initiative (August 12, 1996).

20. Pope John Paul II, *Memory and Identity: Conversations at the Dawn of a Millennium* (New York: Rizzoli, 2005), 73, 77.

21. A key passage: "In 1994, at Castel Gandolfo, a symposium was held on the theme of the identity of European societies (*Identities in Change*). The discussion focused on the changes brought about by the events of the twentieth century in the way European identity and national identity are understood in the context of modern civilization. At the beginning of the symposium, [French philosopher] Paul Ricoeur spoke of remembering and forgetting as two important and mutually opposed forces that operate in human and social history. Memory is the faculty which models the identity of human beings at both a personal and a collective level. In fact, it is through memory that our sense of identity forms and defines itself in the personal psyche. Among the many interesting things I heard on that occasion, this struck me particularly. Christ was acquainted with this law of memory and he invoked it at the key moment of his mission. When he was instituting the Eucharist during the Last Supper, he said: 'Do this in memory of me' (*Hoc facite in meam commemorationem*; Lk 22:19). Memory evokes recollections. The Church is, in a certain sense, the

'living memory of Christ: of the mystery of Christ, of his Passion, death, and resurrection, of his Body and Blood'" (144–145). This is a deep and beautiful meditation on memory and identity that overlooks the second half of Ricoeur's scheme—"forgetting." Forgetting—mercy—is not absent from the mission of Christ or the church. Yet, in John Paul's construction of the church's identity, memory weighs for more and forgetting is not mentioned.

22. "The Roman Rite is itself a precious example and an instrument of true inculturation. . . . The work of inculturation, of which the translation into vernacular languages is a part, is not therefore to be considered an avenue for the creation of new varieties or families of rites; on the contrary, it should be recognized that any adaptations introduced out of cultural or pastoral necessity thereby become part of the Roman Rite, and are to be inserted into it in a harmonious way" (5).

23. See *Sacrosanctum Concilium* 37. Pope John Paul II's years-long reflection on inculturation is too complex for a full or satisfying treatment here, in which, for considerations of space and topical applicability, I have simplified his argument significantly to emphasize the firmness of the church's identity. It is the case that John Paul was eager that the church should "pay heed to the variety or missionary charisms and to the diversity of circumstances and peoples" (*Redemptoris Missio*, 23). Yet, in the same paragraph, John Paul emphasized the "fundamental unity" of the church's mandate "to cooperate in the mission of Christ . . . based not on human abilities but on the power of the risen Lord." In John Paul's writings there is openness to diversity and change, but worldly culture and diversity seem clearly intended to yield to the unifying mandate of the church's identity.

24. One notable exception is the legal provision under the laws of most states that endows a Catholic bishop as a "corporation sole." The concept had deep roots in common law, permitting the transfer of church property from bishop to succeeding bishop by making the bishop the sole shareholder of a corporation that owns all of the diocese's assets. In American law, fifteen states have accommodated religious groups—especially Catholics—dating back to New York Archbishop John Hughes, who seems to have been the first to use the mechanism. See Morris, 118.

25. John XXIII, *Pacem in Terris*, 30.

26. The principle of double effect, long recognized in Catholic moral theology, speaks to circumstances in which an ordinarily bad thing might be done in order to achieve a good outcome. An act can have two effects, one bad and one good. A bad effect never stops being bad, but a good effect is always good. Oral contraceptives offer an interesting example. See M. Dayal and K.T. Barnhart, "Noncontraceptive Benefits and Therapeutic Uses of Oral Contraceptive Pills," *Seminars in Reproductive Medicine* 19, no. 4 (December 2001): 295–303. Dayal and Barnhart report: "The oral contraceptive pill is one of the most extensively studied medications ever prescribed. The health benefits are numerous and outweigh the risks of their use. Definitive evidence exists for protection against ovarian and endometrial cancers, benign breast disease, pelvic inflammatory disease requiring hospitalization, ectopic pregnancy, and iron-deficiency anemia. It has also been suggested that oral contraceptives may provide a benefit on bone mineral density, uterine fibroids, toxic shock syndrome, and colorectal cancer. Minimal supportive evidence exists for oral contraceptives protecting against the development of functional ovarian cysts and rheumatoid arthritis. Treatment of medical disorders with oral contraceptives is an 'off-label' practice. Dysmenorrhea, irregular or excessive bleeding, acne, hirsutism, and endometriosis-associated pain are common targets for oral contraceptive therapy. Most patients are unaware of these health benefits and therapeutic uses of oral contraceptives, and they tend to overestimate their risk." The Affordable Care Act mandated coverage to broaden access to these disease-preventing effects, not to encourage promiscuousness but to achieve the double effect—reduced incidence of disease, reduced suffering, and lower healthcare costs through prevention of diseases that require expensive treatments.

27. The Obama administration offered several workaround compromises to accommodate religious objections to the contraceptive mandate without sacrificing the coincidental medical benefits oral contraceptives provide. In 2012, the administration offered a plan where insurers, and not an objecting religious employer, would provide and pay for oral contraceptive coverage. The only involvement religious employers would have is to provide access to an insurance plan, not to pay for contraceptives and, of course, the decision whether to use contraceptives would be made by individuals, not employers. The compromise was regarded as inadequate by religious groups who felt still they would be complicit in providing abortifa-

cient drugs. Closely held corporations were exempted by *Hobby Lobby v. Burwell* (2004), and litigation is ongoing.

28. Archbishop William Lori preached in a June 21, 2012 homily, "Even if current threats like the HHS mandate were to be overcome, we would still have to face powerful forces which seek to prevent religious faith from exerting an appropriate & necessary influence within our culture. Some would even say that the Catholic Church is a primary obstacle that stands in the way of creating a completely secular culture in the United States." In a 2012 *Meet the Press* interview, Cardinal Timothy Dolan called the contraceptive mandate "a dramatic, radical intrusion of a government bureaucracy into the internal life of the church."

29. Garry Wills, who has been a Vatican critic, called the synods "hollow" and, "window dressing, not real consultation"; Garry Wills, *Why I Am a Catholic* (New York: Houghton Mifflin, 2002), 240. But dissatisfaction with the synod procedures since the 1960s has not been an unusual or controversial opinion to express. Bradford E. Hinze described several "constraints imposed on dialogical procedures" that have grown up at the synods of bishops, such as how, "instead of establishing the synod of bishops as a means of exercising the collegial authority of bishops as full and proper sharers in their own universal pastoral ministry with the bishop of Rome, it has been formed with the sole mandate to assist the pope in his universal pastoral ministry"; Bradford Hinze, *Practices of Dialogue in the Roman Catholic Church: Aims and Obstacles, Lessons and Laments* (New York: Continuum, 2006), 171.

30. Francis, "Address of His Holiness, Pope Francis" (24 October 2015).

31. *The World Over* (15 October 2015)

32. Philip J. Murnion, "Introduction," in Cardinal Joseph Bernardin and Archbishop Oscar H. Lipscomb, *Catholic Common Ground Initiative Foundational Documents* (Eugene, OR: Wipf and Stock, 2002), 18.

Chapter 6—pages 160–189

1. With the Second Vatican Council, the church "proposes, for the benefit of the faithful and of the whole world, to set forth, as clearly as possible, and in the tradition laid down by earlier Councils, her own nature and universal mission" (LG 1). Also: "The one People of

God is accordingly present in all the nations of the earth, since its citizens, who are taken from all nations, are of a kingdom whose nature is not earthly but heavenly. All the faithful scattered throughout the world are in communion with each other in the Holy Spirit" (LG 13).

2. Associate Justice James Iredell of the United States Supreme Court wrote in *Calder v. Bull* (1798) that "the ideas of natural justice are regulated by no fixed standard: the ablest and the purest men have differed upon the subject; and all that the Court could properly say, in such an event, would be, that the Legislature (possessed of an equal right of opinion) had passed an act which, in the opinion of the judges, was inconsistent with the abstract principles of natural justice." Iredell described the inevitable problem when abstract principles of natural law must be translated into the particulars of public policy, especially in a political system that permits widely different opinions about the fundamental questions we would hope for natural law to resolve. Citing natural law does not settle the matter, and people still disagree. A courtroom or a legislative chamber is not a philosophy classroom.

3. In 2012, Chicago's Cardinal Francis George wrote, "What will happen if the HHS regulations are not rescinded? A Catholic institution, so far as I can see right now, will have one of four choices: 1) secularize itself, breaking its connection to the church, her moral and social teachings and the oversight of its ministry by the local bishop. This is a form of theft. It means the church will not be permitted to have an institutional voice in public life. 2) Pay exorbitant annual fines to avoid paying for insurance policies that cover abortifacient drugs, artificial contraception and sterilization. This is not economically sustainable. 3) Sell the institution to a non-Catholic group or to a local government. 4) Close down," quoted in Phyllis Schlafly and George Neumayr, eds., *No Higher Power: Obama's War on Religious Freedom* (Washington: Regnery, 2012), 12–13. Schlafly and Neumayr approved of Cardinal George's "apocalyptic tone," as "justified" (13). Bishop Lawrence Persico of Erie, PA made similar remarks, and for a time the bishops of Illinois did close most of their Catholic Charities operations in objection to the regulations. The US bishops began to step back from this approach at their November 2013 meeting.

4. At the final session of the Second Vatican Council, New York's Cardinal Francis Spellman opposed the recognition of conscientious

objectors in law, arguing that "when one sees an injury done to others, one has a duty to prevent it," and that "if rules of a nation judge that military service is necessary . . . it is a moral obligation for the citizen to obey"; John Cogley, "Spellman Opposes Council Draft on Conscientious Objectors," *New York Times* (22 September 1965): 17. It is not that the church always opposed war, but a tradition of peace and pacifism begins with the Ten Commandments and is as old as the injunction, "Thou shalt not kill." All Christian war making is a compromise—often a necessary compromise—but still always an exception to firm rules. That is why Christian theology has struggled for centuries with the doctrine of the just war.

5. See John Paul II, *Redemptor Hominis*, 14. Also: Pontifical Council for Justice and Peace, *Compendium of the Social Doctrine of the Church*, 126. The *Catechism of the Catholic Church* quotes from the ancient "Epistle of Barnabas" to make the same point: "Do not live entirely isolated, having retreated into yourselves, as if you were already justified, but gather instead to seek the common good together" (1905). It bears repeating, not every compromise is advisable or worthwhile. Still, the history of the church demonstrates forcefully that, as a spiritual community set within a human community, a spirit of compromise and meeting the world is an inevitable part of the church's social ministry.

6. Robert P Jones, *The End of White Christian America* (New York: Simon & Schuster, 2016).

7. Christopher Buckley recalled in a 2008 essay for the *Daily Beast* how his father had once said to him, "You know, I've spent my entire life time separating the Right from the kooks." See Christopher Buckley, "Sorry, Dad, I'm Voting for Obama," *Daily Beast* (8 October 2008), online at http://www.thedailybeast.com/sorry-dad-im-voting-for-obama. That assessment is blunt, but also a fair description of the challenge that dogged Buckley's efforts to bring conservatism to the mainstream from the beginning. In the earliest years of Buckley's *National Review*, he struggled with the John Birch Society's extreme tendencies until firmly rebuking the JBS in 1961. Richard Hofstadter's classic, *The Paranoid Style in American Politics* (New York: Vintage, 1952, 2008) remains the authoritative history of the tendency on the American right to offer a home to "uncommonly angry minds."

8. See Joshua Green, *Devil's Bargain: Donald Trump and the Storming of the Presidency* (New York: Penguin, 2017), 154–155. Bannon had developed the strategy with Peter Schweizer to shape Schweizer's

2015 book *Clinton Cash: The Untold Story of How and Why Foreign Governments and Businesses Helped Make Bill and Hillary Rich* (New York: Harper, 2015). In *Devil's Bargain*, Green recounts Schweizer's and Bannon's "mantra": "Facts get shares; opinions get shrugs" (154).

9. Barack Obama, *The Audacity of Hope: Thoughts on Reclaiming the American Dream* (New York: Crown Publishers, 2006), 36.

10. Antonio Spadaro, SJ, and Marcelo Figueroa, "Evangelical Fundamentalism and Catholic Integralism in the USA: A Surprising Ecumenism," *La Civiltà Cattolica* (June 2017), online at http://lacivilta cattolica.com/june-2017/evangelical-fundamentalism-and-catholic -integralism-in-the-usa-a-surprising-ecumenism/. Spadaro and Figueroa describe a "Manichean language" that evokes the ancient movement begun by the Babylonian prophet Mani during the third century. Mani taught "the existence of two opposing eternal principles, light and darkness, and three stages of a cosmic battle: a preliminary stage, a stage in which both principles become mixed and battle for control of the cosmos, and a final stage in which light will win over darkness" (see Jonathan Z. Smith and William Green Scott, eds., with The American Academy of Religion, *The HarperCollins Dictionary of Religion*, s.v. "Manichaeism"). St. Augustine of Hippo (354–430) may have been a follower of Mani before his conversion, but certainly he wrote against the Manicheans, whose popular ideas challenged the emerging institutions of the Christian Church. Manichaeism remained influential throughout the Middle Ages, influencing the Cathars, Bogomils, and other heretical movements. Needless to say, Manichaeism's all-or-nothing, Good-versus-Evil, black-and-white perspective has its twenty-first century adherents, too.

11. Spadaro and Figueroa.

12. Ibid. Evangelical fundamentalists hold to the "absolute and unerring authority of the Bible," ruling out "scientific or critical study of the scriptures." See *HarperCollins Dictionary of Religion*, s.v. "fundamentalism." Integralists seek the full integration of spiritual authority and worldly authority, a church with political power. Integralism has a long history, and Spadaro and Figueroa describe its most recent manifestations.

13. Ibid.

14. See, representatively: Philip Bump, "Donald Trump Will Be President Thanks to 80,000 People in Three States," *Washington Post* (1 December 2016). Also: John McCormack, "The Election Came

Down to 77,744 Votes in Pennsylvania, Wisconsin, and Michigan," *The Weekly Standard* (10 November 2016).

15. Here I use data from the Bureau of Labor Statistics. I examine average, annual, county-level unemployment data for 2009, the worst year of the economic crisis. I assume that the psychic effects of massive unemployment are felt by communities for a long time after the unemployment crisis has passed. Thus, voters in 2016 may have made decisions based on perceptions shaped by a memory of 2009. The national average for unemployment from that dataset was 9.3 percent. Therefore, unless otherwise noted, this sample only examines counties whose average unemployment rate for 2009 exceeded 9.3 percent. For data on religious participation, I consulted the 2010 US Religion Census, with county-level data as compiled by the Association of Statisticians of American Religious Bodies. Acknowledging that using 2010 religious participation data to discuss voter decisions in 2016 is problematic, I have used the 2010 data because it is the most recent county-level data available. Especially among Catholics, no event like the sexual abuse crisis has provoked a mass exodus from the church since 2010. Thus, acknowledging some weaknesses in the data, this is the best study that can be constructed from what is available.

16. The Wisconsin counties did not reach the 9.3 percent threshold to be counted as above-average unemployment.

17. Charles J. Chaput, OFMCap, *Render unto Caesar: Serving the Nation by Living Our Catholic Beliefs in Political Life* (New York: Doubleday, 2008), 49.

18. Ibid., 227–228.

19. Francis, *Evangelii Gaudium*, 240–241.

20. *Gaudium et Spes* 27, 31.

21. The Second Vatican Council's Dogmatic Constitution on the Church tells us that, "many elements of sanctification and of truth are found outside of its [the church's] visible structure" (LG 8).

Conclusion—pages 190–203

1. Ed Mechmann, "A Political Desecration" (7 November 2016), at http://archny.org/news/a-political-desecration.

2. Canon 1239.

3. On 7 November 2016, Pavone wrote, "The issue is not how I'm treating a baby. (I've been providing funerals and burials for these children for decades, with full legal and canonical counsel, and those

concerned about these things would do well to talk to me rather than the media.) The issue is how the abortionists, supported by the Democrats, are treating these babies. What's sacrilegious is abortion, and voting for those who support it. It's time we get our heads screwed on straight about who the bad guys are." At http://www.renewamerica.com/columns/abbott/161108.

4. This is different from saying that Donald Trump is a racist, a claim for which there would be no evidence in the public record. Rather, Trump has been particularly expert at exploiting the sort of "dog-whistle" politics imagined by the late GOP operative Lee Atwater ("you say stuff like, uh, forced busing, states' rights, and all that stuff, and you're getting so abstract. Now, you're talking about cutting taxes, and all these things you're talking about are totally economic things and a byproduct of them is, blacks get hurt worse than whites" [see https://www.thenation.com/article/exclusive-lee-atwaters-infamous-1981-interview-southern-strategy/]). Trump's refusal to condemn white nationalists and neo-Nazis after the August 2017 violence in Charlottesville, VA, revealed the extent of his dependence on voters who hold opinions that are not only repugnant, but that the US bishops condemned in a 1979 pastoral letter as "a sin that divides the human family, blots out the image of God among specific members of that family, and violates the fundamental human dignity of those called to be children of the same Father" (*Brothers and Sisters to Us*).

5. In a Republican primary debate on February 6, 2016, in Manchester, NH, Donald Trump said he would "bring back a hell of a lot worse than waterboarding." He reinforced that promise throughout the 2016 campaign as late as October 30, 2016, when he asked the crowd at an Albuquerque, NM, rally, "These savages are chopping off heads, drowning people. This is medieval times, and we can't do waterboarding?" About ISIS, Trump told a rally crowd on November 12, 2015, in Fort Dodge, IA, "I would bomb the shit out of them. I would just bomb those suckers. And—that's right. I'd bomb the pipes, I'd blow up the refi—, I would blow up every single inch. There would be nothing left." Weeks later on December 2, Trump said in a Fox News interview that he would "take out" members of ISIS terrorists' families who were not involved in terrorism to bring pressure on those who were, adding that "we're fighting a very politically correct war" in the way that the US was not targeting civilians as

terrorists do. Though it came after the campaign, we should note that Trump urged police at a Long Island rally on July 28, 2017, "not to be too nice," and instead to be "rough" while making arrests. The comments came after a wave of publicly reported incidents of police using excessive force against African American suspects between 2013 and 2016, culminating in the movement known as Black Lives Matter. Trump's comments about Black Lives Matter evoked the "law and order" theme of his campaign, often expressed by supporters as "Blue Lives Matter." Trump drew campaign support from law enforcement, including Milwaukee (Wisconsin) County Sheriff David Clarke and Maricopa (Arizona) County Sheriff Joe Arpaio, both figures who have become known for extreme tactics in law enforcement and who played prominent roles in the Trump campaign. Arpaio was pardoned by President Trump in 2017 after Arpaio was convicted of defying a federal court order concerning his treatment of prisoners, and Clarke reportedly was considered for a subcabinet position in the Trump administration (see Matt Ford, "Sheriff Clarke Joins the Trump Administration," *The Atlantic*, 17 May 2017). Trump made no effort to distance himself from those who favor "rough" police tactics throughout his campaign.

6. The *Washington Post*'s Philip Bump tracks Trump's slippery position on abortion at "Donald Trump Took 5 Different Positions on Abortion in 3 Days," *Washington Post* (3 April 2016), at https://www.washingtonpost.com/news/the-fix/wp/2016/04/03/donald-trumps-ever-shifting-positions-on-abortion/. In an April 2016 interview with the *New York Times*'s Maureen Dowd, Dowd recalled this exchange: "I had to ask: When he was a swinging bachelor in Manhattan, was he ever involved with anyone who had an abortion? 'Such an interesting question,' he said. 'So what's your next question?' " See Maureen Dowd, "Trump Does It His Way," *New York Times* (3 April 2016), at https://www.nytimes.com/2016/04/03/opinion/sunday/trump-does-it-his-way.html. Days later, Trump clarified his response: "The answer is no." See Mary Jordan, "Trump Says He Never Dated a Woman Who Had an Abortion," *Washington Post* (8 April 2016), at https://www.washingtonpost.com/news/post-politics/wp/2016/04/08/trump-says-he-never-dated-a-woman-who-had-an-abortion/. That seems to end the discussion, except for the fact that such ambiguity has rarely before been acceptable among people serious about being pro-life.

7. *Catechism of the Catholic Church*, 2356.

8. The story about Reagan's quip before surgery was widely reported in 1981. See, for example, Marjorie Hunter, "Men in the News: Surgeons to the President," *New York Times* (1 April 1981).

9. Bruce Bueno de Mesquita, "Why Politics Should Not Stop at the Water's Edge," *Hoover Daily Report* (15 November 1999), at https://www.hoover.org/research/why-politics-should-not-stop-waters-edge.

10. Pew Research Center, "Key Takeaways on Americans' Growing Partisan Divide over Political Values" (5 October 2017), at http://www.pewresearch.org/fact-tank/2017/10/05/takeaways-on-americans-growing-partisan-divide-over-political-values/.

11. Michael Sean Winters, "The Sanity Caucus Wins," *National Catholic Reporter* (14 November 2013), at https://www.ncronline.org/blogs/distinctly-catholic/sanity-caucus-wins.

Bibliography

Books

Aikman, David. *A Man of Faith: The Spiritual Journey of George W. Bush.* Nashville: Thomas Nelson, 2004.

Anderson, Patrick. *Electing Jimmy Carter: The Campaign of 1976.* Baton Rouge, LA: Louisiana University Press, 1994.

Bernardin, Cardinal Joseph. *Consistent Ethic of Life.* Edited by Thomas G. Fuechmann. Kansas City, MO: Sheed & Ward, 1988.

———. *Selected Works of Joseph Cardinal Bernardin.* 2 vols. Collegeville, MN: Liturgical Press, 2000.

Bernardin, Cardinal Joseph, and Archbishop Oscar H. Lipscomb. *Catholic Common Ground Initiative Foundational Documents.* Eugene, OR: Wipf and Stock, 2002.

Blanshard, Paul. *American Freedom and Catholic Power.* Boston: The Beacon Press, 1949.

Bork, Robert H. *The Antitrust Paradox: A Policy at War with Itself.* New York: Basic Books, 1978.

———. *Saving Justice: Watergate, the Saturday Night Massacre, and Other Adventures of a Solicitor General.* New York: Encounter Books, 2013.

Brownson, O.A., LL.D. *The American Republic: Its Constitution, Tendencies, and Destiny.* New ed. New York: P. O'Shea, 1865.

Byrnes, Timothy A. *Catholic Bishops in American Politics.* Princeton: Princeton University Press, 1991.

Castelli, Jim. *The Bishops and the Bomb: Waging Peace in a Nuclear Age.* Garden City, NY: Image Books, 1983.

Chambers, Whittaker. *Witness.* New York: Random House, 1952.

Chaput, Charles J., OFMCap. *Render unto Caesar: Serving the Nation by Living Our Catholic Beliefs in Public Life.* New York: Doubleday, 2008.

Clinton, William J. *Public Papers of the Presidents of the United States: William J. Clinton, 1993-2001*, 1996, book 2. Washington, DC: GPO, 1998.

Cuomo, Mario M. *The Diaries of Mario M. Cuomo: The Campaign for Governor*. New York: Random House, 1984.

Curran, Charles E. and Richard A. McCormick, SJ, eds. *John Paul II and Moral Theology*. Mahwah, NJ: Paulist Press, 1998.

Dolan, Jay P. *The American Catholic Experience: A History from Colonial Times to the Present*. Garden City, NY: Doubleday & Company, Inc., 1985.

Doody, Colleen. *Detroit's Cold War: The Origins of Postwar Conservatism.* Chicago: University of Illinois Press, 2013.

Dunne, Matthew W. *A Cold War State of Mind: Brainwashing and Postwar American Society*. Boston: University of Massachusetts Press, 2013.

Ellis, John Tracy. *American Catholicism*. 2nd rev. ed. Chicago: University of Chicago Press, 1969.

Faggioli, Massimo. *True Reform: Liturgy and Ecclesiology in* Sacrosanctum Concilium. Collegeville, MN: Liturgical Press, 2012.

Farina, John, ed. *Hecker Studies: Essays on the Thought of Isaac Hecker*. New York: Paulist Press, 1983.

Furgurson, Ernest B. *Hard Right: The Rise of Jesse Helms*. New York: W.W. Norton & Company, 1986.

Finke, Roger, and Rodney Stark. *The Churching of America, 1776–1990: Winners and Losers in Our Religious Economy*. New Brunswick, NJ: Rutgers University Press, 1992.

Gimlin, Hoyt, ed. *Historic Documents of 1990*. Washington, DC: Congressional Quarterly, Inc., 1991.

Glazier, Michael, and Thomas J. Shelley, eds. *The Encyclopedia of American Catholic History*. Collegeville, MN: Liturgical Press, 1997.

Greeley, Andrew M. *The Making of the Popes 1978: The Politics of Intrigue in the Vatican*. Kansas City: Andrew and McMeel, Inc., 1979.

Green, Joshua. *Devil's Bargain: Donald Trump and the Storming of the Presidency*. New York: Penguin, 2017.

Hastrup, Kirsten, and Karen Fog Olwig, eds. *The Shifting Anthropological Project*. London: Routledge, 1999.

Hebblethwaite, Peter. *Pope John Paul II and the Church*. Kansas City: Sheed & Ward, 1995.

Hennessey, James, SJ. *A National Pastoral Council: Pro and Con*. Washington, DC: US Catholic Conference, 1971.

———. *American Catholics: A History of the Roman Catholic Community in the United States*. New York: Oxford University Press, 1981.

Heyer, Kristin E., Mark J. Rozell, and Michael A. Genovese, eds. *Catholics and Politics: The Dynamic Tension between Faith and Power*. Washington, DC: Georgetown University Press, 2008.

Hinze, Bradford. *Practices of Dialogue in the Roman Catholic Church: Aims and Obstacles, Lessons and Laments*. New York: Continuum, 2006.

Hofstadter, Richard. *The Paranoid Style in American Politics*. New York: Vintage Books, 1952.

Hudock, Barry. *Struggle, Condemnation, Vindication: John Courtney Murray's Journey toward Vatican II*. Collegeville, MN: Liturgical Press, 2015.

Hudson, Deal. *An American Conversion: One Man's Discovery of Beauty and Truth in Times of Crisis*. New York: The Crossroad Publishing Company, 2003.

Hunter, James Davison, and Alan Wolfe, eds. *Is There a Culture War? A Dialogue on Values and American Public Life*. Washington, DC: Brookings Institution Press, 2006.

Hunter, James Davison. *Culture Wars: The Struggle to Define America*. New York: Basic Books, 1991.

John Paul II. *Memory and Identity: Conversations at the Dawn of a Millennium*. New York: Rizzoli, 2005.

Jones, Robert P. *The End of White Christian America*. New York: Simon & Schuster, 2017.

Judis, John B. *William F. Buckley, Jr.: Patron Saint of the Conservatives*. New York: Simon & Schuster, 1998.

Kaveny, M. Cathleen. *Law's Virtues: Fostering Autonomy and Solidarity in American Society*. Washington, DC: Georgetown University Press, 2012.

Kelly, Monsignor George A. *Battle for the American Church (Revisited)*. San Francisco: Ignatius Press, 1995.

Kennedy, Eugene. *Bernardin: Life to the Full*. Chicago: Bonus Books, 1997.

Locke, John. *A Letter Concerning Toleration*. Ed. James H. Tully. Indianapolis: Hackett Publishing Company, 1983.

Mansfield, Stephen. *The Faith of George W. Bush*. New York: Penguin, 2003.

Mastroeni, Anthony, ed. *Proceedings of the Fellowship of Catholic Scholars 20th Annual Convention: Is a Culture of Life Still Possible in the U.S.?* South Bend, IN: St. Augustine's Press, 1999.

McAndrews, Lawrence J. *What They Wished For: Catholics and American Presidents, 1960–2004*. Athens, GA: University of Georgia Press, 2014.

McAvoy, Thomas, CSC. *The Great Crisis in American Catholic History: 1895–1900*. Chicago: Henry Regnery, 1957.

McGreevy, John T. *Catholicism and American Freedom: A History*. New York: W.W. Norton & Company, 2003.

McGuigan, Patrick B., and Dawn M. Weyrich, eds. *Ninth Justice: The Fight for Bork*. Lanham, MD: Rowan & Littlefield Publishers, 1993.

Medhurst, Martin J., Robert L. Ivie, et al., eds. *Cold War Rhetoric: Strategy, Metaphor, and Ideology*. East Lansing, MI: Michigan State University Press, 1997.

Millies, Steven P. *Joseph Bernardin: Seeking Common Ground*. Collegeville, MN: Liturgical Press, 2016.

Milton, J.R., and Philip Milton. *John Locke: An Essay Concerning Toleration and Other Writings on Law and Politics, 1667–1683*, The Clarendon Edition of the Works of John Locke. New York: Oxford University Press, 2006.

Morris, Charles R. *American Catholic: The Saints and Sinners Who Built America's Most Powerful Church*. New York: Times Books, 1997.

Murray, John Courtney, SJ. *We Hold These Truths: Catholic Reflections on the American Proposition*. New York: Sheed & Ward, 1960.

Neary, Timothy B. *Crossing Parish Boundaries: Race, Sports, and Catholic Youth in Chicago, 1914–1954*. Chicago: University of Chicago Press, 2016.

Nevins, Albert J., MM., ed. *The Maryknoll Catholic Dictionary*. New York: Grosset & Dunlap, 1965.

Noonan, John T., Jr. *The Lustre of Our Country: The American Experience of Religious Freedom*. Berkeley, CA: The University of California Press, 1988.

Obama, Barack. *The Audacity of Hope: Thoughts on Reclaiming the American Dream*. New York: Crown Publishers, 2006.

O'Brien, David J., and Thomas A. Shannon, eds. *Catholic Social Thought: The Documentary Heritage*. Maryknoll, NY: Orbis Books, 1992.

O'Connell, Marvin R. *John Ireland and the American Catholic Church*. St. Paul, MN: Minnesota Historical Society Press, 1988.

O'Roarke, Lawrence M. *Geno: The Life and Mission of Geno Baroni*. New York: Paulist Press, 1991.

Phillips, Kevin. *American Theocracy: The Peril and Politics of Radical Religion, Oil, and Borrowed Money in the 21st Century*. New York: Viking, 2006.

Rawls, John. *Political Liberalism*. Rev. ed. New York: Columbia University Press, 2005.

Reese, Thomas J. *Archbishop: Inside the Power Structure of the American Catholic Church.* New York: Harper & Row, 1989.

———. *A Flock of Shepherds: The National Conference of Catholic Bishops.* Kansas City: Sheed & Ward, 1992.

Schlafly, Phyllis, and George Neumayr, eds. *No Higher Power: Obama's War on Religious Freedom.* Washington, DC: Regnery Publishing, Inc., 2012.

Schweizer, Peter. *Clinton Cash: The Untold Story of How and Why Foreign Governments and Businesses Helped Make Bill and Hillary Rich.* New York: Harper, 2015.

Shaw, Russell. *American Catholic: The Remarkable Rise, Meteoric Fall, and Uncertain Future of Catholicism in America.* San Francisco: Ignatius Press, 2013.

Shor, Ira. *Culture Wars: School and Society in the Conservative Restoration, 1969-1984.* New York: Routledge, 1988.

Spalding, Thomas W. *The Premier See: A History of the Archdiocese of Baltimore, 1789–1994.* Baltimore: The Johns Hopkins University Press, 1995.

Steinfels, Peter. *A People Adrift: The Crisis of the Roman Catholic Church in America.* New York: Simon & Schuster, 2003.

Szulc, Tad. *Pope John Paul II: The Biography.* New York: Pocket Books, 1995.

Tanenhaus, Sam. *Whittaker Chambers: A Biography.* New York: The Modern Library, 1998.

United States Conference of Catholic Bishops. *Pastoral Letters of the United States Catholic Bishops: 1989–1997.* Vol. 6. Washington, DC: USCCB Publishing, 1998.

———. *Pro-Life Coordinator Handbook.* Washington, DC: United States Conference of Catholic Bishops, 2005.

Viera, Norman, and Leonard Gross. *Supreme Court Appointments: Judge Bork and the Politicization of Senate Confirmations.* Carbondale, IL: Southern Illinois University Press, 1998.

Vital, David. *A People Apart: The Jews in Europe, 1789–1939.* New York: Oxford University Press, 1999.

Voegelin, Eric. *The Collected Works of Eric Voegelin, Volume 31.* Edited and translated by Detlev Clemens and Brendan Purcell. Columbia, MO: University of Missouri Press, 1999.

Wacker, Gene. *America's Pastor: Billy Graham and the Shaping of a Nation.* Cambridge, MA: The Belknap Press of Harvard University, 2014.

Weaver, Mary Jo, and R. Scott Appleby, eds. *Being Right: Conservative Catholics in America*. Indianapolis: Indiana University Press, 1995.

Weigel, George. *Catholicism and the Renewal of American Democracy*. Mahwah, NJ: Paulist Press, 1989.

———. *Witness to Hope: The Biography of Pope John Paul II, 1920–2005*. New York: Perennial, 2005.

Williams, Daniel K. *Defenders of the Unborn: The Pro-Life Movement before* Roe v. Wade. New York: Oxford University Press, 2016.

Wills, Garry. *Why I Am a Catholic*. New York: Houghton Mifflin, 2002.

Journal Articles

Brownson, Orestes. Review of *The Condition of Women and Children among the Celtic, Gothic, and Other Nations*, by John McElheran. *Brownson's Quarterly Review* 21 (July 1859): 493–526.

Congressional Quarterly. "The Helms Report." *Congressional Quarterly Special Report* (6 March 1982): 499–505.

Cunningham, Maurice T. "A Christian Coalition for Catholics? The Massachusetts Model." *Review of Religious Research* 51, no. 1 (September 2009): 55–70.

Dayal, M., and K.T. Barnhart. "Noncontraceptive Benefits and Therapeutic Uses of the Oral Contraceptive Pill." *Seminars in Reproductive Medicine* 19, no. 4 (December 2001): 295–303.

Dubin, Richard. "The 1968 Confirmation Hearings of Justice Abe Fortas." *Colonial Lawyer* 7, no. 1 (Spring 1977): 10–24.

Finke, Roger, and Rodney Stark. "Turning Pews into People: Estimating 19th Century Church Membership." *Journal for the Scientific Study of Religion* 25, no. 2 (June 1986): 180–192.

Kalscheur, Gregory A., SJ. "Catholics in Public Life: Judges, Legislators, and Voters." *Journal of Catholic Legal Studies* 46, no. 2 (2007): 211–258.

Penning, James M. "The Political Behavior of American Catholics: An Assessment of the Impact of Group Integration vs. Group Identification." *Western Political Quarterly* 41, no. 2 (June 1988): 289–308.

Reher, Margaret. "'Phantom Heresy': A Twice-Told Tale." *U.S. Catholic Historian* 11, no. 3 (Summer 1993): 93–105.

Reichley, A. James. "Religion and Political Realignment." *Brookings Review* 3 (Fall 1984): 29–35.

Stempel, Jeffrey W., and William D. Morris. "Electoral Folklore: An Empirical Examination of the Abortion Issue." *Yale Law & Policy Review* 1, no. 2 (Fall 1982): 1–40.

Voegelin, Eric. "The Growth of the Race Idea." *The Review of Politics* 2, no. 3 (July 1940): 283-317.

Winsboro, Irvin D.S., and Michael Epple. "Religions, Culture, and the Cold War: Bishop Fulton J. Sheen and America's Anti-Communist Crusade of the 1950s." *The Historian* 71, no. 2 (Summer 2009): 209–233.

Government Documents

Committee on Constitutional Amendments of the Senate Committee on the Judiciary. *Abortion—Part I: Hearings on S.J. Res. 119 and S.J. Res. 130*. 93rd Cong., 2d sess., 1974.

Subcommittee on International Resources, Food, and Energy of the House Committee on International Relations. *The Right-to-Food Resolution—Hearings on H.Con.Res. 393*. 94th Cong., 2d sess., 1976.

US Department of Health, Education, and Welfare. Public Health Office. Office of Health, Research, Statistics, and Technology. National Center for Health Statistics. *Contraceptive Utilization: United States*. Series 23, no. 2. DHEW Publication No. 79-1978.

US Senate Committee on the Judiciary. *Nomination of Robert H. Bork to be Associate Justice of the Supreme Court of the United States*. 100th Cong., 1st sess., 1987.

Archival Collections

1976 Campaign to Elect Jimmy Carter Collection. Jimmy Carter Presidential Library. Atlanta, GA.

James M. Cannon Files. Gerald R. Ford Presidential Library. Grand Rapids, MI.

Joseph Cardinal Bernardin Collection. Archdiocese of Chicago Joseph Cardinal Bernardin Archives and Records Center. Chicago, IL.

NCCB Collection. American Catholic History Research Center. The Catholic University of America. Washington, DC.

Magisterial Documents

Francis. *Evangelii Gaudium* (2013).

John XXIII. *Pacem in Terris* (1963).

John Paul II. *Redemptoris Missio* (1990).

———. *Evangelium Vitae* (1995).

———. *Ut Unum Sint* (1995).

———. *Liturgiam Authenticam* (2001).

Paul VI. *Sacrosanctum Concilium* (1963).

———. *Lumen Gentium* (1964).

———. *Dignitatis Humanae* (1965).

———. *Gaudium et Spes* (1965).

Other Periodicals (variously)

America (print and online).

Catholic News Agency (online).

Commonweal (print and online).

CRUX (online).

First Things (print and online).

Human Life Review (print).

La Civiltà Cattolica (online).

Los Angeles Times (online).

L'Osservatore Romano (online).

National Catholic Reporter (print).

National Review (print and online).

OSV Newsweekly (online).

Politico (online).

The Atlantic (online).

The Daily Beast (online).

The New Republic (print).

The New York Times (print and online).

The Wanderer (online).

The Weekly Standard (online).

Washington Post (online).

Index